CONTEMPORARY CINEMA

CONTEMPORARY CINEMA

John Orr

Edinburgh University Press

© John Orr, 1998

Edinburgh University Press Ltd
22 George Square, Edinburgh

Typeset in Palatino Light
by Pioneer Associates, Perthshire, and
printed and bound in Great Britain by
The Cromwell Press, Trowbridge, Wiltshire

A CIP record for this book is available from the
British Library

ISBN 0 7486 0836 2 (paperback)

CONTENTS

———◦◦———

LIST OF ILLUSTRATIONS

(illustrations pages 120–9)

FOREWORD

———◦———

To encompass the infinity of contemporary cinema is an impossible task. To ignore its prehistory is the height of naivety. I have thus combined the best rather than the worst of both worlds by singling out a dominant and guiding feature in the development of the cinema over the last thirty years. This I have called, after Pasolini, the 'Cinema of Poetry'. This book takes its inspiration from his famous essay on the topic in the same way, I hope to show, that the key films to which he referred in 1965 are at the heart of the transformation which has taken place in the art of cinema. His guiding idea has taken off in ways he never imagined, and this study attempts to uncover some of those many paths and directions. In doing so, it sadly leaves out scores of films of this epoch which I have seen and enjoyed, usually again and again. Most of those mentioned have also been seen again and again, but have probably been enjoyed even more.

My enthusiasm for the cinema has at times been carried along quite shamelessly by that of others, and the following are among those whose fervour and critical eye for the moving image have helped to make this book possible, though they are in no way responsible for the outcome. I would like to give special thanks, therefore, to Diane Bell, Mark Cousins, Christophe Dupin, Spiros Gangas, Jennifer Goeppart, Cristina Novelli, Asbietta Ostrowska and Bernard Rudden, and also to Jim Hamilton and all the staff of Edinburgh Filmhouse for making their cinema the most congenial I know in which to watch and talk about movies.

John Orr
May 1997

ACKNOWLEDGEMENTS

———⊃⊂———

I would like to thank the British Film Institute for the film stills used in this book and the following distributors for the permissions to reproduce them:

Artificial Eye for *Raise the Red Lantern, Exotica, La Belle Noiseuse* and *Beyond the Clouds*
Contemporary Films for *Stalker*
Electric Pictures for *Shanghai Triad, Sweetie* and *Vagabond*
ICA Projects for *Chungking Express*
Metro Tartan for *The Adjuster*

Chapter 1

A CINEMA OF POETRY

———

Scorsese recalls that in 1960 New York film students were divided over the respective merits of *La Dolce Vita* and *L'avventura*. By 1965 controversy over film form had spread into the realm of colour as it became standard for features throughout Western cinema. We can note the bold experiments of Jean-Luc Godard in *Le Mépris* and *Pierrot le fou*, but two other films also stand out as markers for the cinema of the next thirty years: Hitchcock's much-pilloried *Marnie* with Tippi Hedren, and Michelangelo Antonioni's *The Red Desert* with Monica Vitti. Like Godard, both directors experiment with expressive uses of colour to explore the world of the senses, a world embodied in the texture of the screen image. Both show a social order seen through the eyes of a young woman who is marginal to it, who is neither pure heroine nor pure victim, but was to the audiences of the time disarmingly neurotic. This foregrounding of female neurosis is hardly box-office unless it is used in a comedy of manners, as by Woody Allen, to brilliant effect with Diane Keaton in *Annie Hall*, or Pedro Almodóvar at his very best. But serious neurosis? And from Hitchcock? He had after all created the figure of the cool blonde as romantic heroine – Grace Kelly, Eve-Marie Saint – or complex victim – Kim Novak, Janet Leigh and Hedren in his previous film *The Birds*. But as Marnie, Hedren was an outsider, a drifter, a man-hating thief. Antonioni's different work follows a similar path with Monica Vitti. In his monochrome trilogy which ends with *L'eclisse*, she was a single woman of sensuous beauty but also the centre of the film's moral disquiet. *The Red Desert* is something else. The disturbed, neglected mother stranded amidst the polluted wastes of industrial Ravenna is not an icon at all but a human eruption who

1

complements the film's controlled but delirious images. By its end, *The Red Desert* is both woman and camera on the verge of a nervous breakdown.

Let us compare the films with two epics which preceded each of them in their respective countries. John Ford's great Western *The Searchers* (1957) and Luchino Visconti's spectacular version of Lampedusa's *The Leopard* (1964) have one thing in common. Both are quasi-mythic visions of remote landscapes in the nineteenth century. Both harness the power of arid landscape as a source of visceral spectacle, Ford in the desert of Monument Valley, Visconti in the interiors of Sicily, and both are films of sublime power. Light and landscape generate a grandeur to match the heroic mission at the core of their narratives as they question the nature of honour and destiny, *male* honour, *male* destiny, on a bold visual plane. *The Red Desert* and *Marnie* deal, by contrast, with the perils of survival in daily life for a modern woman.

Yet neither film is naturalistic. For Marnie, thief on the run, the colour red connotes danger and erotic revulsion. Gladioli blossoms are repellent and she cannot bear to look at them. For Giuliana in *The Red Desert* the colour yellow is the colour of poison and of death, seen first in the smoke of Ravenna's chemical refineries and later in the yellow flag of the quarantined tanker, bringing mysterious disease from the East. The landscape is expressive, but it is also something more and here there is a clear paradox. The shot seems to express the point-of-view of the disturbed subject yet does not operate primarily through the POV shot. The subject is framed within the landscape, not separately from it. Antonioni opens his film with a long shot of Vitti and her son wandering around the perimeter of the refinery. Hitchcock intercuts location shots of the foxhunt with obvious studio process shots, in medium close-up, of Marnie riding her favourite horse, Forio. The artifact of the process shot, cutting from Hedren riding a horse through woodland to Hedren simulating riding on a studio rocking horse expressively conveys the subjective experience of (female) riding with a knowing Freudian subtext. As Vitti and Richard Harris walk down a Ravenna street, they encounter a food stall where the fruit and vegetables are painted grey. In framing Vitti by the stall in long shot, the sequence has a clinical objectivity but the artificial grey colour of the fruit echoes the grey colours of Ravenna's industrial landscape. It is as if the fruit has been seen through Vitti's eyes, yet she herself is in the frame. Subjectivity is conveyed through the objective shot, not through the POV shot.

This has a strange effect, a mind-distortion which is hardly *simpatico*. Hitchcock ends up framing his heroine through the techniques of full-blown melodrama and studio expressionism. The tunnel vision of Marnie is echoed by the painted backdrop of the ship in Baltimore harbour which frames her final homecoming while the mannered unreality of the horse-riding shots has recently influenced the virtual reality style of the car process shots in *Pulp Fiction* and *Natural-Born Killers*. By contrast, Antonioni found exterior equivalents. The over-the-shoulder shots of Vitti with a telephoto lens have the back of her head in clear focus but make her visual field seem blurred and imme-diate, pressing in upon her as if her unseen eyes themselves cannot clearly see what confronts them. We have simultaneously, subjective vision and a clinical distancing from it. That vision is unstable and for that reason a new challenge to film form, a challenge taken up imme-diately by Luis Buñuel in his remarkable study of female subjectivity with Catherine Deneuve, *Belle de Jour* (1967). All three films make an important juncture in the continuous experimenting which charac-terises the 1960s, and *The Red Desert* is a key text in Pier Paolo Pasolini's enduring case for a 'Cinema of Poetry', first delivered to the Pesaro film conference in 1965.

Pasolini's endorsement of a new 'poetic' cinema first pays homage to *Un Chien Andalou*, Buñuel's silent surrealist short of 1929 but equally it prophesies the coming age of what he called 'free indirect subjectivity'. What did he mean by this? Technically speaking, it entails immersion of the filmmaker in the experience of the subject who possesses some clear affinity with the auteur. This cannot operate, like fiction, through written narrative and spoken dialogue. It must be expressed primarily through visual style. Unlike novelists who immerse themselves in both the language and psychology of their central characters – elsewhere Pasolini mentions Italian writers as diverse as Ariosto and Moravia – filmmakers have no abstract language. They must work with concrete images possessing a pre-grammatical and irrational history. The film image is irrational.[1] This does not move the image away from the Real but towards it. Gilles Deleuze has pointed out that Pasolini's critique signalled a shift from the arid formalism of semiology towards a new kind of language system, a language system of reality.[2] Deleuze judges

this 'reality-system' vital to a new understanding of film, where movement and image are inseparable, for the naive critical isolation of
images as 'objects' presupposes an immobility of objects which is not
only misleading but goes against the grain of the film medium itself.
Thus the false semiological distinction between the object as mere
referent and the image as a component of the signified, breaks down.
In film, image and object are inseparable. Film is not a succession of
represented objects but a series of moving images. A film language
exists through its response to non-linguistic material which it then
transforms, and narration is grounded in the image itself. The filmmaker cannot 'use' the character's language in the same way as the
novelist. 'His activity cannot be linguistic,' Pasolini asserts, 'it must
instead be stylistic'.[3]

This is the basis of what he calls a 'free indirect point-of-view shot'
which works, he insists, through analogy in two distinctive ways. In the
first instance there is a juxtaposition of multiple POVs of the same
image, with only a minor shift in angle, in distance, in lens length, or
in some combination of any of these to signify a decentring of the
point-of-view, a technique used recurrently in *The Red Desert*. Second,
there is the further device of making characters enter and leave the
frame in such a way that the picture in the frame gains significance
both from their presence *and* their absence. This, it can be added, was
an extension of the out-of-field techniques Antonioni and Godard
had developed in their black-and-white cinema.[4] For Pasolini this
obsessive framing means 'the world is presented as if regulated by a
myth of pure pictorial beauty that the personages invade, it is true, but
adapting themselves to the rules of that beauty instead of profaning
them with their presence.'[5]

In *The Red Desert* Antonioni moves back and forth from his central
subject Vitti, to the autonomous beauty of things. Moreover he looks
at the world by immersing himself in the neurotic subject (Vitti) and
then re-animating the facts of the world through her eyes. The narrative technique works not through identification or sympathy with
the heroine as it would in melodrama, but by analogy: 'Antonioni has
freed his most deeply felt moment: he has finally been able to represent the world through his eyes, *because he has substituted in toto for the
world-view of a neurotic his own delirious view of aesthetics,* a wholesale
substitution which is justified by the possible analogies of the two

views.'[6] This homology is the key to the double-register of the cinema of poetry, the subject's disturbed vision of the world and, by substitution, the director's artistic representation of it. Neither is possible without the other. Pasolini contrasts this substitution with the different technique of Bertolucci's *Before the Revolution* (1964). Here his assistant director on *Accatone* is seen as portraying a neurotic heroine (Adriana Asti) too close to his own sensibility, a harsh, misleading judgement by Pasolini since Asti is very much the object of the male gaze, in particular that of her nephew-lover, Fabrizio, in this the most dazzling and lyrical of Bertolucci's films. For Pasolini *The Red Desert* suggests in contrast a double reading through homology – the world as subjectively disturbed, the world as deliriously aesthetic. To this we can add our own coda. The historic transformation of the cinema of poetry lies in the world viewed. We see industrial Ravenna of 1965, not a studio facsimile. Through the figure of its disturbed subject Antonioni's camera seeks out the toxic eco-spaces of the 'red desert'.

The camera here is both objective and subjective, a feature of the modern cinema discussed at length by Deleuze and Jean Mitry, whose dissection of the ambiguities in tracking and shot/reverse shot sequences lead him towards the concept of a generalised semi-subjective image. That is to say, the camera is always moving among its characters but is not identical with any one of them. For Deleuze this camera-consciousness is the 'truly cinematographic *Mitsein*' of an unidentified other who bears witness to the events filmed.[7] Yet it is also a filmic artifice which has no status in natural perception. Assessing the films of Godard, Antonioni and Bertolucci, Pasolini had provided a crucial link between the Heideggerian *Mitsein*, the filmic being-with-others, and free indirect subjectivity. The *Mitsein* or witnessing camera enacts homology, the double-register of style and psychic disturbance. Yet as Deleuze points out, Pasolini allows himself the slippage to a technically incorrect term, mimesis, which he uses for a very different reason, but one no less significant. Mimesis connotes the *sacred* nature of filming itself. In making *Accatone* a few years earlier he had already discovered the 'technical sacredness' of the long lens shot, a form of unmediated reality make possible by the movie camera alone. The lens records reality in the raw, without embellishment, and that, for the director of *The Gospel According to St Matthew*, is sacred.

There is a sense here in which Pasolini directly challenges Plato's devaluation of mimesis to the third order of truth in the tenth section of the *Republic*. Plato, we may recall, had seen the craftsman's form as an attempt to replicate the pure form of the object ordained by the Divine and seen art in turn as a third-order praxis, a copy of the crafts-man's copy, an imitation of the craftsman's imitation of Divine form. Film technology affords a unique chance in Pasolini's view to short-circuit this triad. The world captured on film in its raw purity is not mere imitation like painting or mythic narrative. The style of the camera is nourished by sacred immediacy, in which advanced technologies have recovered the possibility of the sacred in a secular world. The power of the Human is made possible by imitating reality in the raw but subjecting it at the same time to the double-register of the cinema of poetry. The auteur attains pure Form by virtue of film's raw content. Pasolini uses a number of adjectives to delineate this ideal cinema – 'oneiric, barbaric, irregular, aggressive, visionary' and crucially, 'expres-sive/expressionistic'. For him, the irrational works through form more than through content. As visual style pursues its free expression, rules of narrative continuity and editing no longer apply.

Although poetry for Pasolini means narrative poetry, and works against Sartre's distinction between prose as writing referring to a world outside itself and poetry as writing referring only to itself,[8] there are still ambiguities over form. Key history films of the 1970s, for example, such as Herzog's *Aguirre*, Malick's *Days of Heaven* and Peter Weir's *Picnic at Hanging Rock*, can be seen as 'poetic' by virtue of their lyric style and sparse dialogue. Equally their narratives convey stories of the past with a precise naturalistic detail, a lucid concern with time, place and culture. For that reason we might place them closer to fiction than poetry, especially in its modernist forms, where in the English language Imagism has had such a powerful impact. The closer analogy in twentieth-century writing lies not with poetry but with the poetic prose of modernist fiction. Here Pasolini argues that interior monologue is the closest literary form to the free, indirect POV shot, and the imme-diacy of the shot would seem at times to correspond to the present tense of the interior 'I' in prose. Yet in English language fiction, the poetic prose which prefigures poetic cinema is a 'third person stream-of-consciousness', described by Banfield as a discourse of represented thought and speech.[9] It makes use less of present tense than of past tense to conjure up the immediacy of the reader's mind. It is less the 'I' of Joyce's Molly in 'Penelope' and more the Stephen of 'Wandering Rocks', more the 'she' of Woolf's Clarissa Dalloway or Grassic Gibbon's Chris Guthrie in *Sunset Song,* more 'The Consul' (Geoffrey Firmin) hallucinating with delirium tremens in Lowry's *Under the Volcano.* In each case narration moves fluidly in and out of consciousness so that Stephen in 'Wandering Rocks' is seen both from the inside and the outside, seeing as he is being seen, an interior protean sensibility but also a figure on a coastal landscape. Yet a crucial difference remains. Film is a medium of the present. It happens on screen. It also has no set discourse for representing thought.

Contemporary film seems closer to this style of writing than it is to the self-conscious fabulating of Pynchon, Barth, Fowles or Calvino. There is no self-conscious author present to play with our response. Or is there? The other pole of Pasolini's double-register is Godard where the camera continually makes its presence felt in its poetic epiphanies. Here free indirect subjectivity is that of the libertarian technicist who makes unpredictable forays in the space of his own narrative. The presence of the camera charges the force-field of the narrative, not least through its recurrent dissonance. In *Le Mépris* Fritz Lang plays himself as a director of a Hollywood movie in Capri based on *The Odyssey* while the journey of return moves on a parallel plane in the modern triangle of screenwriter Michel Piccoli who sees himself as Odysseus to the Penelope of his contemptuous spouse Brigitte Bardot, and her would-be lover, Hollywood producer Jack Palance. The reflexive motif gives us two films for the price of one and for Deleuze Godard becomes the prime exemplar of free indirect vision.[10] In *Pierrot le fou* (1965) he moves more openly into the double-register. Jean-Paul Belmondo is both aesthete and criminal, Godard and not-Godard, aficionado of the quotation and the handgun. His flight south with Anna Karina, shot by Raoul Coutard in brilliant summer colours, is complete with multi-coloured captions, chapter headings, chance digressions and endless quotations to prove Godard is at his best when he combines visual freedom with emotional doom. As the love affair of Ferdinand and Marianne falls apart, the technical virtuosity intensifies, but the presence of the camera does not dilute expressive power. Baudelaire had claimed that the clinical detachment of the artist strolling through Parisian crowds sharpened the visceral power of the artwork. A hundred years later, this is what happens in the cinema of poetry. But it happens because pure form is transcended in the act of filming. Form is born out of the intensity of theme and the irrational, not the aesthetic, remains the raw datum on which the filmmaker works.

Pasolini's Marxist critique is sadly too narrow in its view of bourgeois neurosis as a symptom of class decadence under advanced capitalism. The cinema of the poetry has featured strongly in Polish and Russian films of the late Soviet period, especially those of Andrei Tarkovsky and Krzysztof Kieślowski, and the films of the Chinese 'fifth generation' directors such as Chen Kaige and Zhang Yimou. Pasolini assumes an incestuous kinship between the neurotic bourgeois and the bourgeois auteur. But the parameters of resemblance and difference stretch, historically speaking, much wider. Indeed we can say poetic form is at its best when the auteur *plays more upon difference than upon resemblance*. While gender transference works, as we have seen, through neurosis, class transference (male-to-male) often works through psychosis, thus echoing ironically the sexual difference noted by critics in Freud's casework.[11] While for Freud the neurotic female tries to ignore existing reality but does not disavow it, the psychotic male disavows it and replaces it with a purely imaginary world. Yet female ignoring is also a complex form of resisting the wrongs of a specific male domination. We have already seen this in Vitti and Hedren but we may single out other cases. The most striking which come to mind over the last two decades are Krystyna Janda in the dark reveries of recent Polish history, *Man of Marble* (1977) and *The Interrogation* (1981), Sandrine Bonnaire in Agnes Varda's *Vagabond* (1987), Juliette Binoche in *Three Colours: Blue* (1992), and Gong Li in Zhang Yimou's *Shanghai Triad* (1996). Contrast this with the male-centred subjectivities of the same period. Overwhelming psychosis defines De Niro in *Taxi Driver* (1975) and *Raging Bull* (1980), Martin Sheen in *Badlands* (1974) and *Apocalypse Now* (1979), Jack Nicholson in *The Shining* (1980), David Thewlis in Mike Leigh's *Naked* (1993), Bruce Willis in *12 Monkeys* (1996). Resistance to the psychosis of imaginary worlds, resistance to the lure of the paranoid gaze defines David Hemmings in *Blow-Up* (1966), Jack Nicholson in *Chinatown* (1974) and *The Passenger* (1975), Gene Hackman in *The Conversation* (1974), Griffin Dunne in *After Hours* (1985), Harrison Ford in *Blade Runner* (1982). While paranoia is the resistible temptation of the bemused modern investigator, the psychopathic violence of the socially excluded to which paranoia is integral, becomes a key motif in the nightmare vision of the present and future city.

In *Taxi Driver* Scorsese, Schrader and De Niro constructed through the deranged figure of Travis Bickle a working-class mirror of their complex urban paranoia, the shared paranoia of the streets of Manhattan expressed through the free indirect subjectivity of a Vietnam Vet trapped in the nightmare of his Yellow Cab. In Kieślowski's powerful and savage *Short Film About Killing* (1988), filmed in Warsaw through slime-green filters, Jacek is the country boy adrift and alone in a hostile city which finally makes him homicidal. In *Cyclo* (1996), echoing *Taxi Driver*, the young French-Vietnamese auteur Tran Anh Hung charts the Hadean descent of a Saigon cyclo cabby into an inferno of sexual commerce and multiple murder where East and West, communism and capitalism, insanely collide. The endlessly circulating traffic of the streets with its myriad bicycles, is shot in high-angle from dilapidated balconies to affirm metonymically the eternal recurrence of the hero's bad dream, his Vietnamese *fleur du mal*. In 1993, two American independents forged disturbing poetries of psychosis in a minor key, reminding us further of the sociopathic underside of contemporary capitalism while resisting Hollywood's great mythic temptation, the pseudo-documentary of the serial killer. In Lodge Kerrigan's 16mm feature, *Clean, Shaven*, Peter Greene plays a released schizophrenic in search of his young daughter in a fishing community on the Canadian Atlantic seaboard. Through a mosaic of visual fragments and weirdly strident sounds which comprise his perceptual world, Kerrigan recreates the disintegration of his schizoid subject whose mind is haunted by an unbearable self-hatred, a self-loathing clinched in the image of the razor in the mirror by which he constantly bloodies his own face. In Bryan Singer's *Public Access*, Ron Marquette is the psychotic but well-dressed drifter who starts up his own Cable talk show in the small Western town of Brewster and then murders those he tempts into challenging the official rhetoric of 'our town' which he generates over the airwaves. Looking the spitting image of Clark Kent, the crossover here which comes to mind is somewhat different. Mr Deeds changes into Norman Bates. The contrast between these films and *Three Colours: Blue* is quite fundamental, highlighting the sexual difference in the poetics of psychic disturbance. Here redemption is female. Binoche, amnesiac, traumatised by the crash which has badly injured her and killed spouse and child, is sado-dispassionate, turning cruelly and clinically against grief and compassion. Yet her Parisian journey takes her to the other side of trauma, through the art of music, to a dream of Christian redemption but also a reunion with the daily world of her past life. In the filmic liturgies of male psychosis redemption is impossible.

The essence of the double-register would seem to exclude from Pasolini's poetics the autobiographical cinema so prevalent in Fellini where Marcello Mastroianni proved to be such a brilliant and enduring version of his director's persona. In general, autobiography does not generate sufficient tension between style and theme, the vital spring-board for free indirect vision. One extraordinary exception to this rule is the short episode which Rainer Werner Fassbinder made for the landmark composite of New German Cinema *Germany in Autumn* (1978). Like other episodes in the film Fassbinder lends a distinctive gloss to Germany's terrorist crisis of the time, to the polarised reaction to the killing of Hans Martin-Schleyer by the Baader-Meinhof group. He brings politics back into the home and charts the effect of the crisis on his relationships with his gay lover and his uncomprehending mother. The effect of separation here, between Fassbinder as creator and Fassbinder as subject, is alarmingly schizophrenic but dramatically effective. He turns himself inside out and shows us not only the collapse of the mother-son relationship through the generational impasse in German politics, but also the collapse of the gay intimacy which has no shield to protect itself against the eruption of political crisis. Meanwhile the narcissism of Fassbinder the subject is mercilessly scrutinised by the Brechtian camera of Fassbinder the filmmaker as he rolls naked on the floor with his lover in a fit of paranoia, and then finally kicks out of his flat the degraded object of his self-regarding desire.[12]

This play of identity and difference also operates on the plane of memory, memory as reverie of a lived past not as objective remember-ing. Pasolini points out that in film the present is transformed into the past by the very feature of editing, yet the past still appears as present in filmic projection for the audience by virtue of the immediacy of the image. This immediacy is a poetic affirmation of the presentness of the past unique to the medium. It gives us also a new insight into the 'history' film. For this phenomenology of film form translates reflexively into thematic treatments of history as reverie or history as lived immediacy, into the poetic cinema of Bergman's *Cries and Whispers* or Bertolucci's *The Conformist*. History becomes a dream or a nightmare of difference, in which time itself is an integral part of the double-register. For Bergman in this case the historic other is female and dying. For Bertolucci, the historic other is fascist and repressed. Between the two films another key difference emerges. The singular nature of Marcello Clerici's persona gives us a single poetic subject. By contrast, Bergman's quest to reduce film to pure-dream state, 'a dark, flowing stream' as he puts it,[13] creates a collective subject of three sisters whose emotions merge at times into one another, like the characters of *Persona* and *The Silence*, as aspects of a single soul before they finally hive apart. The legacy of *Cries and Whispers* can be seen most strongly in Terence Davies's *Distant Voices/Still Lives* (1987). Its title split because it had been filmed for cash reasons in two instalments, it emerged as one of the great films of the 1980s. Like Bergman, Davies used the family as collective subject who face a hideous death within their midst, the father-husband dying of cancer. But Davies went further. Family memories are shared by mother and siblings but there is no chronological order to the flashbacks and no ascription of a single point-of-view. The past is a collage of interwoven memories, some individual, some shared, and these spring to life out of still photographs which capture the family rituals of birth, marriage and mourning. These still tableaux, filmed in washed-out sepia and developed in post-production through a 'bleach-bypass' technique eliminating primary colour, then spring into the moving images of shared experiences. The double-register of the collective subject, mother, brother and sisters, from which Davies absents his biographical self is more powerful than his sequel *The Long Day Closes* where he reinstates himself as a young boy at the centre of the narrative. This is because Davies creates a double-register in which the subjectivities of the family weave in and out of one another as phantasmic memories.[14]

Yet there is still a key concept missing. We need to conceive the camera's *Mitsein* or active witnessing more precisely to stress its diffuse and fluid nature, to avoid the trap presented by the lure of that simplistic phrase, point-of-view. We also have to add a key dimension seen by Tarkovsky as linking cinema and poetry – the world of dreams. A reductive discourse of self is no use here since film is first and foremost a visual language. Since 'POV shot' is often an ambiguous term we can adopt Bruce Kawin's more fertile concept 'mindscreen' which interrogates subjectivity from a different angle.[15] Kawin opposes the filmed thought of mindscreen to its verbal expression in the voice-over and its purely subjective point-of-view shot. Here I would disagree that such hard-and-fast distinctions can be made. It seems to me that mindscreen is by its nature fluid and can only work if it incorporates all three, the verbal, the physical and the mental, something which is implicit in Kawin's excellent discussion of subjective sound. Mindscreen, then, has to be a fusion of 'sightscreen' and 'soundscreen'. It would thus incorporate the verbal *Mitsein* or witnessing of such voice-overs as *Badlands* (Sissy Spacek) and *Days of Heaven* (Linda Ganz), whose teenage girls are part of the action they witness but mostly do not make it happen and where, unlike the fall-guy narrators of film noir, they are not ultimate victims but survivors, part of the tragic action but also apart from it. This naive narration is an aural 'following' to match the visual following of the camera which goes beyond, indeed deconstructs the POV shot. The travelling shot, so typical of Kieslowski's work, follows the movement of his central characters yet is never identical with them. In *Blue* for example, the camera tracks Binoche through space and time and films her POV sporadically through the still shot. In Polanski's *Chinatown* there is a similar effect. John Alonzo's camera is right behind the ear of Jack Nicholson (Jake Gittes) as he tracks Mulwray, the city's water commissioner to a dried-out riverbed, then to the Pacific at dusk and onto a rowing-boat on the lake in Echo Park. The *Mitsein* of the camera is thus a form of mindscreen which fuses body, voice and psyche by creating a montage of different shot-sequences of a singular vision. The resulting composite image resembles different aspects of the subject's world, both real and imaginary.

Tarkovsky's poetic logic of dream is a world where landscape, dream, memory and fantasy all have the same ontological status.[16] His own films, *Mirror* (1974) and *Stalker* (1978), show just how much poetic cinema can free dream from the signifiers which, conventionally, would top and tail it, from the dissolve over eyes closing to the sudden start of the frightened subject waking from nightmare. In mindscreen, by contrast, the exterior world is contiguous with the interior world. In this context filmmakers have constantly challenged the POV shot. In Atom Egoyan's *Exotica* (1993) his distressed tax inspector (Bruce

Greenwood) obsessively recalls the pastoral setting of a search party in which he himself is not present. Present in the scene however are the current object of his desire, Mia Kirschner, dancer at the Exotica club who also recalls the scene quite separately, and her slimeball MC, Elias Kotias who is with her in a search party in the meadow (searching, we later learn, for the body of Greenwood's murdered daughter). Both wear the casual hippy clothes of a previous decade. After the recurrent 'flashback' the film usually flashes forward to either Kirshner or Kotias at the Exotica as fashionable black Goths, but never to Greenwood, the tax inspector. The objects of Greenwood's original gaze – is it day-dream or memory? – then become the screen's subjects while the original subject (Greenwood himself) is now completely absent. The puzzle about the origin of the shot increases – whose point of view? In different variations on free indirect subjectivity the point-of-view itself is often rendered problematic, and is no longer a fixed point through which the viewer can read the film.

The cinema of poetry not only presents us with the raw data of the real in its most advanced technical terms, it also provides us, as a con-sequence, with a journey of 'derealisation' to use Virilio's term, which is at its most effective when its found realities are at their most luminous. Of course the found reality in filmmaking is a cultural artifact of its time. It depends on the shapes, the buildings and landscapes which culture bequeaths it, but to which it often adds its own. In *Zabriskie Point*, Antonioni had billboards built on LA streets and an extra storey constructed at MGM's expense onto the downtown Mobil Oil building in order to use a deep-focus shot through a high window of the Richfield building opposite. In *The Long Goodbye* Altman made use of a beach house in Malibu overlooking the shore as a transparent habitat constantly refracting itself through its curved panes, the image of its interior superimposed upon that of the waves so that the perceptual dividing line between them is indistinguishable. In *Wings of Desire* Wenders had a section of Berlin Wall built for the scene where the angelic Bruno Ganz crashes rudely to earth since the border guards at the actual wall were too hostile to the presence of his film crew. In the sublime panning shot between two apartment buildings where the camera looks in turn at the occupants, the crew rigged a chair sliding on pulleys between the two buildings. To save the health of veteran cameraman Henri Alekan, Wenders himself was strapped to the chair

and, fearless, filmed one of the movie's most striking variations on
the angelic point-of-view.[17] Cinematographer Chris Doyle, away on
another assignment, offered his Kowloon apartment to Wong Kar-Wai
as the home of Cop #663 for *Chungking Express*. But the 'found reality'
of Doyle's apartment was not exactly left as Wong had found it. As
sequences in the picture show, the apartment was flooded and the fax
ruined in the absence of its owner, who on his return was reported to
be furious. For Poet's suicide in *Cyclo* Tran Anh Hung got permission
to construct a small building on wastleland in the busy Cholon district
of Saigon, to be torched for the occasion. In long shot, Poet's burning
apartment looks as old and seedy as the rest of the buildings in the
block.

Film location generally has its own 'thereness' and the more extreme
the climate and topography, the greater the sense of risk. This has led
to up-front filmmaking about filmmaking such as the docudramas of
the filming of *Apocalypse Now* (*Hearts of Darkness*) and *Fitzcarraldo*
(*Burden of Dreams*). The danger, the setbacks, the freaked-out actors,
the insane logistics of jungle cinema all make good visual copy, a retro-
promo of the cult of risk and movie delirium.[18] But resilience can often
be more mundane. During the making of *Raise the Red Lantern* (1991)
at the Chou Family Castle Village near Taiyan, Zhang Yimou and his
crew shot sequences only at the Golden Hour in sub-zero temperatures. Unsatisfied with powdered fertiliser substitute Zhang and crew
were camped out in the fierce January winter, waiting for the snow that
was to be crucial in key sequences of the movie, this flair for endurance
in twenty-below-zero temperatures to be repeated during his shooting
of the Communist winter advance against the Kuomintang in his epic
To Live.[19] During the filming of the Dekalog, Kieślowski shows that all
mundane problems can be interesting. During one key shot in *Short
Film about Killing* either the director failed to throw the strangled
cabby's false teeth accurately into the mud or else one of the filters
on the camera would fall out. As a result one brief shot needed any
amount of retakes. In *Short Film About Love* (1989) Kieślowski cheated
on his audience by ostensibly filming through the windows of Magda's
ground-floor Warsaw flat but instead used a small villa twenty kilo-
metres from Warsaw, flanked by a crane for high-angle POV shots.
His ingenuity had its practical difficulties, since he was forced to bark
instructions over a megaphone to his actress indoors at a great distance

in the middle of the night. For the two 'flats', that of the teenage voyeur and that of his adult object of desire, Kieślowski used seventeen different interiors.[20] Yet both films work and the final cut excises the embarrassment of the failed takes. The final seven-minute take of Tarkovsky's *The Sacrifice* (1986) remains, however, the true cause célèbre of complex location shooting, since the effort and expense of its fire and explosions demanded the success of a single well-rehearsed take. Yet as Sven Nykvist's camera failed on its lateral track and he was forced to replace it *in situ*, as the explosive charge on the white Renault failed to ignite the car after Erland Josephson's sacrificial house-arson, most of Tarkovsky's rage was directed not at fatal technical failures but at two of the confused actors whom he accused of running in the wrong direction. When the shot was tried for the second time, the charred house by the shore rebuilt in a single day by the crew in order to burn down again, two separate cameras were used, everything was near perfect and the rest is movie history.[21]

Some films do treat locations as secondary or purely mythic and give us that hyperreal feel we might wish to call the burning intensity of the copy. Sergio Leone's dual 'Once upon a Time' epics use mythic surroundings to echo mythic themes, as more recently do the American films of Philip Ridley and Emir Kusterica, while *Les Amants du Pont-Neuf* gives the look of the built exterior topical valency by recreating part of Paris near Montpellier. The supercharged hyperreal look is also a feature of three Scottish box-office hits, the magic trio of Scotch hyper-reels, *Shallow Grave* with feeble exteriors but a superb studio design of Edinburgh New Town 'surreal', *Trainspotting* where Glasgow doubles for the Leith of Irvine Welsh's novel, and the mythic *Braveheart* where Ireland and the Irish army double for Scotland and the soldiers of William Wallace in Mel Gibson's mega-buck epic. In his current studio recreation of 1950s Paisley for *The Slab Boys* John Byrne has self-consciously recharged a segment of Scotland's urban-industrial past as purely hyperreal.

Yet landscape and found realities remain vital to the cinema. Derealisation is not to be found in Baudrillard's icons, the cockpit computer screens of the Gulf War by which Allied fighters delivered laser-guided missiles onto their 'hyperreal' targets. It is to be found in the chilling aerial shots of *Lessons of Darkness*, Herzog's Gulf War documentary where the camera glides high over surreal desert landscapes of ruined military hardware and burning oil-wells bearing the disturbing imprint of darkness at noon. A more enduring image of the contemporary horror of war comes in *Ulysses' Gaze* (1996) where filmmaker Harvey Keitel walks through the streets of a battle-scarred Sarajevo (actually shot in the ruined cities of Mostar and Vukovar) watching civilians running in all directions to dodge incoming shells and sniper fire which they (and we) hear only too well but whose source they cannot possibly see. This, the invisible enemy, is the true opposite of war propaganda and the Hollywood epic, a physical dislocation of cause and effect that is real and surreal at the same time. Such images affirm the enduring impact of film for our age. Though digital video may soon change things, indeed may be changing them already, derealisation still depends most effectively on the found realities of celluloid and the 35mm images which can then be derealised by other means, both on location and in post-production. For location shooting on *Do the Right Thing* (1989) Spike Lee commandeered a street in the one of the black neighbourhoods of Brooklyn, hired security guards to keep its retinue of drug-dealers off-limits and asked Ernest Dickerson to have tenement walls painted red to connote the summer heat which would help to spark the film's climactic riot. In Lars von Trier's *Breaking the Waves* (1996), post-production was often as vital as the shoot itself. While Robbie Müller shot the film on hand-held Cinemascope with no artificial lighting, in editing von Trier transferred from film to video to manipulate the image, and especially the colour, before transferring back for theatrical projection.[22]

Another form of derealising works most effectively is the mind-screen of the young boy or adolescent. Here the rites of passage from innocence to experience come to have a hallucinatory feel in which, to quote Yeats, the ceremony of innocence is drowned. In the last decade, two outstanding films to work in this way have been Elem Klimov's epic Soviet war movie *Come and See* (1985) and Zhang Yimou's oblique narrative of 1930s gangsters *Shanghai Triad* (1995). Both adapt the *Mitsein* of the camera to the witnessing of the naive youngster, country boys whose presence at events far outstrips their comprehension of them. There are, however, key differences of poetic form. Klimov's abiding images of Flyor the boy partisan tagging wretchedly onto the end of his partisan detachment as they march off through the forests of Bielarus signify humiliation, not heroism. His oneiric journey with the teenage camp prostitute back to his own village where his family has been massacred, is like a sexual dream fused onto an Inferno without hellfire. For the first two-thirds of the film the Germans are an absent presence as planes drone above, bombs explode, leaflets fall to earth, paratroopers float down into trees, invisible German guns fire tracer bullets at dawn from the hillside. This is a reverie of the past as nightmare shot on localities which are tangible, material. But the mindscreen of war Klimov creates through the dense use of a following hand-held camera then makes them seem unreal. Are the Germans really there? Is this an imaginary enemy of ghosts?

The look of the partisan unit – ritually photographed at the start of the film – the torching of the village and the massacre of the villagers in the church by the SS (a reference to the Katyn massacre), all have a documentary feel as if this were a meticulous reconstruction of geno-cide. Yet seen through Flyor's eyes this is free indirect vision of genocidal horror. Moreover Flyor hallucinates terror before he finally faces it, yet when he does face it, it is worse than anything he has dreamed. Escaping from the burning church he becomes at last the surviving witness to genocide. Klimov's film bears intriguing comparison with Claude Lanzmann's brilliant documentary of the Holocaust, *Shoah*. Like Lanzmann in his painstaking interviews with survivors, Klimov at first avoids the direct representation of genocide and his camera obliquely interrogates the evidence of it, the nightmarish piecing together of what has come to pass. But his decisive switch to the village massacre is an opting for full-scale expressionist portrayal in the sure conviction that film really is capable of dramatically reconstructing genocide and must take on the task. The film thus reads not only like a haunting of the Soviet past but a prophecy in 1985 of things to come. With the break-up of the Soviet Union, whole swathes of Eastern Europe enacted their own mini-scenarios of ethnic cleansing based on religious and nationalist feud. What Klimov filmed as past fiction has come back to haunt us as television news of the living present.

The films by Klimov and Zhang Yimou show an oblique awareness of the American cinema from which they also detach themselves. While *Come and See* follows in some degree the open expressionist structure of *Apocalypse Now*, *Shanghai Triad* has that quality of nostalgic pastiche to be found in *The Godfather*. It matches the look which Gordon Willis created for Coppola, the overhead lighting and the dimming of the faces, the gold and ochre hues, the Westernised Shanghai mansion which echoes the Long Island mansion of the Corleone gang. Yet Coppola's film is a conspiratorial melodrama which plots its way through the labyrinth of power at first hand. Zhang Yimou reverses the convention through the mindscreen of Shuisheng, the boy-servant who attends the gangster's moll, cabaret singer Gong Li. Just as Flyor brings up the rear of the partisans so Shuisheng witnesses the tail-end of killings and assassinations, the trails of blood he follows through corridors and around doors where Byzantine intrigue remains elusively out of reach, not only for him but also for us. The killings he can never witness nor understand are the reality which seals his fate as he follows his triad master Tang into island exile. The gangster idiom refers not only to Shanghai of the 1930s as the most Western city in China, but indirectly to present Shanghai which again has become an entry point for the economics and consumer culture of the West with all the glitter and corruption that entails. The iconography of Gong Li is that of the female narcissist linking the past equally to present. Zhang presents her farewell film performance for him as both that of the Westernised star of Chinese cinema – her narcissistic singing echoes that of Monroe – and equally an echo of Shanghai's Westernised past which communism had subsequently obliterated but has now reinstated under its own rule. The narcissistic image oscillates between two male reactions, the naive wonder of the country boy's mindscreen and the cynicism of the gangsters forced to acknowledge Gong Li as Tang's woman, both of them oblique and contrary registers, one suspects, of the director himself.

If we explore further we see that the derealising emerges, above all, from what Deleuze has called the lyrical trip (bal(l)ade) of modern film which meanders, accelerates, digresses and appears to have no fixed goal. Such a film is Agnès Varda's *Vagabond* (*Sans toit ni loi*), one of the defining female films of the late twentieth century which has a defining subject in the figure of its roadside drifter, Mona, played so powerfully by Sandrine Bonnaire. Like Chabrol in his later *La Cérémonie* (1995), in which Bonnaire also stars, Varda suffuses the bleak midwinter with intense and saturated colours to evoke the unremitting coldness of climate and landscape. The filming is more naturalistic than in *The Red Desert* but the zero temperatures of Herault match the icy air and the frozen farm fields to the coldness of the soul. Bonnaire is the unmotivated outlaw *par excellence*, the woman with no past who comes out of the sea (shades of Vitti's technicolour fantasy and in turn of the Aphrodite myth), and goes back to the winter earth as a frozen corpse. In fact the corpse which begins and ends a film told in flashback seems two connected things, the play on circularity and upon the form of representation which Bazin had seen in the historic figure of the Egyptian mummy.[23] The preserved image which holds the power and magic of likeness is derealised. The corpse is Bonnaire mummified, derealised, crucified, unrecognisable but still Bonnaire. The film then springs the corpse to life in two ways. Like *Citizen Kane*, it follows its subject's life back through the connected thread of multiple conversations among locals who have encountered her en route. The narrated 'reality' is thus a synthetic image of the unknown woman given flesh by the actual figure of Bonnaire hitting the road, grimly hyperactive. Here it is made material in a specific way. As Hayward points out, Bonnaire's hammer-stride cuts across the convention of film language, the subject walking left to right across the screen.[24] The anti-clockwise movement cuts across the cultural grain and suggests the Return to a death as yet unconsecrated, but which for the audience is already known. Mona, the undead, remains the unknown, unmotivated woman who must surely die.

The mindscreen of Varda's camera, its determined following shots, point forward to the peripatetic figure of Julie in *Three Colours: Blue*. The cool neurasthenia of Bonnaire and Binoche displaces the earlier 'hot' distress of Vitti and Hedren. A parallel comparison can be made between the heated anxiety of Anthony Perkins in *The Trial* and the affectless kinesis of Jean-Louis Trintignant in *The Conformist*. Bertolucci had based the monumental look of his film and the flattened look of his hero very strongly on the picture of Welles, and yet there is a crucial difference. As Joseph K, Perkins is primarily a character. As Clerici, Trintignant is first and foremost a figure. This points us to a new form of stardom which challenges Hollywood convention, but in the cinema of poetry the first truly defining performance comes in a film which followed very quickly on the heels of *Marnie* and *The Red Desert*, that of Catherine Deneuve in *Belle de Jour*. Deneuve, as Parisian ice-maiden, is not only the glacial reprise of lookalike Hedren in *Marnie* but also, as Vincendeau notes, a perfect hybrid of the virgin killer she plays in Polanski's *Repulsion* and the proper young girl of *Les parapluies de*

Cherbourg.[25] A crucial linking in the French iconography of female stardom, Deneuve-Bonnaire-Binoche maps out one particular journey of the cinema of poetry. Before them we have to add Karina in *Vivre sa vie* and *Pierrot le fou*, in between Stephane Audrun in *Les Biches* and *Le Boucher* and after Emmanuelle Béart in *La Belle Noiseuse*.

In the Deneuve of *Belle de Jour*, Buñuel gives us a form of indirect female subjectivity where expression becomes enigma. The form works so well because Buñuel matches the presence of the camera to the surreal quality of its montage. Take the film's famous opening. On a forest road where in the far distance cars can be glimpsed, the camera tracks towards an approaching landau of an earlier age and cuts to a medium shot of the couple Séverine (Deneuve) and Pierre (Jean Sorel), seated inside. The colours are soft, autumnal. The couple declare their love but Sorel finds Deneuve cold and she in turn rejects his tenderness. The two coachmen stop on Sorel's orders and take Deneuve into the forest to be bound, whipped and finally, we presume, raped by one of the coachmen. A gothic abduction is shot in a naturalistic style after a banal conversation between a modern couple accompanied by two ancient coachmen. From the start of the rape, there is an elliptical cut to a mirror shot of Sorel in the bathroom of a Paris apartment speaking to Deneuve who is in bed in the other room. The cut is cued by his questioning voice-over: 'What are you thinking of, Séverine?' As we cut again to Deneuve her look does not answer. It hints at the prior sequence as daydream but its mystery gives no confirmation. Moreover, the initial cut to Sorel's mirrored image suggests it could equally be his own daydream. In any event, the sado-masochistic passion for cruelty in the daydream sequence, if it is that, is juxtaposed to the loving tenderness without passion in the goodnight sequence. The couple kiss, but Deneuve refuses to let Sorel share her bed.

For Buñuel in his colour films, derealisation is forged through the incongruous cut. He is no longer the maestro of surreal images, of the razor-slit eye and the open-wound hand crawling with ants which define the start of *Chien Andalou*. His camera is natural and his actors are natural. Yet the juxtaposition of shots is uncannily disturbing. While expressionism distorts *mise-en-scène* the surreal deconstructs narrative sequence. By the mid-point of *The Discreet Charm of the Bourgeoisie* (1972) we can no longer pin down the point of descent into a strange imaginary world we have clearly undergone. Not only are we faced by daydream and nightdreams, we are also made to witness mistaken identities, tales-within-tales and dreams-within-dreams which different characters tell. Yet in spite of this – and unlike Hitchcock's gothic horror – Buñuel's characters remain unflappable, acting as if nothing out of the ordinary has happened. Through insult and social disaster, mayhem and terrorist murder, they behave as if life has brought them just another day. *The Discreet Charm of the Bourgeoisie* seems like a title intended to belie its central motif, the failure of an upper-middle-class couple to organise a dinner party for their closest friends. Either the guests arrive on the wrong day or the hosts escape to make love in the bushes while their guests are left waiting in the living-room, or the army invades the dining room on manoeuvres just as dinner is served. Stéphane Audrane is Buñuel's unflappable Parisian straight out of charm school who cheerfully transgresses the etiquette she upholds. While she is the pivot of the series of tales and tales-within-tales which mark the film's narrative maze, the free indirect vision here is collective. Unlike *Belle de Jour*, the double-register here floats incongruously from one character to another so that in the end the film has no nucleus. No more nucleus, that is, in a single subjectivity than it has any anchoring in a primal reality which grounds memories, daydreams, nightmares, tall tales and dreams-within-dreams. Thus Buñuel disperses the cinema of poetry to infinity and makes it great fun in the process.

At the same time he sets an important agenda for contemporary cinema. His colour films in particular reformulate the surreal as everyday and expressive, and redefine the sublime object of desire as everyday and banal. In *Tristana* Deneuve gives to Buñuel's subject heroine an aggravating limp which magically defines her iconic presence for Fernando Rey. In *The Discreet Charm* the dinner party is always prevented from happening and becomes fetishised through its non-occurrence. In *The Obscure Object of Desire* the endless postponement of reunion and of consummation amidst terrorist bombings with the enigmatic woman Fernando Rey so desires, makes him overlook what the audience clearly sees, that she is played in alternating sequences by two different actresses.

In any case the modern Buñuel helps to breaks down the original divide of the 1920s between the expressionist and the surreal aesthetics just as Max Ernst had earlier done in his life and his painting. The

dividing line is never clear. What we have instead is a crucial difference
of emphasis. The everyday surreal deconstructs narrative sequence
while neo-expressionism subtly deforms the *mise-en-scène*. Everywhere
there is a crossing of the line as we watch the very different films of
David Lynch, Tim Burton and Atom Egoyan. In Lynch's *Blue Velvet* (1986)
the diurnal tempo and the opening sequence are Buñuelian. The
bizarre investigations of Kyle McLachlan into the dark of Lumberton
are studies in everyday incongruity. The passing fire-engine and the
watering of suburban lawns, with their winning clash of saturated reds
and greens, provides the surreal prelude to the surreal discovery of
the severed ear. Yet Lynch is no Buñuelian and thereafter gives us an
updated transformation of German Expressionism into American
Gothic especially in the psychopathic figure of Frank Booth. Isabella
Rossellini's bleakly lit apartment is a place of expressive violence but
also a desolate Heartbreak Hotel in which the anamorphic ratio of
Cinemascope and the prevalence of medium-long shots means that
the camera is intimately present but coolly detached. The crossover of
the expressive surreal is equally apparent in *Edward Scissorhands* (1990)
and *Exotica*. Burton matches Johnny Depp as gothic monster with
mutant appendices (hands both sublime and castrating) to the suburban surreal of day-glo homes in identical gardens. In *Exotica*, lighting
and *mise-en-scène* are meticulous in their expressionist look, but the
montage of Egoyan's sexual mystery is spasmodically surreal.

A further cross-over in the expressive surreal which parallels
Egoyan's obsession with video as an instrument of surreal experiment
can be found in the English films of Derek Jarman in the ten frantic
years between 1984 and 1994. Indeed Jarman's expressive surreal is a
tale of two screens, history as pure 35 mm in *Caravaggio* and *Edward the
Second*, the dystopian present as hybrid of video and super 8 in *The
Garden* or super 8 blown up to 35 mm in *The Last of England*. In the
first two films Jarman is the magician of anachronism. *Caravaggio* has
the modern suits of Sean Bean and the roar of passing trains on the
soundtrack, his version of Marlowe the khaki uniforms and accents of
1950s England to disrupt the splendour of court spectacle. Here the
freedom of the camera lies in the aesthetic affront to the history epic,
an imaginary space within a preconceived structure but equally in what
has been the central paradox of Jarman's cinema, its homoerotic bisexuality. What defines the look of Jarman's cinema of the present, which

equally mixes the future and the past, is the expressionist figure of Tilda Swinton. Swinton is at once Madonna and Christ, prophet and tortured victim like the figure in Munch's *The Scream*, the constant female presence of his cinema. There is a visual counterpoint between gay mindscreen and female icon which breaks down and re-forms the double-register. In his history epics the gay figures are famous and title the films. In the present they are diffuse, anonymous, collective while Swinton retains her expressive persona. Often like the contrast of the grappling male couple in *Last of England*, they are either naked and fragile or masked and effaced. With its apocalyptic Isle of Dogs setting the film lent itself very easily to the commodification of designer wasteland images shot at a hundred times the budget for pricey 35mm television commercials. It is, however, the grain of blown-up super 8 which in Jarman's case preserves the validity of the image, and makes the film a genuine updating of Eliot's *The Wasteland*. In *The Garden* the doubled format of super 8 and video reinforce the effect of the schizophrenic surreal to be found in Jarman's gendered differences. The atmospheric locations of Dungeness are given a Blakean overlay with hand-held super 8 while the interior video with its equally unreal colour are the opposite of the frantic Christian apocalyptics on the beach. The video sequences with the gay bathing couple, for example, possess a Warhol cool of studied kitsch. The contrast here is too stark to contain in one film. For many audiences the most satisfying of Jarman's films are paradoxically those which take the fewest stylistic risks. Yet the most exciting sequences within his features are those where he is at his most experimental.

For all the cross-over effects there is still something of a geo-political divide, a north-south split between the expressive and the surreal. Expressionist idioms of Northern Europe also dominate in North-American cinema and especially its science fiction. By contrast, the expressive surreal is Hispanic and Southern European. Following Buñuel it has encompassed directors as diverse as Tenghis Abuladze, Emir Kusterica, Bigas Luna, Victor Erice, Thomas Guterriez Alea and Raul Ruiz. In 1987 two key films were released which epitomise the north-south split, Wenders's *Wings of Desire* and Abuladze's Georgian fable *Repentance*. Both films invoke the metaphysical but to completely different ends. The two angels of Wenders's Berlin, Damiel and Cassiel, are allegorical figures who echo the metaphysical angels of Rilke and

Benjamin, mediators of the human and the divine in what Wenders has wryly termed 'his vertical road movie'. Abuladze's metaphysical tropes by contrast are more chilling by virtue of being more comic, the corpse of Varlam the local Georgian Party dictator constantly exhumed and propped against the tree in the opening sequence; the armoured knights on horseback who accompany Varlam's black Mercedes coupé in the flashback to the time of Stalin's Great Terror. Both images have an effortless comic terror, since they combine the utterly implausible with the most routine and ordinary things. Varlam sports a Hitler moustache and a Mussolini blackshirt while resembling Stalin's most ruthless chief of secret police, fellow-Georgian Lavrentii Beria. His propped corpse is the trauma of Varlam the Undead while his NKVD knights are feudal images of chivalry transformed into guardians of brute terror. Their daily reappearance, their mechanical repetition naturalises their threat but fails to neutralise it. While Varlam is a Soviet Citizen Kane, a retro-image seen backwards from the moment of his corpse's exhuming, the terror of the unexpected turns into the tragi-comedy of the familiar.[26] This mode of Georgian surreal, a landmark of the Soviet *glasnost* period, is far removed from Wenders's humourless allegory of angelic despair. Yet there are parallels. Wenders also uses naturalistic means to harness the metaphysical. Yet because his meta-physical angels offer no threat, neither do they have any comic potential. Inspired by Walter Ruttmann's 1926 documentary *Berlin: Symphony of a Great City* Wenders's camera contains its own topography of the city, clinically observed yet highly fascinated by its subject. The cityscape makes the gaze natural, yet the origin of the gaze is metaphysical, the bird's-eye POV as the nub of angelic mindscreen which hears too the unspoken voices of those it sees. The two angels are observers unobserved, whose eyes function like those of a camera eye using monochrome film. They perceive but cannot intervene since they have no earthly presence.

By invoking the past, Wenders twice invokes the presence of the camera. Damiel (Bruno Ganz) encounters Peter Falk who is directing a film about Nazi Berlin on a set which teems with Nazi uniforms, but the winged Ganz is also a simulacrum of Wenders himself, the director as angel and the angel as director, the Supereye of the city. This is neo-expressionism as a cinema of the Superhuman and with portentous conflation of Nietzsche and Wagner, a new version of the modern sublime. While Abuladze ridicules the politics of the sublime by uncovering its farcical untruths and its practical absurdities Wenders and screenwriter Peter Handke literally elevate the human to sublime status in the final sequence where Ganz and circus acrobat Solveig Dommartin mythologise their aerial grace and pronounce themselves Superlovers destined to produce a new sublime race of metaphysical beings. In the old-fashioned bar of the Hotel Esplanade (a former Nazi meeting place), the couple displace the punk habitués who have been listening to the decadent sounds of Nick Cave in the adjoining room.[26] Passionate Superlove is alternative Nietzsche in the modern city, a rewriting of Berlin's history to displace both its Nazi past and its Punk present. For Wenders the incongruities of life and spirit demand metaphysical redemption. In the surreal *Repentance*, there is a very different concern. Remembrance of political terror demands laughter to staunch the flow of tears.

More recently Wenders has provided a different glossing of the metaphysical in *Beyond the Clouds* (1996). That, however, is because this is a collaboration in film with the ageing, disabled Antonioni whose loose chronicle of four interwoven love stories is set in Ferrara, Portofino, Paris and Aix-en-Provence. The crossing of the north-south Euro-divide provides us with a downbeat cross-over of the expressive surreal. Antonioni's four separate episodes are connected by Wenders's filming of its main subject, film director John Malkovich, whose voice-over contains Antonioni's own ruminations on film from an earlier decade. At one level, Malkovich is a Wenders vehicle, a freewheeling free spirit, a cross between the Friedrich Murnau of *The State of Things* and Damiel the observing angel of *Wings of Desire*. Yet something strange is going on here. The voice-over ramblings seem not only ponderous and banal but incidental, for the look of Malkovich has a different resonance. In one of his best film performances to date, Malkovich observing and acting undercuts Malkovich the auteur in search of his characters since his uncanny searching throws into question the very fact of observing itself. As image, Malkovich comes across as a more sinister figure, a satanic filmmaker, a Mephistopheles in Armani clothes who seeks out with unerring eye the human failures of intimacy while proving himself in his own episode with Sophie Marceau to be a ruthless seducer who rises above human folly but also above human feeling. The auteur-observer mouthing pious humanisms becomes a clinical voyeur and at the end, one feels, a manipulator who has willed Peter Weller and Fanny Ardant into emotional calamity. Antonioni's montage in the Malkovich/Marceau sequence creates superbly the erotic tensions of abrupt consummation. By contrast, in the first sequence with Ines Sastre in Ferrara and the last sequence with Irene Jacob in Aix, the strange failures of Eros come to have the suspended and timeless quality of dream. The film director within the film here is neither God's messenger nor humanist auteur, but is best seen as bored satanic angel playing with images of human frailty as an existential sport. The film also reminds us along with *Sweetie*, *Un Coeur en hiver*, *Cyclo* and *Fallen Angels* that in the freest age of sexual expression the cinema has yet encountered, the intimate mysteries of denial are often more visually compelling than the mechanical couplings of consummation.

In a further variation on the expressive surreal we must look at a key technical development, the standardisation of colour. As black-and-white cinema recedes its look appears more mimetic than its coloured successors even though all the major formats from three-strip Technicolour onwards approximate more accurately to the colour spectrum of the eye. Over the last fifteen years, the monochrome picture has been conspicuous by its rarity. *Raging Bull* works as an homage to the look of 1940s photojournalism, Jarmusch's *Strangers in Paradise* to the existential and shabby feel of its low-budget ambience, *La Haine* to the bleakness of the ghettoised Parisian *banlieue*. The importance of colour can be seen dramatically where it bursts into narrative life out of monochrome. *Raging Bull* reverses our expectations by shooting in 35mm monochrome yet using colour home-movie reels for the respective weddings of the La Motta brothers. In *Stalker* the rhapsodic burst into colour as the three men enter the Zone at dawn is as profound as it is unexpected. The colour burst is repeated in the Estonian heist thriller *Darkness in Tallinn* as the power to the city is restored after the robbery. In *Wings of Desire* colour is the sign of angel Damiel's eventual fall to earth and the dominant colour, the blood-colour of the human body, is red in his terrestrial mindscreen, a red mirrored as vivid scarlet in the lush evening dress of Solveig Dommartin at the nightclub. All these colour bursts draw attention to its basic premise, that colour is never neutral. It has to mean something. Naturalistic colour, prevalent in early 1960s photography, is often so garish it distracts from the shape of objects and the spatial relations of characters. The use of filter and diffusion, of extreme saturation or desaturation, the elimination of primary colours by for example the bleach bypass technique, adopted for Mike Radford's *1984* and for *Distant Voices/Still Lives* as the colours of memory, introduce the subjective elements of mindscreen which mark the cinema of poetry. The more mimetic the possibilities of colour, the greater the manipulation of the image.

Colour has also led to the resurrection of painting within cinema both as inspiration and object. The look of Antonioni's cinema is indebted to De Chirico, that of Bergman to Munch, and that of Herzog to Caspar David Friedrich, while Dali and Ernst have left their surreal imprint on all of Spanish cinema. Greenaway endlessly talks up his debt to Vermeer and Georges de la Tour, while the dining-room of La Hollandaise – the name is the giveaway – in *The Cook, The Thief, His Wife and Her Lover* is framed by the huge canvas of Franz Hals whose flamboyant chevaliers are the golden age prototypes of Albert Spica's garish gangsters. Specific films have a specific painterly look. The Russian winter landscapes of Tarkovsky's *Mirror* are framed through Breughel's medieval figures skating over iced rivers. *Picnic at Hanging Rock* echoes the canvas of the Australian impressionists of the turn of the century when the film is set, the radiant colour of *Claire's Knee* was modelled by cinematographer Nelson Almendros on the colours of Gaugin while the look of life-model Emmanuelle Béart and the ruthless manipulation of her body by painter Michel Piccoli echo the technique of the later Degas and the twisted postures of his female figures. Andrew Wyeth's paintings have been a marker for both Robert Altman and Atom Egoyan while the work of Edward Hopper has had a profound effect on a whole generation of American cinematography from the films of Terrence Malick to those of John Dahl.

In Hopper's case, as with many others, specific paintings stand out as indispensable models, *House By the Railroad* for *Days of Heaven*, *Night Hawks* for *Blade Runner*, *After Hours* and *Glengarry Glenross*, while Dante Spinotti's photography for *Blink* evokes in the look of Madeleine Stowe's apartment a whole range of Hopper interiors from *Room in Brooklyn* to *Conference at Night*. This intertextuality of film and painting throughout the century is affirmed by the heritage of *Battleship Potemkin*. Eisenstein's silent masterpiece gave us the unforgettable cry of the unknown woman whose shattered face defines the horror of the Odessa

Steps massacre, but it gave it not only to us but to Francis Bacon whose expressive reworking of physiognomy has filmic origins. Bacon's framing of the human body in turn inspired the framing of Brando's despairing figure on the floor of the empty apartment in *Last Tango in Paris*. The looping is completed by that picture's self-acknowledged influence on the paintings of Glasgow New Boy Steven Campbell. Colour has a chromatic range of associations which can add indefinitely to the filmmaker's palette. The great colour films of Southern French landscapes are in that sense all indebted to the Cézanne's impressionism which has left its mark on films as diverse as *Pierrot le fou*, *Le Boucher*, *Les Biches* and *La Belle Noiseuse*. Here Pasolini's vision has to be qualified. The raw and sacred data of represented reality is often framed in the *auteur's* mind by the legacies of specific culture. Filmmakers can see the world through the viewfinder, for sure. But they can also see the world through the painted canvas of their own cultural heritage and in the age of colour they have done so more and not less. In that sense, the screen will never supersede the canvas for the simple reason that it does not need to.

Screenwriting is a much a link to the world of the text as cinematography is to the world of painting since both engage representations which are prior to the filmed image. The film director here is at a midway point and collaboration is often vital. Dramatist Jean-Claude Carrière has written most of Buñuel's screenplays while dialect poet Tonino Guerra has established an important pedigree in his scripts for Antonioni, Fellini, Rosi and Tarkovsky. Novelist Angela Carter worked closely and triumphantly with Neil Jordan on the adaptation of her *Company of Wolves* while playwright Peter Handke has collaborated with Wenders. In the 1990s Christopher McQuarrie has written the powerful screenplays of *Public Access* and *The Usual Suspects* for Bryan Singer. In France film theorist Pascal Bonitzer has worked effectively with Jacques Rivette and André Téchiné, while film theorist Paul Schrader's transition to director only makes sense in terms of his early screenplays for Scorsese. In Poland the legal background of screenwriter Kryzstzof Piesiewicz was an invaluable resource for Kieślowski. Moreover a number of screenplays stand out in their own right as powerful fusions of the verbal and the visual dimensions of the feature film. Four which spring immediately to mind are Carole Eastman's writing for *Five Easy Pieces*, Robert Towne's magnificent screenplay for

Chinatown, Caroline Thompson's witty and devastatingly precise script for *Edward Scissorhands* and Alan Sharp's acerbic re-visioning of history in adapting *Rob Roy*. Meanwhile we must never forget that in his dazzling career Pasolini was poet, critic, filmmaker and philosopher all rolled into one.

On the visual side collaboration is equally vital and enduring. Almendros worked successfully for Truffaut, Rohmer and Malick, while Sacha Vierney has worked for Resnais, Buñuel and Greenaway. Carlo di Palma now provides the invaluable service for Woody Allen he once gave Antonioni, while comparisons between Bergman and Tarkovsky are surely enhanced by Sven Nykvist's stunning visual contribution to *The Sacrifice*. The Hong Kong imaging of Wong Kar-Wai has been worked out in close collaboration with designer William Chang and cinematographer Christopher Doyle. In the United States New Yorker Gordon Willis has provided an unforgettable look for the New York films of Coppola, Allen and Pakula while Michael Chapman has done likewise for Scorsese. The transatlantic bridge in cinema which so many Europeans cross is best illustrated by Vittorio Storaro who photographed two of the most visually dazzling films ever made in colour, *The Conformist* and *Apocalypse Now*. The Europeans, moreover, can also make banal Hollywood melodrama seem dazzling, witness the architectural bravura of Dante Spinotti's LA photography amidst the various bloodbaths of *Heat* and the silver heat of expressionist inferno forged by Darius Khondji for the serial killer number-crunching of *Se7en*.

Since Pasolini wrote of it, the cinema of poetry has journeyed in ways he never imagined. In the 1990s one of the most powerful variations has been the use of parallel subjectivities, inaugurated in 1988 by the triple narrative of *Short Film About Killing*. Kieślowski's masterpiece is extraordinary because what seems primarily the story of the socio-pathic Jacek, is equally a story of his taxi-driver victim and Piotr, the lawyer who defends Jacek in his murder trial. In the triplicate narrative of the single day so fateful to all three lives, there is a near-perfect fusion of movement through space and movement through time. Before the time-switch to the trial at the end, the film begins at dawn and ends as night falls. Jacek drives his victim's taxi back to the apartment block from which the action had started earlier that day. It is a day in the life not only of the three men, but also of the peripatetic taxi in which the brutal murder takes place and finally of Warsaw itself, a city made strange by the lime-green haze of Idziak's unsettling filters. Kieślowski's three males, on different rungs in the social order, are all isolates in their own way. Jacek has no real place in the city which remains strange to him. The cab driver has a sure place but the glass and metal cage of his machine isolate him from all his fellow-beings whom he views with contempt. The young lawyer is the opposite, triumphantly putting his faith in human nature but at odds with the cynical, jaded profession which he has just joined.

We see a destitute atomistic Warsaw through the eyes of each male subject in turn, each of them making a journey through the city which seems circular and futile, constantly turning back on itself. Jacek moves on foot, Piotr on his moped, the cabby in the cab, all three of them negotiating the same world and the same space by different means. The first two moments where paths cross are dryly comic. The cabby laughs contemptuously as Piotr's moped pirouettes through traffic in celebration of entry to the Bar. Later Piotr is seen declaiming his future visions to a girlfriend in a different part of the coffee shop where Jacek is gleefully flicking cream from his éclair at two young girls looking at him through the window. These rare moments of light relief come before the two encounters which are so deeply tragic, the meeting of Jacek and his victim in the cab which ends in a relentlessly slow and brutal murder, one of the longest in screen history, and the final meeting of Jacek and Piotr, now his defence lawyer at the end of the trial where the drifter is sentenced to death, soon to be hung. Obliquely the politics of the film start to make themselves felt. Jacek's case is one in which the law condemns and then takes life but is also seen as powerless. For Kieślowski, the cement of social solidarity has cracked and crumbled in a country in the grip of martial law. Communism, which prides itself on the sovereignty of the social, has divided and isolated its subjects and is ideologically bankrupt.

Kieślowski's film disperses the mindscreen in such a way that it is separated, shared, overlaps and interweaves without disrupting the time-space rhythms of his intricate narrative. Afterwards, we somehow feel we have seen everything from Jacek's point of view since his is clearly the most desperate and most powerful. But the mindscreen is spread three ways and the tension Kieślowski creates comes precisely from this triangulation. The obsession with the single subject or with the shared experience of the bonding couple is dispersed into a set of poetic intersubjectivities. Elsewhere the sharing of mindscreen has been strengthened by the doubling or tripling of voice-over. Here one of the vital uses of voice-over has been to free the camera even further in its pursuit of visionary images, but it remains one option among many. As an inner voice which speaks outwards to the audience but not to the other characters in the film, the voice-over radically extends Kieślowski's vision of modernity in his cinema of solitude.

In the 1990s we see this diffusing of the intersubjective in world-cinema right across the board: in Scorsese's dynamically voice-overed gangsters of *Goodfellas* and *Casino*; in the alternating mindscreens of Laura and Leland Palmer in Lynch's *Fire Walk with Me*; in the double-register of Kurosawa and his oneiric subjects in the many episodes of *Dreams*; in the fluid and breathtaking poetry of Wong Kar-Wai's Hong Kong stories which have revolutionised film language for our time; and in the Taiwanese *Vive L'Amour* of Tsai Ming-Liang where spatial rivalry and doubling are such intricate themes in the lives of the young unloved. Among cult Western hits we see it in the tripled mindscreen of Gabriel Byrne, Chazz Palminteri and Kevin Spacey in *The Usual Suspects* where Spacey ingeniously doubles as unreliable narrator 'Verbal' Kint and the demonised object of his story-telling, Keysar Soze, while on a lighter note the scabrous mindscreens of narcotic schemies whiz mindlessly but cunningly through the film of Welsh's inspirational *Trainspotting*. Lastly we must go back to *Cyclo*, possibly the most complex and challenging film of the decade, which charts parallel descents to the inner circle of hell for Saigon cyclo-cabby Kien and ruthless gangster Poet, a visceral degradation ceremony which changes the meaning of cinema and ends in the purgation of fire. In general, the speed of filming which has kept pace with the increasing speed of our daily existence and with the increasing speed of the electronic image in all media, is increasingly the greater speed of the subjectivities in many of these pictures. But some of film's journeys take place in slow motion and so confound the tendentious. We must now look at some of these journeys which have given flesh to Pasolini's revelation. Some will be familiar, others surprising. The chapter headings which follow are at best cryptic clues to the mysteries of cinema which have never been fully solved, and may never be so.

Chapter 2

THE SACRIFICIAL UNCONSCIOUS:
The Red Desert to Three Colours: Blue

—⊃⊂—

Pasolini's cinema of poetry defines the encounter between the expressive irrational and bourgeois culture, but the idea had its origin in the distance that he felt between himself as Marxist director and the demythicised Christ of his *Gospel According to St Matthew* (1963). This is the source of the double-register which matches delirium of form to free indirect subjectivity. It thus originates for Pasolini in sacrilege, the sacrilegious image of a simple peasant Messiah who is beautiful but not divine, or rather whose divinity dwells for the director in his beauty. Pasolini's conscious demolition of Christian myth did not, however, eliminate his fascination with the sacralised subject as pre-rational. If anything, it intensified it. After 1965 he decided the pre-rational needed a more primal foundation, one he explored through a series of surreal polemics against modern taboos on sexuality and sacrifice. His work bore mixed results. *Theorem*, whose title may show the film to be a 'theorem' for his cinema of poetry, pits bourgeois pretension against angelic sexuality, the normal against the polymorphous, the civilised against the irrational. Yet more is at stake. His bourgeois Milan family are the beneficiaries of the God of Eros whose angelic messenger is Terence Stamp and while Stamp's bisexual seductions have a satirical edge, the beautiful Angel is an idealised figure of Pasolini's homoerotic imagination. *Theorem* ends up as comic and surreal and it draws its power from its cool Buñuelian regard, not its portentous metaphysics. The serious quest for the irrational then took Pasolini back into classical tragedy where he explored a poetry of archaic sacrifice, culminating

32

powerfully in *Medea* and aided by the astonishing performance of Maria Callas. The locations for his classical tragedies – *Edipo Re* in Morocco, *Medea* in Anatolian Turkey – also took him away from European landscapes.[1] Yet in looking for new themes Pasolini was never entirely happy with either the present or the past. *Il Porcile* matches medieval cannibalism with modern bestiality but for all the ferocious savagery of its satire, it still suggests intellectual contrivance. When he finally returned to the twentieth century in *Salo*, the result is disastrous. Yet his desire to experiment with the taboos of his own time had set an important precedent which others would soon follow.

It is precisely those filmmakers who stay with modernity and discover traces of the sacred in material, secular culture, that take film into new dimensions. To illuminate this we can look at the perceptive gloss of Raul Ruiz on Walter Benjamin's concept of 'the photographic unconscious'. For Ruiz and Benjamin the term has evoked a distinctive but unrecognised feature of the still photo in the age of mechanical reproduction.[2] It produces a set of signs hovering like ghosts around the still image and evoking an uncanny conspiracy of absent meanings which intrigue but elude us. This, I would argue, recurs in contemporary cinema in the filmic projection of a *sacrificial unconscious*. Here Pasolini's double-register is the medium through which the sacrificial trace is crystallised as moving image. It brings forth a spectral presence, the ghost of the past which hovers over the modern and it produces that uncanny paradox of recent cinema, the profane sacrifice, the trace of the sacrificial experience lived without ritual in the absence of the divine.

Nietzsche prophesied that twentieth-century art would be founded on a very specific wager. 'To sacrifice God for nothingness,' Nietzsche wrote, '– this paradoxical mystery of the ultimate act of cruelty was reserved for the generation which is now arising.'[3] The Pasolinian aesthetic explores its own exchange of the sacred for the profane, and in so doing rediscovers sacrifice at the heart of nothingness. In other words, it explores Nietzsche's 'paradoxical mystery' only to find nothingness in the place of rational progress, and within that nothingness the uncanny presence of sacrificial remains. This sits uneasily with the ethos of modernity where, after all, sacrifice is the downside of the sacred. We now live in an age where the discourse of human rights, always multiple, fragile, betrayed, contradictory and unresolved, has

largely prevailed. While literal sacrifice is seen as an archaic relic the
metaphorical discourse of sacrifice, however, is still with us as a material force. As noun and verb, it has a use in common language verging
on the indispensable. Simmel, indeed, had said that sacrifice was the
basis of all modern economic exchange since the transfer of objects
means giving up one thing for something else. Here we sacrifice
objects, not living creatures, and it is we the sacrificers who suffer. We
make sacrifices not to the Gods but to others as a means to material
gain. Yet the priority of value – the thing gained is better than the thing
relinquished – at times cannot alter our pain at what is lost. There is a
rationale to the judicious weighing of means and ends which means,
it would seem, that sacrifice becomes endemic in the modern psyche.
If sacrifice is inseparable from scarcity in this respect, then it is inherent in our culture as the pragmatic attribute of a profane experience,
inseparable from rational calculation. But rational ethics often introduce
a stress on altruism in moral discourse which in turn bears echoes of
the Christian Passion, the historic substitution of self-sacrifice for
others in the place of both the sacrificing of others and the meaningless sacrifice of self. The Passion in turn has been one of the incubators
of the modern visual icon.

In this context, Christ has been a central figure in the transformation
of religious imagery into Renaissance art. But this iconography merely
intensifies the imagistic enigma of the Passion. Zizek has contended
that Christian myth provides an answer to the enduring puzzle of Judaic
belief, an answer to the unanswerable question 'Che Vuoi?' What does
our absent, invisible God want of us? The icon fills in an absence which
can be unendurable, the absence which is 'the desire of the Other in
its terrifying abyss, with the formal prohibition to "make an image of
God"'.[4] The Christian myth propagated by Hellenised Jews can thus
be read as a doubled resolution of God's absence which works simultaneously as spirit and image. An inspired local prophet, Jesus, becomes
the universal Son of God, the divine Christ. At the same time and in
the same mythic breath, the prohibition of images appears to be eliminated. The image of his divine presence is exalted, and the crucifixion
becomes the enduring visual moment of sacrifice visually implanted in
the collective memory. For Zizek, the heretical Lacanian, it becomes a
fantasy-scenario, a 'fascinating image which cancels all other images'.[5]
Technically, the prohibition remains but the Passion is exempted. The

sacrificial unconscious of modern cinema echoes this uncanny fusion of divine spirit and divine image with its uncanny fusion of destitute spirit and moving image. It also provides a vital context for Adorno's notorious critique of Enlightenment which, perverse and cranky at times, pinpoints the mythic undercurrents of modern rationality, first in the renunciation ethic of salvational Protestantism so important for early capitalism and later in the sacrifice of autonomy to the fetishes of consumer capitalism. Here a further paradox ensued. Greater freedom from material sacrifice has been achieved only by sacrificing self-autonomy to a consumerism controlling human need. One form of sacrifice is expiated but only through another. Soviet communism, by contrast, sacrificed autonomy to the fetish of industrial production. Under both systems, East and West, renunciation has been inseparable from the cult of the machine. From *Metropolis* and *Modern Times* to *Blade Runner* and *Apocalypse Now* that fetish has been a source of constant movie fascination. Here is an even darker way to look at the twentieth century, the machine as source of the various sacrifices of humans to war, production, nation, empire. Soldiers, workers, civilians must die in order to guarantee the future of others, or so the rationale of sacrifice, that unerring logic of perverse substitution would have us believe. If we are the beneficiaries, so be it. The sacrificing Other was, therefore We are. The sacrificing Other no longer is, therefore We shall be. But things change. The mass slaughter of two world wars, the Holocaust, organised bloodshed in Korea, Vietnam and Afghanistan have all had their impact. The wars of the advanced industrial powers in the nuclear age are now fought by professional armies. For who wants to sacrifice themselves in distant lands?

The experience of Vietnam, as *Apocalypse Now* demonstrates, was one in which sacrifice did not come easily for American soldiers who took into combat most of the values they had absorbed from a consumer society back home. Coppola's film is pathbreaking for two reasons. It creates superb melodrama out of its central conflict of renunciation and consumption, brutal death in the jungle versus drugs, sex and rock-'n'-roll, and as in Greenaway the modern passion for consuming is the objective correlative of baroque flamboyance in the *mise-en-scène*. The second reason runs deeper. The war is seen and displayed as insane, as devoid of principle, of lacking clear relation in its rhetoric of cause and effect, and thus failing the guarantee that combat will be

construed in retrospect as heroic sacrifice. Indeed, by the time of
Coppola's film, it was clearly not. The vain search for heroic action, we
may recall, had sent Kurtz, insane Green Beret and Willard's military
alter ego, over into Cambodia to continue to fight the guerilla war with
the tribal Montagnards. If combat has been made profane because it is
insane, part of Kurtz's insanity is to sacralise combat through the most
barbaric means, to regress to the primitive. The guiding idea of the film
which Coppola fails to realise in its excessive ending, is this regression
to primitive sacrifice when rational sacrifice – the defence of a 'democratic' South Vietnam against 'Charlie' – has become a meaningless
charade. As Willard seeks to terminate Kurtz without prejudice, he is
killing his double who instead of rejecting military sacrifice for R & R
like his enlisted troops, seeks it out in a deeper form.

This updates what Girard has grandly called 'the sacrificial crisis' of
the modern age.[6] With the rise of universal law sacrifice has long lost
the troubled function that it had in the ancient world where, Girard
claims, it aimed to control violent reciprocity through presenting the
surrogate victim for slaughter. Instead it now centres if anywhere on
the figure of Christ, the final substitution of self-sacrifice for blood-
sacrifice in the modern world. Yet in a consumer age the growing
divorce of culture and Christianity has largely transformed the figure of
Christ into an effigy of seasonal consumption, his birth travestied in
the spending spree of 'Christmas' while he appears to have died at
Easter in order that we may consume all the more. Crucifixion in the
shopping mall. A film which explores this surreal incongruence and by
so doing has struck a chord with audiences around the world is Denys
Arcand's French-Canadian fable, *Jesus of Montreal* (1989).

Arcand's Jesus (Lothaire Bluteau) is an actor, Daniel, who watches a
failing Passion Play and recruits other actors to develop a more Brechtian
performance in the grounds of Montreal's Mon Royal Cathedral. He is,
literally, an imitation of Christ, recruiting players and not disciples, but
in such a way that analogy takes hold. His Brechtian preference for
research into the historical Jesus over the myth of a Divine Christ leads
the play into trouble with the Church authorities who decide to ban
it. Before then Daniel has rescued Mireille, his 'Magdalene', from an
audition for a sleazy beer commercial where his angry destruction of
the studio and its electronic gear is analogous to the cleansing of the
merchants from the temple. Later after notoriety has brought him

media attention, a sleazeball entertainment lawyer tries to seduce him into a package deal to do tours and television spots with a glossier, more spectacular production of the Passion. As they stand in a glasstop restaurant overlooking Montreal he declares 'The city is yours'. In this version of Matthew 4, the Satanic temptation takes place not in the desert but in a sleek post-modern building at the centre of a North-American city.[7] Material corruption is presented in contemporary terms, the glitter, luxury and decadence of objects desired and the desire consummated. Arcand combines satire with tragedy in the sequence where Christ's crucifixion leads to his death. As Daniel acts, strapped to a cross in the Cathedral grounds, a spectator clashes with the police ordered to the performance. In the melée the cross crashes to the ground and Daniel is knocked unconscious. As in Pirandello's *Henry IV*, the actor's injury precipitates the illusion that he really is the historic figure he is impersonating. Delirious, he becomes the 'Jesus' he has performed. When he dies soon after in a Jewish hospital his internal organs, in mimesis of the transcendence of the Holy Spirit, are taken from his body as possible transplants to 'save' the lives of others. *Jesus of Montreal* is a powerful film because it was a conscious trans-position of myth to the present which also awakened a sacrificial unconscious through homology, finding topical settings for the narrated incidents of the Gospels and following the pattern of that narration without overt signifying. Within Christian cultures, audiences are vaguely conscious of the allusions, and this is enough to give the parallels their narrative power.

Cinema has rarely played so directly upon the secular imitation of the Christian Passion. We can note here two films by Christian directors which are self-conscious imitations of the Passion-within-modernity, but without the Brechtian distancing of *Jesus of Montreal*. In place of spectral haunting, so to speak, we are given the explicit sign. Tarkovsky's aptly named *The Sacrifice* and Von Trier's *Breaking the Waves* oscillate between the lure that sacrifice has for the Christian soul and its absurdity to the secular eye. Tarkovsky's last film, made in exile, highlights that oscillation in his fable of impending apocalypse. Faced on a remote Swedish island with the threat of nuclear war and alarmed by the constant whine of unseen jets flying low over his summer house, theatre director Alexander (Erland Josephson) makes a pact with God to become a recluse in order to save his family. But the framing of

the pledge has the look and structure of a dream, connoting hallucination both under the mental pressure of impending breakdown and
through the effect of a playful blow to the head by his son, Little Man.[8]
The transition from the real to the hallucinatory is signified by the
zoom into a reproduction of Leonardo's *Adoration of the Magi*, and
through the change of colour in Sven Nyquist's photography, black-
and-white for the hallucinations of apocalypse – city crowds fleeing
in terror – and desaturated low-lit colours for the nocturnal sequences
in the house. Like Buñuel, Tarkovsky creates the oneiric spiral of a
dream-within-a-dream. He later repeats the zoom shot on the painting to signal the alternate desire of the dreaming patriarchal brain
when Alexander is tempted by Otto his eccentric postman to meet a
foreign woman named Maria and secretly seduce her. The plea of the
God-dream is transformed into the pleasure of the desire-dream as the
last night on earth. The second 'sacrifice' is a wish-dream which his
dreaming brain scrambles through the dubious rationale of desire as
carnal sacrifice. At dawn, when the nuclear crisis has passed, he keeps
his side of the hallucinated bargain with God and turns his summer
house into a blazing pyre. His distraught family think him insane and he
is bundled into an ambulance to be driven away. We are left divided
between two readings. The sacrifice is real yet mysterious, or else it is
the fantasy of a deranged mind. It is the oscillation between the two
readings which creates our distance from the subject. At one level there
is a conscious exoneration of divine sacrifice by Tarkovsky, at another an
undermining of it through the profane concerns of modernity-at-risk,
whose pressures are unendurable.

Tarkovsky distorts the distancing Pasolini double-register since he
immerses himself in his imploding patriarch to the detriment of his
female characters. Indeed his conscious agenda is to contend 'God's
silence', that powerful trope in those films of Bergman which influenced
him most, *Through a Glass Darkly*, *The Silence* and *Shame*. As an Ortho-
dox believer, Tarkovsky polemically reinstates God's presence but it
remains ambiguously the presence of hallucinated voices and images.
The Sacrifice is a haunting film because of the tension between explicit
polemic and the power of dream. Yet a vital paradox remains. Sacrifice
is made too explicit at times and too melodramatic to do justice to its
mystery or to its aesthetic form. Where Tarkovsky's film rides out its
weakness, *Breaking the Waves* capsizes for the same reason. It has the

same Christian agenda in condoning the pain of sacrifice but though inventively filmed, its surrogate biblical narrative is put through the mincing machine of hospital melodrama and ends in explicit vindication of male power. Beth, brilliantly played by Emily Watson, is the True Believer on Skye who sacrifices body and life for Jan, her Danish husband paralysed by an oil rig accident. Conveniently, the miracle of his subsequent cure allows him to attend her funeral. Von Trier uses Free Church dogma to kickstart hospital melodrama so that Beth expiates her guilt by obeying Jan's perverse demand that she sell her body to others in his absence. Religious anguish, Von Trier admits, is a tactical device to trigger the hospital conflict between patient, wife, nurse and doctor.[9] Watson plays the sacrificial victim with the radiant righteousness of a justified sinner and many viewers have responded strongly. Yet unlike Bill Douglas who portrays childhood destitution in a religious culture as a sacrificial unconscious that cannot be named, and unlike Bergman who bases sacrifice on God's 'silence', Beth's child-like sacrifice is explained away by the fanaticism of the righteous few.

As a modern image of female crucifixion, this pales in comparison with *Vagabond*, which makes no concessions to male power. The abiding image of Beth is of the desperate sinner running frantically to the door of the unrelenting Kirk in high boots and hot pants, a truly kitsch, late 1960s image of female wantonness. The remarkable zoom which opens *Vagabond* upon the distant frozen corpse of Sandrine Bonnaire has a different resonance. With luminous pale blue lighting upon a rounded hillock it has been framed, Hayward has suggested, with reference to Piero della Francesca's fresco, *Resurrection of Christ*, and the zoom moves forward through this Quattrocento perspective on deep space which had transformed Christian myth.[10] Thus the naturalistic shot in a winter landscape of the frozen corpse of a female drifter is itself framed through a painterly representation of a crucifixion myth. But there is no cross, no crucifixion, only a blood-red stain which we discover through flashback is paint forcibly daubed on her in town as a pagan rite of male possession during a local wine festival. Narratively the film moves forward from pagan to Christian myth but its flashback form sends it in the opposite direction. We regress through sacrificial traces until the films loops itself in the rediscovery of death.

Let us probe here more deeply into film form. Eisenstein once noted a powerful bond between sacrifice and the sacred image. As mimesis, film is more than just a form of mechanical reproduction. Imitation becomes, as he points out, not just mastery of form but at the same time mastery of the object. While Christ is said to have sacrificed himself for the world, his sacred image can be seen as quite the reverse, a model of imitation, an idealised human resemblance of oneself for which one is prepared to sacrifice one's own self-image. 'The sacrifice of one's own image in the form of human likeness in order to achieve eternal life: does not the same idea,' demanded Eisenstein, 'also lie at the basis of the Christian myth?'[11] Communion may be a sacrament by which believers can 'share' in salvation, but it is also a sacrament in which they retrospectively sacrifice themselves to the image they wish to resemble, and which image they hope to appropriate by losing their own. To 'represent' here means to re-present oneself through the likeness of the ideal other, not to show the world as it is. The sacred doubling of communion has its profane equivalent, its Nietzschean mimesis, in film where the auteur of the feature passes over into the screen character through the medium of the actor sacrificed to the persona of the fiction. To lose oneself in the ideal image is a form of relinquishment whose final goal is mastery. There are intriguing historical comparisons of the preserved image. In prehistoric burial rituals the mummy was sometimes intended to preserve the image of the sacrificed creature for the pleasure of the Gods, while some critics have conjectured that animals on prehistoric wall-paintings are sacrificial icons. Today the film process preserves the represented image, Bazin's 'mummified image', for the pleasure of spectators who are lured by the mirage of transparency, who see the imprint of the will-to-mimesis as moving image but not its power source. In film, the mimetic image is never pure. Where the reflexive camera reveals itself, it disavows mimetic purity by its intrusion. Where the camera hides itself as 'invisible' it disavows mimetic purity through disguise – disguise, that is, of the filmed object as sacrificial offering to the eternity of art. This is surely the central theme of Rivette's *La Belle Noiseuse* (1991) in which the act of painting is an act of power exercised over painter Michel Piccoli's life-model, Emmanuelle Béart, whose likeness in the finished canvas, unseen by the audience, he then bricks into the wall of the studio, never to be seen by anyone. The buried image of Béart, inverted over the previous image on the same canvas from years before of Piccoli's wife (Jane Birkin) who had also been his life-model, is an uncanny echo of the ancient mummified image. But as the cruel spread-arm posture of Béart at one point makes clear, something else is happening too. The sacrificial image – the crucifixion pose – becomes the sacrificed image – the image buried from sight – sacrificed not to God but to nothingness.

A grouping of features around profane sacrifice allows us to illustrate its course over the last thirty years. *The Red Desert* and *Stalker* deal with the modern ecologies of destruction and their human impact. *Apocalypse Now* and *Blade Runner* explore the connections between sacrifice and paranoia in the world of advanced technology. *Aguirre, Wrath of God* and for Antipodean cinema, *The Piano* and *Picnic at Hanging Rock*, probe the colonial histories of sacrificial intent as founding myths. Tarkovsky's *The Sacrifice* and Greenaway's most powerful films *Belly of an Architect* and *The Cook, The Thief, His Wife and Her Lover* highlight the sacrificial crisis through the crisis of modern patriarchy. *Three Colours: Blue* and *The Adjuster* explore the relationship between catastrophe and redemption in the modern secular city, respectively Paris and Toronto. The nuclei of the sacrificial unconscious are *Stalker* and *The Red Desert* which seem on repeated viewings to illuminate the point at which modernity and sacrifice intersect. Yet this collision has better-known dystopian echoes in the genetic engineering which governs human destiny in Ridley Scott's *Blade Runner* released in 1982, just three years after the appearance of Tarkovsky's dystopian masterpiece. If the modern world is a synonym for sacrificial crisis, these three films point to the nucleus of that crisis. It is to be found, as Calasso has stressed, in a modern discourse devoted to experiment and technology, the nuclei around which the various rhetorics of sacrifice has constantly revolved. 'The central role that sacrifice played in archaic societies has been assumed by experimentation,' Calasso asserts, 'the richest of which is war.'[12] People in the twentieth century are periodically sacrificed to the technologies which are supposed to help them. Profane sacrifice is the warped teleology which emerges from the breakdown of progress and reason. Injury, loss, destruction, death are both regrettable accidents and human offerings to the silent Gods of technology. But if technology and experiment were simply profane processes the rhetoric could not be sustained. What contemporary film has shown is the awe and wonder which is attached by its audiences to advanced inventions, the seductions of the technological sublime. Here the sacred is preserved in the celebration of the power of speed, both as delirious motion and destruction. It comes in the worship of cars and planes, jets, rockets and helicopters, and since the Gulf War, laser-guided missiles. The opening shot of *Apocalypse Now* with its silent, gliding fleet of jungle choppers, rotor blades whirring, connotes a visitation of avenging angels upon unseen defilers of an unknown God. In *Blade Runner* the superb studio model of the neo-Mayan skyscraper which houses the Tyrell Corporation, world-hub of genetic engineering, has the uncanny look of a futuristic temple of sacrifice which echoes the sacrifices of the past. In both films the awe and wonder of the widescreen sublime envelop their audiences as a terrible beauty of technologies out of control. The Replicants who are dumped on the sacrificial altar of genetic engineering plot to take their murderous revenge. Since this after all is LA, it can be seen as the revolt of the beautiful people who are perfect products out of Central Casting but not, however, all that human, the casualties of advanced plastic surgery with punk deformities. Here the film spotlights the direct line between sacrifice and paranoia which suffuses recent American cinema. If the replicants have escaped and can go undetected, can act normal, then who in Los Angeles in 2019 is to know if they too have not been replicated. If Darryl Hannah, why not Sean Young? If Rutger Hauer, why not Harrison Ford?

In *Stalker* and *The Red Desert* the destructiveness of science is conveyed differently and with more enduring power. It is destruction as absent presence, as the uncanny, the unspoken, never explicit, never obvious. Consequently it is anathema to myth. It is sacrifice as unspoken experience, a sacrifice degree-zero. Its aesthetic parallel lies in Robert Bresson's encounter with tradition, the rural cruelty with direct human agency but no final cause we find in *Mouchette* and *Au Hazard, Balthazar*. Mouchette is the young, abused victim of village ridicule yet she is the quintessentially Bressonian figure, who as Tarkovsky notes, does not for one minute reflect on her predicament or convey it to the audience in the style of Hollywood melodrama.[13] We can attribute her suffering to the cruelty and neglect of others, as we can with Bresson's hapless donkey, Balthazar, and thus to unrecognised sacrifice. With Antonioni things are more complex. *The Red Desert* contains no overt cruelty. Instead, Giuliana (Monica Vitti) suffers incomprehension by her bourgeois circle, with the result that the collective gaze of the Other deems her embarrassing and hysterical. In *Stalker* the maverick guide to the mysterious, forbidden Zone is under no obvious pressure to continue his dangerous work, if anything the opposite. Both Giuliana and Stalker can be viewed, objectively, as victims of what Ulrich Beck has called 'risk society', of the abstract nature of technology's greatest dangers. But the audience must fill in that enigmatic 'victimhood'. In both films, the querying 'how' and 'why' of action are subordinate to the questing 'where', to a visual questioning of time and place, Heideggerian 'thereness' of Being which the camera must seek out and find. The sources of danger confronting the subjects are partly unseen, often unspecified, the blight of toxic invisibility, poisonous residues, detritus on a landscape they must daily navigate, and which the cinematic image brings forth.

From the opening sequence where the figures outside the factory walls wear ghostly capes transparent in the rain, colour is a defining quality of *The Red Desert*. But the real shock is Giuliana's bright green coat, arbitrary and distracting, until we notice the colour green is virtually absent from the landscape around her. Through a strange anthropomorphic switch her figure seems to have taken on in garish hues the normal colours of trees and plants which are now black and withered in their winter setting. When she turns to see yellow spurts of poisonous flame come out of the refinery's stacks, the yellow seems a further dilution of the green which is not there, a travesty of nature like the colour of the coat she wears.[14] In the soot-grey winter wasteland with its smouldering dumps, colour inverts nature and culture. Yet this is not the unrelieved wasteland of *Stalker* where the inside seems merely an extension of the outside, but a juxtaposition between polluted exterior and sealed-off interiors of office and apartment, a sealing off from consequence through cool abstract design and misplaced sophistication. While nature and culture at times cross over and merge, hygiene and pollution are a binary motif throughout the film. The white interiors of the refinery complex, filmed as an abstract labyrinth in which all the characters seem to lose themselves, connote a purity made false by the refinery's effluent. Yet still the size and power and noise of the complex give rise to a sense of awe and wonder, clinched in a sequence where husband Ugo (Carlo Chionetti) and Corrado the visiting engineer (Richard Harris) are enveloped in a massive discharge of steam which gushes out of the side of the refinery and fills the screen. Everywhere discharged vapours merge with the mists of the polluted river in telephoto shots to create a veil which blocks the power of the gaze. The swirl around the two men is a defining image, visual testimony to the power of technology and the energies it unleashes. By comparison, their conversation is banal.

Giuliana's apartment seems entropic, abstract and sterile, designed by her in blue, in 'cold, undisturbing colours' as she calls them. Their coldness is accentuated by her son's toy robot which walks mechanically back and forth across the room, and the void is conveyed further by the empty shop where she hopes to sell ceramics. The sexual double life of the provincial bourgeois is reduced to a play upon colour. The apartment blue is contrasted with the red alcove in the river hut, signifier of fertility and scene of the 'orgy' with husband and friends. The 'orgy' which ensues is an orgy of touching, not coupling, a ritual charade in which the couples play at promiscuity until entropy sets in. The hut with its log fire, red mirror and red wall is a mock incubator of fertility and to make the point Giuliana eats 'fortified hen's eggs' as an aphrodisiac for the love-making which never takes place. The major act of passion here is not the group's eruption into group sex but the hut's eruption into the colour red, as they wantonly pull down a blue partition to feed the fire in the stove and open themselves up to the redness of the alcove. Red floods the interior but has little resonance, for the exterior will always intrude. The hut window acts as a screen onto which is projected the telephoto image of a large ship passing along the canal, a hallucinatory image which becomes real when they go outside and the ship hoists a yellow flag to signal an infectious disease on board. Smallpox, cholera, leprosy? We never know. But yellow, the colour of poison, has superseded red, the colour of desire. Giuliana's madness lies in the immediacy of the gaze upon blurred objects of disaster to which she has no resistance. 'What do people expect me to do with my eyes?' she pleads, 'What should I look at?'

As the film charts her relapse, it uses a series of doubling images. She tells Corrado the story of a woman in the hospital where she was treated after her car crash, a patient advised by her doctors to learn to love her husband, son, dog, and mother, but who still feels she is on the verge of dying. She later tells her sick son the story of a girl on a beach in Sardinia who sees a sailing ship as she swims amidst the blue coral and wishes to join it on its mysterious journey. Both the woman and the girl are versions of herself, one the self from which she cannot escape, the other a portrait of herself as young girl longing to escape her present life. She voices the Sardinian story over incandescent images of the coastline under a summer sun, the antithesis of her everyday world, a mindscreen of escape and mystery, a longing for the harmony with nature she can never possess, speaking of a mysterious voice singing a mysterious song across rocks which look like flesh. 'Who was singing?' her son asks. 'Everything was singing,' she replies. If industrial Ravenna is her *Inferno* then coastal Sardinia is her imaginary *Paradiso* – but merely a passing imaginary in her daily world.

Her breakdown is not framed in terms of the Cure which heals all, as it is for Hedren in *Marnie*, but in terms of the sacrificial unconscious to which circumstance gives no obvious clues. She inhabits the same world as others who do not suffer the same symptoms. Her husband was in the same accident, her friends walk through the same polluted landscapes with their bourgeois normality of working hard and playing hard, and blithely ignoring what she cannot. 'We all suffer it a little,' Corrado tells her. 'We all need to be cured.' But the cure is even more elusive than the illness. 'There's something terrible in reality and I don't know what it is.' The reply reveals her as the exception, the one who cannot accept what others suffer lightly. It is almost as if she must suffer greatly, therefore, in order that they suffer little. But the *as if* remains an *as if*. There is no confirmation. It is hovering, indefinable, the ghost of a sacrifice which dare not speak its name.

Three American films of the 1990s echo different aspects of this oblique connection of trauma and mindscreen: Peter Weir's *Fearless* (1993) with Jeff Bridges, Todd Haynes's *Safe* (1995) with Julianne Moore, and Michael Tolkien's *The Rapture* (1991) with Mimi Rogers. All are films about the New Age textures of southern California. Bridges survives a plane crash in the desert near Bakersfield in which his best friend dies, then suffers through his guilt at surviving a compulsion to repeat the disaster he escaped. Still traumatised, his obsessive compulsion to repeat turns him into a sacrificial victim in the stakes of air travel, one of the unfortunate few who died at the hands of a technology which affects us all and normally works. A suburban wife and mother in the San Fernando valley, Moore suffers a mysterious respiratory illness, a multiple chemical syndrome which forces her into an oxygen mask and finally to leave her family for an eco-treatment commune in the New Mexican desert. Rogers is a telephone operator into clubbing and casual sex who forsakes promiscuity for evangelical religion after her husband's murder, a fatal swap which leads her to sacrifice her daughter in the Californian desert to the coming Apocalypse.

All three films echo the plight of Vitti. A crucial member of the nuclear family, openly prosperous, endures breakdown through the breakdown of the technologies which help to make their families prosperous. While the dilemma is constant, the breakdown has different consequences for all three and their stories are told through forms of the free indirect subjectivity which Antonioni had forged in *The Red Desert*. But all three films indicate the difficulties of sustaining the link between social critique and poetic mindscreen. New age discourse – the spoken language of therapy and conversion – is part of the New Age culture the films try to satirise, but the sense of balance between involvement and mockery is often difficult. It tends towards a flatness of melodrama. In *Fearless* the weakest sequences are the survivor sessions run by company therapist John Turturro. In *Safe* they are the New Age sequences in the remote therapy centre in New Mexico, which oscillate uneasily between seriousness and satire, and in *The Rapture* the evangelical therapy which weans the traumatised Rogers, whose husband has been murdered, away from her promiscuous life. The conflict between objective and mindscreen narratives has to do with the culture of American melodrama which affects even autonomous filmmakers like Weir, Haynes and Tolkien. The spoken discourse becomes a crucial plot element which mars the considerable visual imagination in all three films. When we are no longer shown what is happening but told, discursively, in a basic visual surround, poetic mindscreen gives way to the telling of the tale. Yet it is in the showing, not the telling of the tale, that the social referent remains more powerful.

Stalker takes the sacrificial unconscious into even deeper territory than *The Red Desert* and contrasts with the later ideology of sacrifice Tarkovsky explored with mixed results in *Nostalghia* (1983) and *The Sacrifice*. Though adapted as a screenplay from their science-fiction *Roadside Picnic* by the Strugatsky brothers, Tarkovsky's shooting script eliminated most of their futuristic references and dissolved their concept of the fantastic. The film minimises plot and plays on the paradox at the heart of the sacrificial unconscious, the dystopian present.

The future is here and now and its terror lies in the ordinary. Given the aristocratic precepts of Tarkovsky's elevated idea of modern art and the difficulties he actively imposes on the viewer, a hostile critic might want to call this a film about three men and a dog which deserves to be watched by only three men and a dog. But it should be seen by everyone who goes to the cinema. With the autobiographical *Mirror* it was that part of Tarkovsky's work most rooted in the experience of everyday Soviet life. Whereas *Mirror* had been an intimate memory-film which mixed documentary and dream and juxtaposed organic images of rural life against the modern destructive technologies of war, *Stalker* has a greater unity of time and place and a more coherent vision of the world. Because it is sparse and minimal – it *is* largely about three men and a dog – it evokes a world in macrocosm, as if the boundaries of the Zone are the physical boundaries of the Soviet Union itself. Moreover it matches its political concerns to a delirium of form. 'Poetry is not a genre,' Tarkovsky has stated, 'but an awareness of the world.'[15] This is evident in the terrible beauty of *Stalker's* aesthetic, so different from that of *Mirror* which seeks and finds solace in the remembered wheatfields of childhood swept by a gentle and silent wind.

The contemplative camera of both films with their long takes and slow gliding tracks is the opposite of Eisenstein's concept of montage which had been such a driving force in Soviet cinema. Tarkovsky's stress on time and rhythm was an alternative view of the realities of existence established by the frame and not the montage. That frame is the vessel of mindscreen since it has to encompass the interior world of the character. The mindscreen of *Stalker* is the shared experience of its three males in which the Stalker, once more repeating his dangerous journey into the Zone, is the dominant figure, the guide in a spiritual as well as a physical sense. The Zone in *Stalker* is an arena of mystery shadowed by Soviet history. It is not, as Tarkovsky stresses, in any way allegorical. It is itself and does not stand for something else. Shot largely on location in Estonia, it is a recreated dystopian landscape into which its audience can read an infinite number of things. The Zone is forbid-den but never fully known. The introductory scientist's caption tells us 'we sent in troops . . . None returned. What was it? A meteorite?' The question is one the film never answers. The Zone is both wasteland and, miracle of miracles, a green desert and a place of hope. What shadowed it during the Cold War were the real forbidden zones of the

Soviet state, from the protected cities like Mayak and the prison Gulags to nuclear complexes like Chernobyl. To say that *Stalker* prefigures Chernobyl – literally 'Wormwood', the star of Revelations – is true enough. But it also comes in the wake of Mayak, that incubator of unreported radioactive disasters, the nuclear city guarded by barbed-wire and internal security troops.[16] *Stalker* is not so much art imitating life as art bridging the time-span of nuclear accidents. Its dystopian present looks forward and backward at the same time. Its presentness is never overtly futuristic, while its references to the past are always oblique.

We never fully know what the Writer and the Scientist seek from the Zone nor why the Stalker, to the despair of his abandoned spouse, enters once more into the obsessive rites of danger which govern his life. 'How can I put a name to what I want?' the Scientist asks. The Zone is thus a realm of indeterminacy across which float endless possibilities, including the Scientist's apparent attempt to destroy the Zone with a bomb. The Writer too denies seeking poetic inspiration from the Zone, so that it comes to mean all things to all adventurers, and the Stalker himself is the servant of this indeterminacy, the guide to that which cannot be named. Yet destiny, we feel, is ineffable. The opening sequence connotes this very strongly in the Stalker's dawn awakening, a Heideggerian call to danger. The camera tracks forward through half-open doors into the room where the family is sleeping, pans across the faces, showing wife and daughter asleep while the Stalker stares upwards with open eyes. It then cuts to a glass on the table vibrating with the sound of a passing train, whose rhythms are a call to the journey the Stalker must undertake once more. The 'waking' is almost a waking into nightmare, a nightmare of repetition which seems like an extension of what Hobson has called the 'dreaming brain', where the thought structures of dreaming are a distorted continuation of those in waking life, no longer nourished by the external stimuli of the senses.[17] The Heideggerian waking achieves the dreaming state in the oneiric narrative by reversing the falling into sleep. For this is a 'falling' into danger. The camera tracks back with the Stalker as he leaves through the door, but in a single take it also records the despairing rage of his abandoned spouse as she keels over and falls to the floor, cursing him. Her pleas for his safety go unheeded. 'Jail?' he queries. 'But I'm imprisoned everywhere. Let me go.' Alexander

Kaidonovsky's shaven head suggests a Gulag inmate. There is a cut from the inert body of the deserted woman to the speeding train – a moment of stasis succeeded by the rush of mechanical motion. It is this sound which governs the Stalker's destiny.

The harsh angular features of Kaidanovsky's face suggest heroic invincibility, Soviet-style, but this, like *The Red Desert*, is a narrative of breakdown, that of a war-scarred veteran whose compulsion to repeat has destroyed all resilience. The journey to the Zone is both linear and circular. There is a beautiful 180-degree panning shot which captures the circular movement of the jeep as it carves its way through warehouse junkyards to jump onto the rail track and cross the forbidden border behind a goods train, fired upon by unseen guards. The deep-focus of the border zone is replaced by telephoto profile shots of the men now on a flatcar passing through a blurred landscape. As the flatcar reaches the Zone at dawn the screen explodes into the deep saturated greens of open landscape. Yet the dawn mist works as a shroud which conceals the shapes and objects of the Zone, adding to its mystery. It is pure mindscreen.'It's just as if at each stage,' the Stalker remarks,'we've made it by our state of mind.'The Stalker's dream by the pool of water adds to this, where he dreams in gold of the place at which he sleeps, so that dream is contiguous with waking reality. Thus the black mongrel silhouetted against the water who goes up and sits next to his prostrate figure is both of his dream and his waking life. Coming as if out of a dream it eventually returns with him back from the Zone to the city. The Stalker also hears voices, warning voices and voices of the prophecy of Revelations which have no clear source. Sound becomes as phantasmagoric as image as the three men make their way to the threshold of the mysterious room which they never enter. Here the elliptical cut from the threshold of the room to the bar in the city from which they have started, is also a dream leap in time-space made more pointed by the earlier shot of the disappearing trolley which the Stalker has sent back along the line. How did they return? The question is never answered for the narrative has already assumed the logic of dream and the question, though never superfluous, can never be answered.

In the convoluted journey through the Zone where the Stalker throws metal nuts tied in bandages to uncover radioactive waste, he gives the appearance of the sacrificed who wishes to be the sacrificer, the endangered lackey who wishes to be king of the Zone and decide the fate of its unwelcome visitors. Thus he prompts the Writer to lead them through the curving underground pipe topped by icicles, the most dangerous part of the journey, and hides behind the taller figure of the Scientist as he watches from afar, the guide being guided, a stalker who has lost his nerve. The role-reversal is a signifier of substitution, the secret desire to sacrifice the interlopers to the purity of the sacred Zone, and thus end the addictive pattern of repeated journeys which make of him the Zone's most likely victim. As Turovskaya points out, Tarkovsky dispenses with the overt theme of sacrifice in the Strugatsky text, where the Stalker sacrifices the Scientist to the Zone in order to gain from the Golden sphere the prize which might heal his mutant daughter.[18] We have instead the oscillation of identities where all three men are placed in the position of sacrificer and sacrificed but none carries through any action to consummate the buried rite. All survive the absurdity they experience, but that absurdity consists of scaling the ruins and scars of a military-industrial landscape, with the tiled floors and syringes at the bottom of the pool suggesting an abandoned laboratory of deadly experiments. If Heidegger once said the modern fate is that of technology's danger, Tarkovsky re-invents that fate as the ruins of its disaster, experiment as destruction and absurd sacrifice.

The poetics of sacrifice in *Stalker* and *The Red Desert* bear the imprint of experiment and advanced technology and have a sense of civilisation's ending. *Aguirre* (1972) and *Picnic at Hanging Rock* (1976) both have a sense of civilisation at its beginning, but a civilisation which is bracketed and questioned and found wanting, the vision of a civilisation founded on a sacrificial act. In this respect Herzog's film of sixteenth-century Spanish Conquest is by far the more violent and more extreme. It recreates the journey of Lope de Aguirre to find the legendary city of El Dorado among the tributaries of the Amazon, a journey which later prompted Walter Raleigh to initiate the English search for El Dorado. Though Aguirre is doomed he sets an example to other adventurers, but Raleigh's own adventure comes in the wake of his own rejection by the English crown. The Americas are the site of English and Spanish conquest, a prelude to empire but also of that rebellion which takes the new countries of the New World away from their imperial source. Aguirre sacrifices his followers to an imaginary kingdom but his journey is one of defiance in which he wishes to merge with the land-scape which in turn defies him. His journey is thus an absurd sacrifice but also a precedent for wholesale colonisation.

The alternation between long-lens shots of Aguirre's party travelling downriver and the low-angle close-ups of the rebel leader himself, often shot on the rafts with hand-held camera, sets up a tension between the objective and subjective poles of the film which, however, Herzog skilfully navigates. The telephoto shot, which opens the film, of the Spanish adventurers and their Indian porters descending the mountainside out of the cloud – an echo of the Expressionist mountain movie of the 1920s – captures a fantastic moment of conquest, a mix-ture of the sublime and the ridiculous, of exaltation and absurdity. The film begins and ends with the circular motion of rafts trapped help-lessly in whirlpools and the journey downriver is a journey towards death in which Aguirre styles himself 'the wrath of God'. The mind-screen is a collective one which Aguirre dominates. The voice-over is provided by the diary of the priest, which distances us from the figure of the Basque tyrant, but the shaky hand-held camera on the swirling raft seems again and again to focus on Kinski's face, the face of cruelty. Aguirre's look dominates the film, predatory, conspiring, ultimately insane. The jungle imposes its own tyranny to match that of the inter-lopers. It rains down arrows from the bows of unseen Indians. It gives rise to thirst and fever and hallucination – witness the famous shot of the boat stranded in the upper branches of a riverbank tree. Herzog's jungle is like Tarkovsky's Zone, landscape as source of fascination and horror, miracle and danger. The adventurer's movie, where film-making reflects the risks of its theme, is also the movie of a university graduate who has read Heidegger and decided two things. Pre-war Germany was too unspeakable ever to film while post-war Germany was too dead to film in, and certainly no place for his esoteric vision of the destructive sublime.

Herzog's picture has in common with Weir's the device of the mis-leading caption. *Aguirre* informs us that the Indians invented the myth of El Dorado in order to trick their Spanish invaders. Adapted from Joan Lindsay's novel, *Picnic at Hanging Rock* tells us the victims who disappeared on Hanging Rock were never found. The film caption, usually treated as truthful, in both cases is mythical. We are inside an illusion which has real parameters. The Rock in Weir's film is as real and incandescent as the Amazonian jungle in Herzog's. But it is also a zone of disappearance. In Herzog's films we see the seeds of imperialism but also the seeds of its destruction. In Weir's film we see at a later stage of history the limits of empire. The early limitations lie in barbarism and plunder, the later Victorian ones in repression and gentility. The linking factor is the Christian God who is invoked to condone both of them. Just as Aguirre's revolt is a threat to Empire, Weir is concerned more obliquely with the cutting of the umbilical cord. As the Victorian period comes to an end – the film is set on St Valentine's Day, 1900 – the disappearances at the Rock become a defeat for a particular English way of life, its grip ever loosening on the colony which threatens to escape it. Here the pivotal figure is not that of a military commander but a teenager at a select girls' school, whose presence and charisma come in a rather different way to dominate Weir's film.

Miranda, like Aguirre, is a magnet for all those around her, but where he repels, she attracts. The mystery of the Rock is sustained first through her eyes, then through her absent presence in the eyes of those she has left behind. Here Weir matches pre-Raphaelite notions of female beauty to the female look of the 1970s, particularly in the combination of the white diaphanous dresses and the long flowing hair. There is a double-register of attractions since Miranda (Anne Lambert), attracted to the Rock – a visual trope of romantic fate – then attracts her admirers in turn to the Rock at Mount Macedon by attracting them to her. The Rock and the girl share the mystery and the beauty which merge with her disappearance into its volcanic heart. Weir plays on Miranda's aura through the narcissism of this double attraction, through mirror images of narcissistic self-regard. As spectators we too are narcissistic in finding the visual pleasures of our own age in the mirror of history. Narcissism creates an endless circle of mimetic rivalries as resemblance of costume gives rise to the resemblance of personas. The image of the semi-circle of girls dressing for the picnic by simultaneously pulling tight each other's identical corset illustrates perfectly what is to come, the mirroring of Miranda's gaze at the Rock through the gaze of others at her and because of her, at the Rock itself. Just as she is loved by her best friend, the orphaned Sarah Waybourne who is punished by being refused a chance to picnic, so she is also loved by the young French teacher, Diane de Portières, who in turn loves Sarah because of Miranda. Hence Miranda's words, which are doubly prophetic: 'You must learn to love someone else apart from me. I won't be here much longer.'

The doubling and resemblance of the girls is intensified by the duality of their male admirers, English teenager Michael (Dominic Guard) and Bertie, a young Australian coachman to Michael's uncle, an aristocratic English colonel. Weir echoes the stress on class difference in Lindsay's novel and the anomaly of stuffy English colonials, the Fitzherberts, on lush Australian landscapes. Much later, after Miranda's disappearance, we realise Bertie is the brother of the orphaned Sarah and this hints at a further doubling. If the two boys, like Sarah, are attracted to Miranda, there is a sense in which they are also attracted to each other through their attraction to her. Teenage female attraction is an affection which dare speak its name, but homoerotic longing is a love which dare not. By adoring the girl, both males suggest after her disappearance a growing affinity for each other and for the Rock. Thus Guard returns to the Rock to look for Miranda but the groom finds him there exhausted, and thus rescues the would-be rescuer, fulfilling the romantic adventure by default. Suspicions linger about the nature of the disappearance. Have the girls been attacked by unseen aboriginals? Have they been sexually assaulted by the two boys whose consequent anxieties are those of unburdened guilt? Have they been molested by the tyrannical maths teacher, Miss McGraw, who vanished with them? Or have they simply disappeared? The absence of any clear answer does not preclude any of the questions but makes them circulate in the spectator's mind as riddles never to be solved. Weir is more interested in the consequence of the disappearance. The Victorian age is at an end, the headmistress takes to the bottle and Appleyard College is doomed. Disappearance leads to disintegration, a shock to the collective moral consciousness from which it never recovers. This gloss on the frailty of Empire has a strong element of anachronism, of pointed retrospective comment in a decade when Australia clashed with its Commonwealth head over the peremptory sacking of its Labour prime minister, Gough Whitlam, by the Governor-General, Sir John Kerr, and the seeds were sown for a new, popular Australian republicanism. It seems no coincidence that Weir's film came out in the year of that traumatic dismissal.[19]

As many critics have noted, the journey to the Rock pits culture against nature, which is both a source of ambiguous attraction to the schoolgirls – the vaginal and phallic shapes of the rocks – and horror of horrors, the poisonous ants eating the leftovers of picnic cake. The journey involves a gradual disrobing, starting with the gloves removed after the girls passed through the local township and ending with the stripping away of shoes and stockings as Irma, Marion and Miranda ascend the volcanic Rock. The sensual motif foregrounded by Weir's camera, is juxtaposed to the parallel transition from cultivated land to prehistoric territory. As prehistoric landscape, the Rock is 'aboriginal', but it is equally so in the political sense. Ayers Rock, for example, has been the subject of vocal territorial claims by Aboriginal groups. As Hughes has noted, within nomadic Aboriginal culture, the sacred was not something confined to a special revered set of objects but inherent in landscape itself.[20] The land is sacred, and plundering or invasion of it is a violation. The movement from repression to sensuality, the liber-ating moment of the picnic, is equally something quite different, an involuntary profaning of sacred land. The camera's poetic licence in exploring the Rock works as a mirror of sexual licence and sacrilege, neither of which can be separated from the other. On this reading, Marion and Miranda are devoured by the Rock, and thus sacrificed to the mismarriage of nature and culture, the colonial and the aboriginal. The new world is different from the old and the ties must be broken. Just as Herzog injects into Aguirre's demented tyranny traces of the German trauma of Hitler, so Weir brings out the consciousness of contemporary Australia towards its colonial past.

The question of colonial sacrifice is also invoked in *The Piano*, yet in its vision of Victorian New Zealand, Jane Campion's film seems almost consciously to go against the look of *Picnic at Hanging Rock*. Its exterior light, blue, violet and purple is threatening and wintry. Like Altman's *McCabe and Mrs Miller*, it seems to exclude the presence of sunlight. Its female costumes are appropriately black and severe. The blazing summer light and white dresses of Weir's picture are inverted in the studied bleakness of setting and settlement, the mud and rain and timber cabins, the perennial forest overhang. Yet resemblance is a key motif, shown in identical costumes and bonnets of the mute Ada (Holly Hunter) and Flora, her talkative daughter, a resemblance broken only in the episode where Ada begins her affair with Baines (Harvey Keitel), and the excluded Flora is dressed in lighter clothes.[21] Thus Flora is Ada's diminutive double and since Ada's voice is only on voice-over, the daughter literally becomes Her Mother's Voice. Like *Picnic at Hanging Rock*, the film pits sensuality against Victorian repression as Ada forsakes a marriage of convenience with a conventional settler (Sam Neill) for a passionate affair with an itinerant Scot with Maori markings on his body. While Weir deconstructs romance through narcissistic mirrors, Campion reinstates it through pointed tropes, the piano as civilising instrument, Keitel as Antipodean Heathcliff, the muteness of Ada as a metaphor of truncated sense akin to the blindness of Rochester in *Jane Eyre*. Though Campion may aim for the wild and uncompromising, the sensibility here is nearer to Charlotte than it is to Emily Brontë. The clothes are a practical hindrance to love-making where disrobing has the power of fate. The hooped skirt forms a tiny tent on the beach and later prevents Ada from marital rape. Its final removal in the nude scene with Baines becomes the romantic centrepoint of the film. In *The Piano* passion negates human sacrifice since what is sacrificed is the cultural artefact, the musical instrument itself. Ada miraculously resurfaces to escape against all odds from the fate of drowning, breaking free of the piano's trailing rope. The civilising instrument is thus sacrificed to the wildness of passion and the raging sea by a device of plot, as earlier Ada's gift for playing it is sacrificed to forbidden passion when her husband amputates one of her playing fingers as the price of her infidelity. The piano and the means of playing are both sacrificed to the triumph of romance, which anyway signifies a new beginning. Ada recovers the speech lost as a child and Baines makes her a silver finger to enable her to play again. The sacrifice of breaking free is romantically redeemed where in *Picnic at Hanging Rock* it had previously been denied.

If Campion explores in miniature the flaws of Victorian patriarchy, Greenaway's most powerful pictures invoke the male predicament in the contemporary age, the waning of authority as the evanescence of power. A comparison suggests itself between *The Sacrifice* and Greenaway's film *The Belly of an Architect*, released a year later in 1987. Both centre their narratives in the unstable mindscreen of middle-aged intellectuals who feel themselves to be in a world which has reached crisis point. Both invoke the connection between personal and public crisis in different ways. For Tarkovsky it is future threat which precipitates personal disaster. In Greenaway, it is the tragic resolve to make the present live up to the past through the architecture of Rome.

Tarkovsky's theatre director and Greenaway's Chicago architect (Brian Dennehy) fail to accomplish their respective pledges. Josephson sets fire to the family home as a deluded 'sacrifice'. Dennehy, setting up an exhibition of his favourite architect, Etienne-Louis Boullée, is doubly betrayed by his young wife and her architect lover who takes over the exhibition. Josephson is taken away from the burning wreckage of his home, insane. Dennehy, dying of cancer, expedites his own end as the exhibition finally opens in the Vittoriano gallery.

A common motif of both films is death and both had a personal dimension. Tarkovsky made his film knowing himself to be dying, while Greenaway's father had recently died of stomach cancer, the fate which awaits Greenaway's failing architect. A common stylistic feature of both films is the extended deep-focus single take, as oneiric as it is naturalistic, which links realities of time and place to the world of dreams. Both films use Bazinian methods to go beyond Bazin's aesthetic, but at the same time bear out in ways he never imagined the ongoing relationship between theatre and cinema. Here the *mise-en-scène* is literally scenic. Both films theatricalise a found reality. Tarkovsky turns Gotland into a theatrical arena. More ambitiously, Greenaway does this with the architecture of Rome where he films in turn seven key buildings of the Eternal City which inspired Boullée, and another Boullée could have inspired, the modernist EUR building known as the 'square Colosseum'. All now act as the backdrop for Kracklite's ignominious fall. This is architectural theatre. Where Fellini's *Roma* used ingenious studio facsimiles to recast the pre-war Rome of the director's imagination and rebuilt a section of the Autostrada in Cinecittà for its 1970s epiphany of traffic chaos, Greenaway takes reality as found and recreates it as nemesis. While Fellini had charted a phantasmagorical *rite de passage* for his autobiographical young hero through the apartments, streets and theatres of wartime Rome, Greenaway is concerned more intimately with the relationship of start and finish, beginning and ending, birth and death. Kracklite kills himself an instant after the premature birth of his first child. His backward fall through the balcony window of the Vittoriano is a staged spectacle to outrival the one below – the exhibition which has been taken from him. But unseen, his gesture is witnessed by the cinema audience alone. Its grandiloquence has a pathos which is highly unusual for Greenaway. It is a monumental gesture in death which expiates the dwarfing of Kracklite's persona by the Architecture of Rome, that multitude of shapes in the course of the film which elude, dominate and devour him. Here Greenaway's static wide-angle takes give both height and depth to the towering edifice, notably in the framing of the floodlit Pantheon sequences which begin and end Kracklite's Roman adventure. Both are shot from exactly the same angle after being prefaced by the same backward track, both invoking the ritual of feasting, the first to com-memorate Boullée, the second a sort of drunken Last Supper in which the dying Kracklite disrupts the dining of bemused locals by displaying his cancerous belly and demanding that the nearest woman diner touch it. Exact repetition shows how far Kracklite has fallen.

Height and depth are given vertical structure by the daring use of the long-shot. Greenaway frames his characters through windows and doorways tightly against vertical designs which tower over them, so that they are as distant as they are distinct. Dominated by the mind-screen of Kracklite the narrative has this remarkable alienation effect of distant seeing, in which point-of-view shots are rare. Kracklite's free indirect subjectivity is captured through objective embodiment. Where POV shots do come into play, as in the peephole shot where Kracklite discovers Louisa making love to Caspasian in his apartment, they are deliberately voyeuristic and undermined by high farce. A boy and his mother from the next apartment watch bemused as Kracklite pulls up a chair to see all the better through the keyhole, only for the chair to collapse beneath him. The studio interiors in Kracklite's apartment, the cavernous Vittoriano basement, Flavia's photographic studio, are all contiguous with the exterior look. Except for the Vittoriano's claustrophobic toilet where Kracklite first vomits up his lunch, the rooms all tower over their occupants.

It is through the powerful physical presence of Dennehy that Greenaway is able to illuminate Kracklite's journey of resemblance and imitation. As a visionary architect he compares himself to his hero, a more famous visionary architect, but also undergoes other resemblances. When the stomach pains first hit him, he compares himself to Augustus whose tomb he can see from their bedroom window and who was poisoned with figs by his wife, Flavia. Soon he will accuse Louisa of doing the same to him. Even his belly which painfully reminds him of his own mortality, becomes a replica. At a photocopier whose eerie green flashing suggests the colour of death

and echoes the colour of the unripe pears which earlier repelled him,
he produces huge blow-ups of the belly of Augustus from a postcard
and places the largest in front of his own, replica upon flesh. He has
thus become Augustus as he was once Boullée, and in between the
hostile Italians suggest other unflattering models of comparison. Flavia
tells him that Boullée designed not buildings, but in typical totalitarian
manner, pre-fascist monuments, while with true sibling rivalry her
brother Caspasian asks Kracklite if he thinks Mussolini admired his
hero. Flavia adds Albert Speer to the list, and the fascist coding is
fleshed out by the EUR building of the fascist period which echoes
Boullée's designs. As if to add insult to injury, money is siphoned off
Kracklite's project by Caspasian to finance the restoration of Mussolini's
Fore Italico. Later, Kracklite finds another model of resemblance in
Bronzino's portrait of the middle-aged Andrea Doria, modelled on
Neptune, in whose image he then poses at Flavia's studio and whose
belly he churns through the photocopier.

The monumental structures of Kracklite's Rome are not those of
its Christian heritage. The Catholic iconography we see in the films of
Fellini, Visconti and Pasolini are conspicuous by their absence. Yet
neither is this the abstract and secularised Rome of Antonioni's *L'eclisse*
with its EUR setting. Greenaway's monuments retain the aura of their
history as part of the lineage of a pagan and pre-Christian *civis*. From
the Pantheon to the Public Baths at a spa outside Rome – again echoes
of Fellini – they have the look of pagan temples and his interiors too
have the uncanny feel of temple interiors which combine worship and
animal sacrifice. But these interiors are also unrecognisable through
ruin and decay. As Pally has noted, these sequences are 'littered with
scaffolding, dropped clothes, plaster, dust and large crumbling halls
leaking water and mud, which Greenaway attempts to choreograph
into elegant symmetries . . .'[22] There is an objective correlative to
Kracklite's unrealised present – that of the architect whose plans often
come to nothing – in the realised past of Rome which finally over-
whelms him. The temple experience is a visual phenomenology on
the vertical, one of sacrifice simulated and yet unrecognised. The narrative's paranoid structure of feeling is guided by this motif through the
labyrinth of persecution, real and imaginary. The canopy of conspiracy
theory explodes, however, as Kracklite's sensibility mingles persecution
with self-sacrifice. On his drunken return to the Pantheon, the most

powerful sequence in the film, Kracklite turns to face his pursuers from the restaurant he has disrupted with the words 'I'm sure Jesus Christ himself would have died of stomach cancer if he hadn't been crucified first'. Unlike Christ he will die for nothing and have no legacy, except his fatherless child. His tragedy is to be lost in the place on which he wished to leave his imprint. Why do we feel this? One answer lies in film technique itself. Greenaway has admitted that the camera made the feel of the Roman architecture vertical and all key horizontals sag in key wide-angle shots, unlike painting where the painter can invent multiple vanishing points.[23] The other crucial answer may be buried in the genealogy of the city. Sennett has analysed the key role of the sixteenth-century designer Sebastiano Serlio in linking Renaissance and baroque components in the social design of the early modern city.[24] Serlio's theatrical design *The Tragic Scene* is a triumph of receding perspective which takes the eye down the end of a long street to an Imperial Gate topped by a heroic warrior and flanked by an off-centred obelisk. The absence of Christian icons and the off-centred obelisk are a model, Sennett suggests, for other designs by Palladio and Scamozzi which move the eye to the limits of perception. In portraying Kracklite's fall, Greenaway uses the long shot to take his spectator's eye to the limits of perception. But those architectural limits, limits of shape and place, are also the limits of his subject's mindscreen, seen by the spectator when the subject, Kracklite, is in the frame. This is Green-away's 'tragic scene' and Kracklite is sacrificed to our sense of limit, as well as his own. Not only is he watched, conspired against, cuckolded and betrayed. He is also dying and also lost in the architecture of the Eternal City whose scale eludes him. Through place alone, his suicide becomes a form of classical tragedy, more a facsimile, a simulation, as his backward leap through the window of the Vittoriano balcony is literally a leap out of the architectural frame, a disappearance beyond the limits of the eye to instant death. Through simulating architecture, he simulates sacrifice. Yet his death is real.

Two years later *The Cook, The Thief, His Wife and Her Lover* (1989) is more explicit about the sacrificial urge but in it Greenaway substitutes baroque excess for poetic ambiguity and the talent of tyranny for the talent of vision. As Albert Spica, Michael Gambon is a melodramatic rogue and East End villain whose performance builds on that of Bob Hoskins in *The Long Good Friday* and *Mona Lisa* but whose psychopathic

urges seem more attuned to those of Frank Booth in *Blue Velvet*. The
element of simulation is still there, the present which cannot live up to
its past captured in the huge painting by Franz Hals of *The Dining
Burghers of St. George* which hangs behind Spica's table in Le Hollandais,
the vast restaurant whose lateral space is the entire cinematic space of
the film's action. The thief's gang are also dressed in black and red but
their actions are a travesty of the figures which frame their disgusting
table manners. Their conspicuous consumption in the Thatcherite
decade of the 1980s is a travesty of early bourgeois consumption in the
Dutch Golden Age, an age of invention, exploration, discovery and art.

Like all of Greenaway's films, *The Cook* has its elaborate, at times
over-elaborate dialectic of order and chaos. The screened menus set the
tone for the day. The food viewed is a mixture of gourmet delicacies
and maggot-ridden offal, cueing us into to Greenaway's love-hate of
the physical, his Epicurean overstatement riddled with a Swiftian dis-
gust of the body, human or animal. The colour-toned rooms, green
kitchen, red restaurant, white washroom and colour-toned clothes,
where Helen Mirren's dress changes from red to white as she walks
from dining-table to washroom are distancing devices to prevent both
empathy and mimetic continuity. Yet spectators here still consume the
sumptuous and extravagant. At one level, the love-making in the
washroom bears out Albert's leering lavatory humour which conflates
the excremental and the erotic. At another the sheer style and elegance
of the design softens the location so that we can after all believe in
the affair. Yet 'the drivel' which according to the screenplay Albert
incessantly speaks, has an unintended power, the power of contemptuous naming which seems to determine the lovers' fate. They end up
hiding from him, naked, first in the kitchen refrigerator and then the
meat truck where they are reduced to the state of the animal flesh
which surrounds them, live carcasses among rotting carcasses. The
hiding places are in part phantasmagoric emanations of the vengeful
mindscreen of the gangster-cuckold, but also of the director himself.
Greenaway's wish to show us 'a very unsentimental love affair' is
reductive in a different way.[25] His lovers are what they eat.

There is then a reflexive component in the film crystallised in its
ending. Having followed Buñuel in the fetish of feasting on animal
flesh, Greenaway then follows Pasolini in the fetish of roasting human
flesh. Cannibalism is the last taboo, an oblique metaphor perhaps for

the Big Bang of Thatcher's deregulated City which turned the Square Mile from an English Old Boys Club into a globalised network of electronic greed. If the signified is thoroughly modern the signifier is thoroughly archaic. The endless feasting which culminates in the thief unwittingly eating a cooked morsel from the dead lover, is a ritual of sacrificial excess. The cathedral-like green of the vast kitchen with its strange soprano choirboy and the sizzling hymns to high cuisine sung on its cooking ranges suggest yet another of Greenaway's 'temple' interiors. If cannibalism is a way in sacrificial societies of possessing absolute power over the dead victim, this is seen as the final consequence of Spica's reign of terror and one which brings about his downfall, a revenge plotted in the spirit of excess which has governed not just his life but Greenaway's own imagination.

The film demonstrates both the power and the pitfalls of the cinema of poetry. It shares with *The Sacrifice* an ambivalent focus on the besieged patriarch, Tarkovsky seeking to re-establish lost authority in divine visions, Michael Gambon enunciating it in the language of a lavatory humour which becomes his profane liturgy. The strength and weakness of the film can be seen by comparing it with an earlier film which highlights the moral violation of crossing over from animal to human flesh. This is Claude Chabrol's *Le Boucher* which, in its naturalistic psychology and autumn Dordogne setting, is worlds apart from Greenaway's colossal studio artefact. Yet the differences are deceptive. Schoolteacher Stéphane Audran's naturalised perception of unnatural happening – witnessing the bodies of young murdered women – is observed with scrupulous mimesis. The murders erupt within the normal. Likewise her growing suspicion of Jean Yanne is free of excess or melodrama in its assiduous understatement. Yet the narrative is a long day's journey into night. The return of the butcher to the schoolroom at night marks him out as a nocturnal monster who turns his knife upon himself, the demon consumed by love for the woman he cannot therefore make his victim. As Yanne comes towards her, Audrane blacks out and gains consciousness only to witness the knife sticking out of the stomach of her would-be murderer, his face drained of blood. The night-time drive to the hospital with the dying murderer is shot in conscious homage to Fritz Lang with its Mabuse imitation of the onrushing roadside trees caught, black and ghostly, in the car's onrushing headlights. The sacrificer sacrifices himself for the love

which cannot be requited, and 'love' here means an end to the impact
of the Algerian war. Yanne can once more, in the moment before death,
make fateful distinction between human and animal flesh. The film
begins with the lamb he has cooked rare and carve for the wedding
feast – the 'normal' trace of ritual sacrifice – and ends with the 'carving'
of his own body – the abnormal trace of ritual self-sacrifice.

At the start of the 1990s two key films have defined the sacrificial
unconscious in opposing ways: Kieślowski's *Three Colours: Blue* and
Egoyan's *The Adjuster*. One invokes the spectre of redemption, the
other the spectre of catastrophe. Yet both directors share similar preoc-
cupations. Their respective subjects are atomistic, not organic, the lone
woman, the disoriented male, the bemused immigrant family. And
both explore the inability to mourn. The dread of isolation hangs over
the daily lives of their characters and is compounded by the inventions
of late modernity. The technologies of communication of which film is
a part are glorified as progress and the greater ease of living. Yet here
the car, the telephone, the camera, the computer, the video image are
brooding threats which close us off from one another. People's lives
intersect but are elliptical. For Kieślowski, the accident is the atomic
instant which confounds the ideology of a determinate world. Here
Blue follows the pattern of his Polish films in the 1980s but takes the
theme much further. Julie (Juliette Binoche), the injured victim whose
car crash has killed spouse and daughter, must henceforth live through
the filter of a new experience of absence, technically the blue filters of
Slavomir Idziak's camera. These signify an ambiguous freedom, liberty
of movement and lack of obligation but also loss of family, which
creates an immediate void and triggers an inability to mourn.

Kieślowski codes mindscreen through the peripatetic figure of
Binoche on the streets of Paris shot by a following hand-held camera
which echoes the street life of Anna Karina in *Vivre sa vie* and clings to
the hyperactive Binoche like a limpet. In *The Red Desert* the car crash
had been the trigger for Vitti's mysterious illness before the film starts.
Here it is seen, unforgettably, in the opening sequence where the
dominance of blue is first established by Idziak's filters. If the camera
later clings to Binoche, initially it clings to the car itself where only the
daughter is visible. The sequence, credits over, is instructive. A close-up
of the rear wheel is followed by a close-up of blue paper floating out of
the car window, and a medium shot of the daughter looking out of

the rear window at the backrushing lights of the subway tunnel. As they stop at dawn in the countryside, a close-up of the rear wheel reveals the dripping brake fluid beyond which in the near distance, the daughter is seen walking back to the car after urinating. The first long shot of the car is a POV shot of a nearby teenager hearing the sound of the crash and looking too late to witness the moment of impact as it hits a roadside tree.

Uncannily mindscreen is situated in the car before it is displaced by the mindscreen of its sole survivor, Binoche in close-up in a hospital bed. Here as mindscreen switches from machine to victim, Kieślowski's use of the camera is startling in its technical innovation. After the fade from the crash we have a close POV shot of Binoche becoming conscious, then we see her damaged arm, then a reverse angle telephoto into her eye so enlarged it exposes a reflection of her doctor in the pupil. Kieślowski's clinical power of observation benefits here from his early documentary experience, and his short film, *Hospital*, much praised by fellow-Poles, comes to mind. Yet this is the objectivity of the documentary style turned inside out. The telephoto shot uses the extreme magnifying power of the latest 200mm lens, so that the reflection in Julie's enlarged eye fuses the natural with the impossible, since this eye could never be seen in that detail by any other human eye, including the eyes of the doctor whose face we see so clearly as a reflection on her pupil as he looks at her. We see what she sees on waking – her unnamed visitor – reflected in her eye. The extreme magnification of the lens also evokes the illusion of seeing through the eye into the soul. What we see and hear for the rest of the film is her soul. Visually everything is out of kilter, off-centre. There are few eye-level shots, even fewer medium shots and even fewer eye-level matches. Imperceptibly the camera is always too high or too low, too near or too far.

Visual dominance of blue and extreme sensitivity to sound reinforce that disturbance of soul conveyed through the tunnel vision of the survivor bereft of the ability to mourn. Binoche sells the family home in the country, changes her name and lives in a small flat within a childless tenement near Rue Mouffetard, where in her fear of all off-spring she borrows a cat to kill the baby mice lurking in her kitchen cupboard. She discards love for perfunctory sex in her fling with her spouse's best friend, Olivier (Benoit Regent), and exorcises the past by dumping the master-copy of her dead husband's new symphony into a bin, pausing to watch as a garbage truck grinds it up. When she meets the teenage witness to the crash she refuses to take back the crucifix necklace he has found by the wrecked car. The yellow and green walls of the apartment echo through proximity the blue which she sees everywhere and simultaneously loves and hates. In the local swimming pool the colour of involuntary freedom connotes something else – the colour of drowning. With defective mourning go the perverse pleasures of denying compassion. When she sees a beating in the street from her window and the victim breaks free to escape up her stair and knock on the door, the sound of the steps and the knocking are magnified and ear-splitting. This is mindscreen as soundscreen, evoking the paradox of an unbearable closeness to the immediacy of things, whose response is a cold refusal to get involved.

It is through music that Kieślowski opens up the route to Julia's redemption. Equally he leaves the meaning of that fraught passage open to doubt. As in *Fearless*, the narrative can be read both ways, as the way out of trauma and defective mourning or as the hallucinating vision of the dying accident victim who dreams their return from the edge of death. The dominance of blue and the constant fade to black where sound alone takes over suggest a drifting in and out of consciousness. The water of the blue pool is a recurrent motif of surviving and drowning. After Binoche confronts her husband's lawyer-lover in a café near the law courts and discovers, to her apparent joy, that she is pregnant with his child, there is a straight cut to the silent, empty pool. The camera pans around the pool as if failing to find signs of life until Binoche suddenly surfaces in front of it, an ascent evoking equally resilience or the conquest of the temptation to drown. The image is echoed in the final sequence when the film shows us in sequence epiphanic images of all its isolates, the fleeting encounters of Julie's life in mourning, now united in spirit. But that transcendental union is a fusion of montage and music, the final version of the dead composer's concerto which Julie and Olivier have completed. The motif of the concerto is love and the first image in the sequence, the entwined bodies of Olivier and Julie seem framed as a romantic trope to trigger the union of the grand finale. But a closer look suggests the movement of horizontal bodies squirming in slow-motion, Binoche's lip pressed and squashed as if against glass. This looks like underwater consummation where the motions could be read as a desire to escape in the final convulsion of drowning.

We are told her husband's 'lost' concerto has been commissioned to mark the Unification of Europe, which for Kieślowski would mark the end of the Cold War and Poland's communist past. But the finished concerto marks something else, the transcendental union of the lost and lonely as if all art – film, music or anything else – was the sole expiation of this unendurable state of modernity, that ineffable isolation also prevalent in the Warsaw apartment block of the Polish *Dekalog*, an isolation which lies for Kieślowski behind all rhetoric of community. Thus we might see this as the vindication of Adorno's modernist aesthetic, Kieślowski the atheist showing us a modern artwork which preserves against the odds the aura of the sacred in the secular world. In full romantic fruition Julie is spiritually resurrected by resurrecting with her lover the lost masterpiece of the dead genius. Yet this is a *trompe l'oeil*. For if we listen as closely as we watch, the aura of art is actually guaranteed by the aura of the sacred. It does not displace it. It ascends into it. The key motif of the concerto which we have previously heard on the soundtrack but also on the recorder of the mysterious vagrant in Rue Mouffetard is only a precedent to what the soundtrack has withheld, its choral hymn from Paul's gospel. The intervention is very apt for Preisner is not Mahler. The concerto does not displace the choral hymn as it might for Adorno, but the very opposite. It ascends into it as the climactic moment of collective hearing, that of character and spectator alike. The power of music to save is itself 'saved' by its sacred text, the scoring of Paul's Tenth epistle to the Corinthians for chorus and soprano, and a reference back to the Polish Weronique of his previous film who hits a high note in a Krakow concert and dies.

But music alone cannot provide the transcendent plane which unites a world of solitary persons in a community of love. Or, more accurately, it cannot create its illusion on screen. Something else must. Kieślowski gives us the words of Paul's Epistle to the Corinthians, 'If I have not love, I am nothing . . .', made over into lyric and doubly rendered by female chorus and solo, a soprano which could well stand in as Julie's inner voice. The choral hymn floats over a panning and lyrical montage of all the film's subjects recalling them to the screen and wrapping them in the canopy of its sound, the lovers, Julie's senile mother, the pregnant lawyer with unborn child as foetal image on an ultrasonic scanner, the teenage witness wearing Julie's abandoned crucifix, the prostitute downstairs, the Pigalle strippers, and once more Julie herself, tearful yet radiant as a tree-like shadow moves upward over her face before the screen cuts to blue. The sequence is one of two things, the inspired delusion of a dying consciousness or the eventual grieving so long deferred and triggered by the musical power of the sacred text. We shall never know which.

The Paris of *Blue* is precise and selective. The hospital, the country house, the pool, the lone apartment, the strip-joint, the law courts, the narrow enclosed world of Rue Mouffetard. So is the Toronto of *The Adjuster*, where locations are chosen for their precise expressive force. We accrete images of place through sparse repetition, the multi-coloured motel, the lone house in the abandoned tract on the edge of the city, the underground censor-temple of the Film Board, the subway train and the football stadium. Playing games with names, Egoyan conjures his central couple out of contrary myths. His insurance adjuster is called Noah Render (Elias Kotias) after the Judaic saviour of life from the Deluge and his film censor, movie 'adjuster', is called Hera (Arsinee Khanjian) after the wife of Zeus, God of thunderbolts which produce fire out of the storm. The linking of opposites here, male and female, flood and fire, Judaic and Greek myth, and finally insurance and censorship also act as a binding of the mythic and the modern. But if mythic naming gives a helping hand to critics, Egoyan soon takes it away again. For we can never work out what the relationship of the couple who share the same bed is. Are they married and living together with Zora's Armenian sister and her son in the model home? Or has Noah, the adjuster, installed them there and then temporarily installed himself as an afterthought? It is never clear and critics have reached different conclusions.[26]

One thing is clear. Noah is a profane saviour, a vehicle of the rational impetus of a capitalist modernity which adjusts its losses and makes money out of the process. Not only does he adjust the losses of his clients, he persuades them to adjust to their losses. His angelic profile is much indebted to Terence Stamp in *Theorem*, with one vital difference. He is a bureaucrat first, a seducer second. His 'ark' is a painted motel where even the colours of the parked cars seem to match. Inside and out the two dominant colours are red and blue, red for fire and blue for water. But given the ubiquities of desire which run through this picture, red also signifies the sensuality which Noah anticipates in the rooms of the motel where he seduces his clients while blue, as in 'blue movie', is the pornography of the moving image which Zera 'adjusts' in her daily sojourn at the Film Board. Here in the viewing theatre the raised dias of Bert, chief censor and patriarch, contains a colour reflection of cultural attribute – his face still and colourless but framed by a beam of blue light which could well be that of the projected film. Bert is the high priest of censorship, forcing a new censor to classify all the categories of the out-takes of sin in Egoyan's parody of the Ten Commandments and presiding over a vast hall which is a cross between a postal sorting office and a converted church. Here the sign of the blue movie is not arousal but immobility, the robotic classification of the sinful moving image a judgement in stone.

Unlike *Blue* the process of defective mourning here is in part satirical. While the priest would normally lead the bereaved in mourning their lost loved ones, the adjuster leads his clients in mourning their lost loved objects. But the value of property has an exchange equivalent so that coming to terms with loss – the burnt-out house, the charred possessions – cannot be extricated from the claim for monetary equivalents, unlike the lost loved one who is invaluable. Administration of the claim is also inseparable from the adjuster's administering of compassion. Yet the compassion is a simulacrum of the compassion for the lost loved one, and defective mourning becomes mourning the loss of objects as if they had been living beings. Claim and compassion are equally robotic, the bureaucratic detail of the former matched by the care clichés of the latter, each given an identical delivery by Kotias, an insistent but mechanical tone of voice. Yet the pay-off for him is never in doubt. The 'ark' in which the homeless victims are briefly housed is a temple of bureaucratic lust where the adjuster ends up in bed with his clients if they are female, or their wives if there are male, or more reluctantly with male clients if they are gay. If the Gods of fire have sacrificed the worldly possessions of their victims the adjuster administers comfort of varying degrees, and seems better at this than sorting their claims, which in a Kafkaesque twist 'never come through'.

Here compassion seems to cut across the grain of gratuitous sacrifice, so that Egoyan links two levels of meaning. The adjuster is the concerned bureaucrat who provides rational compensation for irrational accidents, but he is also the pseudo-biblical saviour who picks up the pieces after the gratuitousness of sacrifice, where the house fire is treated in the compassion routine as a force of nature. Still the spectre of fire-raising hovers uncannily over the charred ruin and the unusual suspects are the wealthy couple, Mimi and Bubba, whose obscene charades are seemingly its other plot, but in fact an extension of the main one since they cast themselves as demi-gods to whom their fellow humans are wanton sport. In the parallel narratives of the film where the adjuster is also the existential seducer, Bubba and Mimi are the existential pornographers who try to rouse their jaded appetites with a variety of soft-core escapades, one of which, a 'tramp gropes businesswoman routine', Hera witnesses on the subway. Their voices are also, it appears, on all the soundtracks of the hard-core porn we hear but do not see and which Zera watches and illicitly videos at the Film Board, raising the prospect of their simultaneous authorship of all the films and fires in the film.

The denouement where film and fire coincide, this eliding of the parallel momentum which has driven the narrative, is ostensibly a backyard motif. Noah it seems is punished for being a compassion junkie who ignores his family to fulfil the needs of his clients, leaving his home loveless and his 'wife' neglected. But it may well be that his wife is not his wife but a client from a previous fire whom Noah has dumped with her Armenian sister and nephew in an unsaleable 'home' in suburban wasteland for a cheap rent, and joined for convenience. When Bubba chooses to photograph and then film in the house he does so to bring the game of movie pornography to a grand finale. Thus the comic scene where he politely confronts the Armenian sister who speaks no English with his filming request may have a sting in its tail. She may after all have seen him on the video copies of the hard-core which Zera brings home to her every evening to 'show her what job it is I do'. Bubba's appearance could then be the materialisation of the monstrous video image on the front doorstep and the mute silence of the sister not incomprehension but absolute shock. Later, having made his 'film' with Bibi, he fills the house with gasoline as Noah returns and burns it down with himself in it. Egoyan cuts into his final sequence of local apocalypse with flashback masquerading as flashforward. The adjuster steps back from the blaze in his neat bureaucratic suit and after a reverse angle of the burning house we cut to a night-time shot of Hera and her sister watching the conflagration. They are approached in the darkness by a long-haired man in leather-jacket who starts talking insurance, and recognise the voice of Kotias before identifying his image. The implication is clear. We have flashed back to the first time around and the homeless, peripatetic Noah is landing on his first client as an adjuster. Through his later intervention his client who becomes his 'wife' witnesses the repeat of 'home' as a funeral pyre. The pure image of Egoyan's cinema here asserts itself – rational intervention as sacrificial repetition. To echo McLuhan as he clearly does is also to transform him. The communication delirium of the global village has given way to the catastrophe of the local cosmos.

Egoyan's local cosmos has all the entrapment of the Expressionist cage reframed in mythic delirium. Bubba's burning down of the model home is the self-consuming wrath of the wealthy porno clown pretending to be Zeus. His own doubling rivals that of his biblical rival, robotic saviour Noah seducing clients with the assuring rhetoric of the insurance industry. As the myths collide, there is a primal recognition in the gesture of Noah's hand shielding his face from the flames, a recognition that fire is not flood, that it comes not from the earth beneath but the heavens above and that he is defenceless against it. On the other hand it ensures his constant existence through the sacrificed other's constant need. He cannot stop catastrophe but only care and adjust. The travesty of redemption depends upon the travesty of sacrifice. Hera, perhaps here – but who knows? – the estranged wife of Bubba/Zeus the wanton pornographer, witnesses a return of the repressed in a houseburning the second time around, since the film's paranoid structure of entrapment evokes constant repetition of the same. Has this been done before? Was it Bubba the first time? Is it an endless cycle of travesty in which one burns and the other adjusts in the farcical battle of sacrifice and salvation? One thing is sure. If there is no grandeur in being sacrificed by Bubba, there is even less in being saved by Noah. Yet something is happening and very disturbing it is. For Egoyan the mystery of it is beyond all myth.

Chapter 3

THE SCREEN AS SPLIT SUBJECT 1:
Persona's Legacy

The connecting link between the screen image and the poetics of sacrifice can be summarised in a single word: imitation. The process of imitation, however, cannot be summarised so easily. It is a key variation on the motif of the double which informs expressionism, Hitchcock and film noir, as well as the romantic novel of the nineteenth century. But it goes further in connecting the archaic to the existential. Take, for example, the question of twins. In primitive societies, Girard contends, twins are often a threat because their physical resemblance symbolises that 'dissolution of difference' of rank which is so much feared because of the violence that often results. Twins are thus made scapegoats and deemed polluted outcasts.[1] The trace of this ritual horror becomes part of the scenario of the horror genre, seen for instance in the chilling portrait by Jeremy Irons of twin gynaecologists obsessed by the same woman in Cronenberg's *Dead Ringers,* which provides us with a perfect image of the screen as divided subject. Uncannily Irons's appearance seems to reinforce his specialism. His hands have the power to heal but also to pollute and contaminate the female womb and, in a favourite trope of Cronenberg, impurify the defenceless body. Yet the stronger dimension still than mere horror is the filmic translation of the sacrificial source into the general fear of losing one's identity in the chaos of the modern world, and the particular fear of self-annihilation through resemblance to the Other.

Since 1966, the year of *Persona*, film has gone further then ever before in its exploration of the dilemma. In one sense the visual spirals which introduce *Vertigo* were its founding image. In another *Persona* is equally momentous and has defined the course mimetic dilemmas have run. Here the psychoanalytic readings of the double, now endless in film criticism, have their obvious limits, since the question of identity of the subject goes beyond standard readings of neurosis, sexuality or the primal scene. In film today the doubled subject connotes not so much a schizoid condition as a form of fear about resemblance and thus of extinction. Film challenges that belief in the autonomy of the self which rightly defines the current discourse on intimacy but wrongly has high hopes of its outcome.[2] That challenge is very much a preoccupation of Western cinema and derives most significantly from Western Europe and North America where individuality has been most nourished and most cherished. In the last decade, however, it has been equally prevalent in the cinemas of the Pacific, especially Australia, New Zealand, Taiwan and Hong Kong.

The gloss on selfhood or its lack, when taken up by semiology, only goes so far or sometimes too far in its vast reductive claims. The screen's divided subject is present initially in something very simple – the cinema's own history of stardom.[3] Here the heterosexual norm of idolatry is well-established in the Hollywood canon – identification with the star of the same sex, desire for the star of the opposite sex. The former is the fantasy role-model, the latter the fantasy love-object. In heterosexual romance, gay and lesbian crossovers merely bring into relief this binary opposition by ringing the changes on it. The straight male, for example, may identify with Bogart and desire Bacall, the female by contrast may imitate Bacall and desire Bogart – for *The Big Easy* substitute Quaid and Barkin, for *Pulp Fiction* Travolta and Thurman. The gay spectator by contrast might identify with Garland or Monroe, both gay icons, while the lesbian viewer, attracted to Kathryn Hepburn, might imitate the role of Spencer Tracy in desiring her. In heterosexual crossovers, still uncharted territory, we might find similar viewing attachments to the diverse gay intimacies, for example, of *Caravaggio, Desert Hearts* or *My Own Private Idaho*. One of the most erotic films of the modern period is Weir's *The Year of Living Dangerously* where diminutive photographer Billy Kwan vicariously emulates journalist Mel Gibson in his open desire for beautiful English spy Sigourney Weaver. But Billy is played by a woman, Linda Hunt, and her/his screen persona is visually androgynous, thus calling into question any fixed relation between sex and identity. A recent piece of film erotica which plays reflexively on stardom is the Wachowski brothers' heist thriller *Bound*, where Gina Gershon and Jennifer Tilly play out butch and femme passion roles in clear pastiche of James Dean and Marilyn Monroe, again undermining sexual identity and the gender divide. Meanwhile all movie stardom can be summed up in the mystic faces of Dietrich and Garbo, the supremos of bisexual iconography, who can be desired or imitated by male and female alike. So much time and space can be wasted trying to locate any of this in the Oedipal crisis of infancy. Adult thrills and traumas of imitation and desire lie as much in the present as in the past. As living culture cinema testifies to this as much as any other medium.

Here the cinema of poetry has taken up the challenge which Girard sees as central to the modern novel, the conflicts between resemblance and identity generated by the incestuous kinship of imitation and desire in the relation of Self and Other.[4] As a visual medium film has now given that conflict a new dimension. Here resemblance has a double focus, the relationship of subject to subject on screen, and the relationship of star to spectator in the act of viewing. The double focus is by its very nature reflexive, and *Persona* signals that in its electric opening sequence where the movie projector literally wills its human subjects into life through film. The birth of the film lies in the birth of the images of its twin personae which alternate on the wall doubling as a screen above the hospital bed of the unnamed boy. The huge close-ups of Liv Ullman and Bibi Andersson flash alternately before the boy, and then from his POV, before us. When he disappears after the credits, never to return, we remain substitutes in his place, trapped within the focus of the gaze after the gaze has departed. Seeing the figures as substitute viewers, do we emulate or desire them? Meeting for the first time, do they emulate or desire each other? Bergman makes the connection clearer in the next voice-over sequence where we are told that Ullman (Elizabet), stagestruck while playing Electra, has a breakdown and cannot speak. We see her for an instant as stage star in the fixed mask of make-up and costume, the mute icon as pure enigma, before she is transformed into sick patient, pale and plain, dethroned. Sister Alma (Andersson) who nurses her is also the one who becomes starstruck by her.[5] So it begins, the vicious spiral of imitation and desire.

In a way it has not yet ended. *Persona* has inspired so many powerful film from *Les Biches* and *The German Sisters* to *Fire Walk with Me*
and *Exotica*, that metaphorically speaking the projector which gave it
life is still running. We can note, to start, its major difference from the
romantic fiction of the double. The theme of the mimetic male has
given way to the place of the mimetic female, the resemblance of
brother and brother to the resemblance of sister and sister. In that
sense the literary epoch of doubling from James Hogg and Hoffman
onwards was largely male.[6] In the film epoch from Bergman onwards
it becomes largely female. Lest this be taken as a sign of cultural
progress, a warning should be heeded. The triadic worlds of class,
sexuality and power do not simply fade away through this transition.
In affairs of the heart, it is usual for identity to be sacrificed on a triangle
and not a cross. It is largely within this triangle, where class at times
entails race, that narrative dramas of doubling are played out. Here
imitation is at the heart of cinema. Is it pure coincidence, for example,
that one of Pedro Almodóvar's transsexual stars, playing in very
unBergmanesque movies, has chosen to call her/himself 'Bibi
Anderson'? Above all, filmic doubling has become a vital register of the
changing role of women in the Western world. With it, alas, is borne
the psyche's poisoned chalice, the bitter privilege for male and female
alike of asking the elusive question 'Who am I?'.

If imitation and resemblance form distinctive chains of connection,
how is it possible to generate free indirect subjectivity? The answer is
complex and uncertain. Yet it does seem that intimacy is part of an
existential game with no closed or predictable outcome. The prize of
possessing the other is fiercely sought but the signs of victory are
seldom explicit and never final. In *Persona* Alma seeks to model herself
on her more talented patient, witness the transition to the wearing of
identical clothes, but also subconsciously desires Elizabet for the aura
of her celebrity. Elizabet by contrast desires to expropriate Alma's
persona to fill in the emptiness of her own being – she is after all an
actress. But the tactic of the mute listener who forces her carer to
confess all, and her vampirish intent, enacted in the sucking of blood
from Alma's wrist, suggest a simultaneous possession of body and
soul. Alma's being is sacrificed to Elizabet's predation and sacrifice is
inseparable from seduction. In the mind-games of modern intimacy, to
sacrifice is to seduce, to be seduced is to be sacrificed. From this springs

Persona's masterly paradox. The fearful symmetries of role-reversal frame the delicate ambiguities of the soul but cannot render them unambiguous.

Yet even this is not final. The enacted role-reversals of domination and submission tell us that both women end up at the same point in the film from opposing directions. Complete opposites in status and personality, they are nonetheless both seducer and seduced, sacrificer and sacrificed. Each woman possesses the plenitude which the other desires, and each trades it in at a price. The third figure of intimacy, for every intimacy here is a ménage à trois, seems to emerge only in dream where Elizabet's husband appears as the seducer of Alma, yet we cannot ever know whose mindscreen it is. Bergman films the sequence so that it appears to start as Alma's mimetic fantasy of stealing her rival's husband and ends up as Elizabet's dream of casting her nurse as pure prey, sharing her with her husband and watching her, along with us, being shared. The male presence is then vital, not to remind the two women in some fake melodramatic way of their 'basic' heterosexuality, but to return their relationship to the difference which precedes and surrounds it, their intimacies with men.

Les Biches (1967) pinpoints the male object of desire (Jean-Louis Trintignant) as the source of rivalry through imitation of the two female lovers, Stephane Audrun and Jacqueline Saussure. Chabrol's film is the first of the explicit reworkings of Bergman which are followed in the next decade by Fassbinder's *Petra von Kant* (1972), Altman's *3 Women* (1977) and Von Trotta's *The German Sisters* (1981). All four introduce different variants of melodrama into the diegesis and thus provide different closures of the aporia, or lack of closure, which lies at the heart of Bergman's masterpiece. Bergman's two woman go back, we assume but are never certain, to their previous lives. In the four films which copy it, the momentous events which mimesis generates make the consequence of resemblance irreversible. Interestingly the European films possess as their dominant figures the new, independent woman of advanced modernity, the celebrity actress (Ullman), the successful businesswoman (Audrun), Fassbinder's Petra (Margit Carstensson) as fashion designer and Von Trotta's Juliane (Jutta Lampe) as radical editor. The importance of resemblance is grounded in social power. The exception is Altman, whose three women are socially subservient, so that Pinkie's naive emulation of the subservient Millie (Shelley Duvall) gives Altman carte blanche for his comic irony. Mimetic desire among women is thus a function of social success but also of differing fortunes between those who have made a niche for themselves and those who have failed to do so. Through possession of the other both the fortunate and the insecure stand to gain, but also to lose.

The pick-up by the Seine which begins *Les Biches* stresses the point. The poor pavement artist trades insecurity to be a kept woman, kept that is, by another woman. Audrun as lesbian predator (Frederique as conscious feminisation of the male name) exerts sexual domination through financial power. She recreates the mannish look of Dietrich for the late 1960s, but this merely stresses her attraction to both sexes. Though Chabrol uses the winter setting of St Tropez very effectively, there are no visual explorations of mindscreen to rival Bergman, where conflict between the two women often turns, reflexively speaking, into a struggle for the filmic point-of-view. Instead Chabrol fashions an existential play of imitation and desire. Audrun's lesbian affair is doubled by the gay couple who act as docile houseboys and spy on Sassard's blossoming tie with Trintignant until Audrun throws them out. Seeing Sassard's attraction, Audrun herself seduces the male object of desire, scooping her lover and thus turning her into a rival. Sassard reciprocates the rivalry by desiring Trintignant through the eyes of her rival lover, dressing up in Audrun's clothes and playfully taking on the role of the other woman as dominatrix in her imagination. This is made clear in the desolate scene where she sits outside the bedroom door while Audrun and Trintignant make love. She wishes to be in Audrun's place but only as Audrun herself. The melodramatic ending, typical of Chabrol, where she takes on Audrun's persona by murdering her, is a chilling but wilful resolution of endless repetition, and contrasts with *Persona* where both women survive the experience of conflictual desire to lead separate lives once more.

For Chabrol the Southern winter is a trope for the icy calculation of sensual game-playing. This leads to a further difference. Both Sassard and Bibi Andersson play the roles of women who emulate other women, but the subtlety of Bergman lies in the disparity of knowledge. Alma realises the invidious pull of emulation only when it is too late to resist while the mute Elizabet knows it only too well, and plays it to the hilt. Chabrol's Why (the English name of Sassard's character which consciously poses sexual motive) perversely seeks out emulation as part of the game, but the game becomes serious over the question of possession, and Chabrol, the French auteur closest in spirit to Hitchcock, ends with a motif common to the modern melodrama of jealous revenge.

In his distinctive exploration of mimesis and desire, Fassbinder pulls melodrama in a very different direction. It is the studio drama of the room which he inherits from Douglas Sirk, a metonym of claustrophobic intimacy, but the emotional frame is still that of *Persona*. Like Bergman, Fassbinder is concerned with the terror of mental survival not the flourish of narrative resolution, and while Hollywood directors use excess to intensify emotion Fassbinder uses it to pull back from emotion. Petra (Margit Carstensson), a lesbian designer whose deep voice offsets a dress sense best described as ornamental feminine, uses and abuses her sexual power. She shows us in the process, like Bergman's Elizabet, that the joy of domination is often expiated by the desire for hurt. Here Fassbinder is more overt and less complex in his exploration of masochistic domination, since his Brechtian aesthetic distances the camera from the heroine's simplified gestures, which embody the paradox. Pain is more hysterical in order to alienate the spectator from its impact. The single set concentrates the obsessions which form a structure of feeling later to be visually dispersed and weakened in *Fox and his Friends*, the gay movie seen by many critics as having biographic kinship to the director's own lifestyle of daily risk.

This leads us onto the other crucial dimension of mimetic desire in modern cinema. This is the cult of ex-tase (or stepping out of oneself) which, as Kundera notes, is now endemic within consumer culture. This being-outside-of-oneself, whose sexual form is usually orgasm and whose religious form is often the witnessing of miracles, has its correlative not only in art but now in the delirium of spectacle and technology, 'ordinary vulgar ecstasy'; Kundera notes, 'the ecstasy of speed at the wheel, the ecstasy of ear-splitting noise, the ecstasy in the soccer stadium', which means in effect that 'living is a perpetual heavy effort not to lose sight of ourselves'.[7] In film, mimetic desire becomes a mirror of everyday ex-tase through the transference of self into the Other, the escape from the 'heavy effort' to remain contained within the self. Here we have a specific variant of Pasolini's double-register, the gender transfer of director into subject which complements the simultaneous transfer of the subject into the Other. This double-register of ex-tase in male director and female star is central to the films of Bergman, Chabrol and Fassbinder, but less so in those of Altman which actively pursue a clinical detachment in the midst of melodrama. Meanwhile in Von Trotta the ex-tase of transfer, sister to sister, is inseparable from sacrifice.

In *Petra von Kant* mimetic desire works rather differently than in *Persona*. Petra has rejected her marriage because of her husband's tyranny, his oppressive control over her mind and body. In rejecting male power, however, she replaces it with a female power which is equally power over other women. Her docile secretary, who is treated no better than one of the mannequins which line the wall in Petra's all-purpose room, is evidence of her contempt for the inferior female whom she turns into a slave. Her seduction of Karin (Hanna Schygulla) is a repetition of her ex-husband's seduction of her while Karin's final rejection of her (ironically to go back to her own husband) mirrors Petra's previous rejection of her spouse. To a point, power relations between women resemble power relations between men and women, and Petra ends up feeling the sting she has earlier administered to male and female alike. In *Persona* the seduction of Alma is enacted as visual mesmerism but in Fassbinder's film seduction becomes a showy form of theatricality. In contrast to the bleak walls of the Faro summerhouse, we sense in Petra's enormous living-room, which doubles as office and bedroom, the oppressiveness of the ornamental baroque, a trap which cannot be sprung. In being stranded between the mannequins at one end of the room and the vast Poussin reproduction with its mythological figures along the other wall, Petra's persona seems metaphorically stranded between the devil and the deep blue sea, between the poles of dead representations of the human figure which have a life uncannily greater than her own. Fassbinder's lovers consume themselves narcissistically in mirror images on which they gaze as fashionable commodities. The Other must be possessed, but only as an extension of the self-consuming self. Here in his use of cinematic space, the camera's recurrent movement of track and zoom is more dynamic than the physical movement of its sated subjects.[8]

Altman's *3 Women* poses a different kind of dilemma. In its triadic gloss, not two women but three, on resemblance and desire, how far are the poetics of free indirect subjectivity possible? To what extent does one more woman make a difference? The answer, sadly, is that the triple effect proves too difficult to accommodate. Altman largely abandons Pinkie's mindscreen after her drowning attempt, and his inspired narrative starts to unravel. While the look of Altman's film is extraordinary, the reversals in role and in power become too melodramatic for the oneiric structure of the images. The trauma of the suicide attempt sees the girlish Pinkie attempt to take over Millie's role as a manhunting woman but a sudden nightmare sees her relapse into her former self. The further trauma of Willie's childbirth, where the baby is stillborn, springs the final change in which Millie takes on the matriarchal role of the older woman who in turn becomes an ageing grandmother figure to the regressive Pinkie. By this point, all erotic and psychological sense is destroyed by dramatic contrivance and Altman's insistence on a highly fudged dream sequence lacks the visual conviction of its Russian contemporary, *Stalker*. For nearly a full hour Altman is on the way to making one of the most compelling pictures of its decade and then it all goes horribly wrong.

First, what is right? The sharp powers of observation, the discerning eye of absurd Americana which only needs the slightest of surreal tinges. The dominant colour scheme of mustard and purple, highlighted by the Purple Sage apartments where the two women live – sage being a well-known species in pulp Westerns – is used as the incongruous meeting-place of nature and culture on the edge of the Californian desert. It has a surreal edge embellished by the yellows of Millie's clothes, car and decor which Pinkie, called after her own dress sense, seeks to emulate. Millie in turn emulates the landscape, and for her pains is seen by everyone but Pinkie as ridiculous. Altman thus delights in embarrassing imitations and also bumps up the surreal through the hyperreal. The guys whom Millie chases hang out at a shooting range in the desert called Dodge City, a crude copy of the old Western town, complete with bar run by Willie's stunt-double husband and a dirt-track circuit for bikers. The poetics work because Pinkie's dreamy mindscreen is offset by the meticulous kitsch of Millie's feminine yellow and dainty junk food and because the images of doubling and difference are at first immense. Witness the doubling at the health spa caught in a backtrack shot of her and Millie walking side by side followed by two women workers, probably lovers, followed in turn by identical twins Polly and Peggy, also side by side. This is Altman's darkly comic play on resemblance, in which those with a psychic union are followed by those with a sexual union and then by those with a biological one, prompting us to make connections through images. Thereafter the twists in the plot, Pinkie's near-drowning and character change, her frothy nightmare and regression to type as a girl-child, Millie's delivery of Willie's still-born child and her own character change, are sudden switches which work against the laconic tone and free indirect style of Altman's filmmaking. They end up as shlock reversals because Altman wishes for an ending that is not there, and then contrives it, turning his three women into figures of different generations, bonding portentously into an all female family. A film which tries to explore through visual dream-work the fusion of female mystery and psychic truth ends up as neither truthful nor mysterious.[9]

More than any film which bears *Persona*'s legacy, the film by Margarethe von Trotta loosely based upon the lives of Gudrun and Christiane Esslin, *The German Sisters*, is closer to the original through its fusion of austere detail and psychic intensity. As Seiter points out, it is not strictly melodrama at all.[10] Instead it can be seen as a form of psychodrama which echoes Bergman's oneiric mindscreen but replaces it with a more detailed poetics of memory. Von Trotta echoes her earlier theme of contrary sisterhood in *Sisters* while earlier still she had explored similar ambiguities of political terror with Schlöndorff in *The Lost Honour of Katherina Blum*. Her film also inverts another key intimacy in New German cinema, the male bonding of *Kings of the Road*, a feature stressed by her casting of Wenders's hero Rüdiger Vogler in the secondary role of Juliane's lover, Wolfgang. Yet the inversion does not simply replace male by female. Male bonding is replaced in turn by female symbiosis. Von Trotta substitutes for the male reticence of confessing little, the sister's dilemma of knowing too much. Wenders's road males meet up as unknowns and break up as soon as they establish intimacy. Von Trotta's sisters cannot escape the shared childhood which tells them how much they have grown apart. The existential role-reversals of *Persona* are replaced by reversals of time. A series of flashbacks from Juliane's viewpoint, presented as a collage of non-linear fragments, tell us that the rebellious daughter has become the accommodating adult, while the obedient daughter who sat submissively on her father's knee has become a political terrorist. Juliane, delinquent during the leaden 1950s, the *'bleierne Zeit'* of German history (witness her dancing alone at the School dance), finds an uneasy niche

in the 1970s as dissident within the law. Marianne, brilliantly played by
Barbara Sukowa, makes no such compromises. Juliane's mindscreen
dominates both present and past, and also signals in Von Trotta's difference from Wenders. Whereas his male bonding is a journey through
space and territory her female intimacies are more a journey through
time and memory, a gloss on the non-identity of West Germany for her
own generation.

The series of meetings which takes place between the sisters defines
the film. These encounters are eruptions of pathos often bordering on
bitter farce, honed moments of mutual despair which contrast with
childhood memories, as the film creates a balance between the tense,
secret encounters before Marianne's arrest and the prison visits which
follow it. The major instance of Marianne's challenging eruption into
her sister's orderly life is the secret night visit with terrorist comrades.
After arrest all intimacy is regimented through the state and its continuous surveillance, the searches and the continuous monitoring in
which privacy no longer exists. The Foucaultian transparency of austere
institutions, bleak and demeaning, is the abiding image one takes from
this film and cues in the ruthless methods of incarceration which
marked the German state's treatment of the Baader-Meinhof group in
Stammheim jail.[11]

This is not, however, prison melodrama posing the stock questions
of fate. Will Juliane's love for her make Marianne a changed woman?
Might she, as a Hollywood remake might surely ask, renounce terror
for love and return to Jan, her neglected son? Von Trotta takes the film
beyond such sentimentality into a key variant of the sacrificial unconscious where there are no easy solutions, indeed no solutions at all.
Instead of the Bergmanesque struggle between sacrificing and being
sacrificed where each woman experiences both in turn, resemblance
here is different. Juliane wishes to maintain her political distance from
the sister who demands she resemble her. But that distance is the
source of the endless guilt upon which Marianne plays. Juliane's tortuous
strategy is to make sacrifices in order not to be the Other, the price she
must pay to ward off resemblance and maintain autonomy. This creates
a strange form of active passivity. It is the paradox of ruthlessly exer-
cising one's will in order to place oneself in the position of victim, and
this is what Juliane does. Her self-sacrifice revolves around the role
of the abandoned son who is directly sacrificed by Marianne to the

impersonal cause of terror. In the unmotivated sacrifice of son by mother, we find a powerful echo of the sacrificing Medea but also, as Zizek stresses, in the sister relationship a powerful echo of Antigone and Ismene, strengthening the parallel Schlöndorff had made earlier (Ennslin= Antigone) in his allegorical episode of *Germany in Autumn*.[12]

Von Trotta starkly presents us with the alternatives of sacrifice, Marianne the sacrificing mother versus Juliane the childless, self-sacrificing aunt-mother who humbles herself before her nephew by mythologising his sacrificing mother as the murdered martyr, killed while in prison and hence sacrificed to a pure cause. The mythology arises from the pure ambivalence of the radical sister, the editor who challenges the law but does not violate it. It is the same ambivalence of the Fassbinder persona in *Germany in Autumn* but the film avoids the deliberate histrionics of Fassbinder's cameo. Juliane is the embodiment of a critical reason as well as a woman of conscience. The anguish over her sister lies in her fear that Marianne is beyond reason, her abandonment of husband and son no more explicable than her descent into terror. At the end she is forced emotionally to find a cunning of reason in history. For others, however, the mythology does not take. The boy is bewildered, the public indifferent and the press cynical to the myth of the murdered martyr. The world wants no more of the terrorist figure it buries in actuality and must also bury metaphorically as a forgotten episode of German history. There is a Bergmanesque reflection shot during a prison visit, where Juliane's image is superimposed by natural reflection of glass upon that of Marianne as they sit opposite one another. Here we have an image of the mimetic trigger, the 'good' sister's wish to copy the inaccessible sacrifice of the Other she resembles, but who is more reckless and more terrifying. Thus Juliane takes on in vain Marianne's role after her mysterious death. The fragments of flashback, showing the Protestant pieties of a shared childhood guided by a father-preacher, are the foundation of her sacrificial ex-tase, her profane transubstantiation whereby she 'becomes' the memory of her dead sister. In a word, she wants to become her sister when she has gone, when the promise of the world of childhood is finally shattered by death.

In the history of cinema's divided subject the male gaze is increasingly turned on itself via the medium of the camera. Here the difference of the sexes has a common denominator, the constant struggle between narcissism and autonomy. In a culture of individualism these are the two sides of the coin which defines the polarities of identity.[8] The lure of narcissism leads to the delusion of greater autonomy and key failures of recognition. Here the failures of autonomy are two-fold, no recognition of self-autonomy and little recognition of the autonomy of others. The visual iconography of doubling testifies to this deficiency in the male gaze. Often the effect is surreal. In Bertolucci's *The Spider's Stratagem* Athos Magnini is the spitting image of his 'anti-fascist' father and moreover shares his name. In the flashback sequences which go back over thirty years, the same actor, Giulio Braga, plays the father while barely changing his appearance. The same is true of his father's anti-fascist comrades who appear in both 1936 and 1970 played by the same actors in identical look and dress. The film works at two levels, the historical flashback to the sordid 'truth' underlying the heroic legend, and the oneiric mindscreen of the Oedipal son masochistically imagining his father's humiliation and murder as his own. The film however is less the psychoanalytic rebirth of the Oedipus myth Bertolucci wished for, and more the reframing of mimetic desire on two polar planes, the sadistic desire for revenge against the revered father and the masochistic sharing of his degraded fate to expiate the guilt rebounding from the desire.

The erotic limitations of the male gaze are equally apparent in the failure to recognise female autonomy. In Tarkovsky's *Mirror* where change of generation is again a central theme, the autobiographical hero's mother and wife are played by the same actress with no semblance of disguise. In *The Obscure Object of Desire* Fernando Rey recognises his elusive love under a single name, Conchita, but the single 'character' is played by two different actresses each with a different style and look. In *Ulysses' Gaze* the three love affairs of Harvey Keitel in three different cities, Salonika, Skopje and Sarajevo, are conducted as part of his Balkan odyssey through troubled times, but he cannot see beneath the visual disguise of triplicate passion to Maïa Morgenstern who plays all three parts. In *The Passenger* Jack Nicholson meets Maria Schneider for the first time sitting on a bench inside the Palais Guell in Barcelona but he has already seen her earlier sitting in the same position on a bench outside the British Museum in Bloomsbury. Or has he? In *The Crying Game* Stephen Rea's identification of the feminine is fatally undermined by doubling and resemblance. His love of Dil (Jaye

Davidson), the dead Jodie's lover, is an escape from Jude, the bait in the IRA honey trap through which Jodie was first kidnapped, and from the IRA itself. But the mysteries of the metropolis in which he finds himself are reflected in the mysteries of the Metro, Jodie's regular East End pub which he now inhabits. The play on the homoerotic becomes clear when Dil's sexuality is revealed. The love of Fergus (Rea) for Dil, the feminine transvestite, is a love for Jodie's love and which becomes by analogy a love of Jodie himself. The desire to copy the other is transformed into the desire for the other once the other is dead. The real affair, one might argue, has already taken place in Ireland between the IRA volunteer and his captured black squaddie. What Jordan creates so well in this film is the symmetrical inversion of appearance and reality. For Jodie (Forest Whitaker), the black squaddie from North London, Ireland is never what it seems, but for Fergus, ex-Provo volunteer, London is never what it seems either. The film's mystery lies above all in the dark side of London, nocturnal, Dickensian, corrupt yet haunting where nothing is at it seems, an outsider's vision of London which Jordan excels at evoking, both here and in his earlier *Mona Lisa*. In that film, minder Bob Hoskins's obsession with upmarket escort Cathy Tyson foreshadows the obsession of Fergus with Dil, repeating the colour attraction of white for black. It is also an unconscious male desire for the beautiful 'she' who desires perversely. In terms of the male psyche, that is, whose sexual identity has been weakened, it becomes an unconscious desire for perverse desire. Jordan's gloss on male sexuality also echoes that earlier London gem of gangster attractions, *Performance*. This extraordinary collaboration by Donald Cammell and Nic Roeg doubles the persona of wounded East End gangster James Fox with retired rock singer Mick Jagger, whose Notting Hill pad services bi-sex, drugs and rock-'n'-roll in great quantities. Through his attraction to the bisexual lovers of Jagger, Anita Pallenberg and Michelle Turner, Fox becomes attracted to Jagger himself (as well as to the endless mirrors by which Cammell fractures his persona) and the two finally trade identities. Hard man becomes hippie, hippie becomes hard man as Fox involuntarily bridges the East End/West End divide of Swinging London. The old and reassuring hiatus between machismo crime and wimpish decadence is lost forever.[13]

In *The Passenger* the male gaze turns in on itself in a different way, when Nicholson as David Locke first contemplates the corpse of his double, the English arms dealer in the North African desert. Locke's trading in of identity, reporter for gunrunner, observer for actor, takes him to all the destinations in his double's diary. Yet with the first buzz of ex-tase, the transfer into the risk of the Other then encounters a deeper resistance. Locke, who has failed to watch closely as reporter, continues to watch idly while playing at impersonating a man of action so that in a way he watches his own inept impersonation. This is the detachment of nightmare and the inversion of all reporter thrillers where the observers of crisis are driven to act. Locke, cast in the role of the risk-taking actor, is driven to observe and chased into the bargain by those inhabiting his former life. His vicious circle of mimesis is acted out in the circular route which takes him from Africa to London and then back south via Munich and Barcelona to Andalusia, ready to cross back to whence he came. No melodrama is needed as the mindscreen lingers on the gaze through the hotel window while the gazer lies, no longer gazing, on his bed and then in a single shot the mindscreen camera loops back to observe him through the collective gaze of his searchers, as if through them he was witnessing his own death. The greater nightmare than the triumph of the Other into whom one is absorbed is to end where one began, before starting off a copy of the Other who acts. One ends up like Locke as a watching copy of oneself and at the same time as the self who watches the copy.

We must now look further at key variants on the female gaze which directly address the sensibilities of female bonding, emulation without rivalry. In European cinema the strongest film form to rival Bergman's aesthetic legacy was that of the French New Wave, and its theme of female friendship has been taken up since 1980 in films such as Diane Kurys' *Coup de Foudre*, Bertrand Blier's *Merci la vie* and Martine Doug-owson's *Mina Tinnenbaum*. Yet the key film of modern French cinema to set up a new kind of dangerous liaison between women was surely Rivette's *Céline and Julie Go Boating* (1974). It was an existential colour movie shot in Paris on 16mm with much street footage and hand-held camera. As such it provides a key link between the New Wave and the more diverse French cinema of the 1980s. As a Rivette film it links the four decades from *Paris nous appartient* (1963) to *La Belle Noiseuse* (1991). Like most of Rivette's features it is provocatively long at 193 minutes, challenging the convention of the ninety-minute feature and highly theatrical in its *mise-en-scène*, challenging many of the false distinctions between cinema and theatre.

Theatricality matters as much to Rivette as it did to Renoir, but he views it in a distancing manner. Above all, he seeks out the playfulness inside mimetic desire. In so doing, he keeps faith with the New Wave and provides an alternative aesthetic of doubling to that of Bergman, an alternative equally apparent though in different ways in the later work of Eric Rohmer. Céline and Julie are the historic source of the narrative move into female bonding – *Thelma and Louise* and Bertrand Blier's *Merci la Vie* are recent examples – but also of emulation, Rosanne Arquette's starry-eyed emulation of Madonna in Susan Seidelmann's *Desperately Seeking Susan* and the imitation of city girl by country girl in Rohmer's *4 Adventures of Reinette and Mirabelle* which uses, like *Céline et Julie*, improvised encounters between its two females; and finally, *Single White Female*, written and directed by Barbet Schroeder who had acted in Rivette's film.[14] In all these films there are forms of closure which distinguish them from *Céline et Julie*. The latter is remarkable for two things, the interchanging of emulator and emulated and the mystery of their personae. Who are they? Where do they come from? The later films all fail to some extent in their heroines' naturalistic profiles of origin. Here there are no origins. They are conjured out of thin air, which is how Céline appears in front of Julie in the first sequence. Morever, the film starts by Julie imitating Céline and ends with Céline imitating Julie. But then we are never sure of the real identity of either, since both are also players in a melodrama in a mysterious old house, where they break the theatrical frame by each playing the role of the maid and finally rescuing the young girl who is poisoned in the repeat performance of the play by one of her father's rival lovers. This rescue is directly inverted, we could argue, in Chabrol's *La Cérémonie* where the illiterate maid (Sandrine Bonnaire) and her pal from the post office (Isabelle Huppert) conspire to murder the family for whom Bonnaire works. In Rivette, the household melodrama is invented, a fantasy scenario by the two women which has the same status as the director's invention of the two women as characters in his film. To make the point, Julianne Berto and Dominique Labourier invent their own dialogue in the same way that the female rivals in the melodrama, Bulle Ogier and Marie-France Pisier, invent theirs, creating a ceaseless circle of invention for the play within the play within the film. For Rivette, cinema is not a pure visual medium since it must explore the theatricality of everyday life in which people constantly invent and re-invent their personas, and which in turn merges into stage performances of all kinds.

Anyone, therefore, who mistakes *La Belle Noiseuse* for a naturalistic art movie would do well to look at the fake blackmail game being played at the very start by Marianne and Nicolas, a charade which echoed the start of Rivette's earlier film, and sets up their visit to the painter's chateau as yet another escapade, a charade to be acted out, this time with unpredictable consequences. If Rivette deconstructs the Bazinian aesthetic in unlikely ways, Rohmer also changes it out of all recognition. For sure, he maintains the techniques inherited from Renoir and adds his own, natural light, natural sound where possible, the eye-level camera, the location shot both inside and outside, the found reality. But his best films also respond to the force of free indirect subjectivity, particularly in the 'Comedies and Proverbs' series where he twice confronts head on the female gaze and the dilemmas of freedom for a single woman. While *The Green Ray* (1986) charts amusingly and infuriatingly the perils of Marie Rivière's singles holiday, *Full Moon in Paris* (*Les Nuits de la pleine lune*, 1984) was more complex in its construction and deals with a form of splitting which is not so much that of personality as of place, the double life of the Marne suburb and Paris. It is also the first film since *Claire's Knee* in which Rohmer fully confronts mimetic desire.[15] What distinguishes him here from many of his contemporaries is his continual emphasis on the autonomy of the self. Reinette and Mirabelle do not, for example, swap identities even though each does a swap by living in the other's home. The same is true of Louise (Pascale Ogier) in *Full Moon in Paris*. She remains herself but inhabits two contrary spaces, the two homes which threaten to make her lose her mind. This is free indirect subjectivity but without the delirium of Pasolini's aesthetic, the derealising we have already found elsewhere. Louise starts as an autonomous woman and ends as one. Yet the process devastates her. Rohmer's exploration of subjectivity lies in talk, similar to Woody Allen in its frankness but injected by a rhetoric of subjectivity at which Rohmer, in following French literary tradition, is so adept. It is not feeling as a resource for confession, as it is with Allen, but philosophical speculation about the consequences of feeling, to translate them to daily actions. In Rohmer that translation is constantly amusing but endlessly difficult. For just as there are limits to the power of the self so there limits to the power of perception.

Louise's wish to live in two places is doomed for two reasons. Her double life is again divided in Paris between her constant companion, Octave, and her transient lover. Equally, she cannot fully predict the consequences of her actions. The lucidity of the plan takes no account of human fallibility. The party sequence soon after she has moved into her Paris flat concentrates the essence of the whole narrative into a handful of crucial takes. Rohmer films the sequence of the party with three long takes in deep focus photography and no reverse-angle cutting. Bazin surely would have approved. Moreover Rohmer himself has spoken of film as a window opening onto the world and here there are open doorways opening onto the dance-floor, a room inviting and evenly lit, no shadows, no distortions. Everything can be seen yet nothing is what it seems. Louise attends with married companion Octave and confides in her friend Camille about her new double-life in city and suburb only to find to her dismay that her boyfriend Rémi is also at the party. The rivalry centres on the dance and Rohmer uses the convention of partner-swapping during the dance to present us with the fundamental irony of displacement which will take place in the course of the movie. Of course, Louise does not realise this and neither in fact do we since we see things largely through her eyes. Only when she finds out at the end that Rémi has been unfaithful and fallen in love with someone else can we think back to what has happened, and even then we are faced, like her, with the vagaries of memory. While the cool jazz musician with whom she dances then and later sleeps is a passing fad, Rémi falls in love – later, we presume, but nothing is certain – with Marianne, the woman in the white dress dancing with the musician in the first place before Louise 'dispossessed' her. While Louise divides her Parisian life between the platonic existentialism of Octave and the raw sex of the young musician, Rémi simply swaps his allegiance from one woman to another, whom Louise mistakenly fears is her friend Camille, but instead is the woman to whom Camille introduces him at the party. If Louise has 'dispossessed' Marianne in the dance, Marianne 'dispossesses' Louise in the suburbs, with more serious consequences. The dual pacts of infidelity are sealed on the same night, but Louise is too busy negotiating hers to recognise the threat.

The crisis of self for Rohmer is not only one of identity but also one of mistaken identity. To see is not necessarily to know and transparency is in the eye of the beholder. Free indirect subjectivity is the freedom to speculate on the nature of one's existential condition, but not the key items of knowledge which inform it. The self-conscious element of fable in Rohmer's work becomes a moral critique of the existential structure of feeling in his cinema. Moral convention finally punishes the freest females in his canon for their existential boldness, but it is that boldness which fascinates him and defines his best films. What is it that Louise sees and yet fails to see? What is it that we see and fail to see? That her future lover and her partner's future lover are in fact dancing together before either meets their future paramour. Rohmer gives us no signs, but creates a dance rotation with *à la ronde* effect. It is a motion which defines the rest of the film. The dance sequence is important in Rohmer because it gives a purely visual rendering of the forms of doubling and imitation which define the film. If, as Deleuze claims, his work is an exemplar of Pasolini's free indirect subjectivity, it usually lies in the power of the spoken word, in that beautifully ironic mismatch between spoken intention (highly attenuated) and subsequent action (rather brief), which is Rohmer's trademark.[16] If Rohmer follows in the Enlightenment tradition in a way not so different from Godard, it is because everyone is her or his own philosopher. If Allen has made Manhattan an island city of DIY psychoanalysts, Rohmer has made Paris a city of DIY *philosophes*. If Allen's comedies pose as their first question 'How do you feel?', Rohmer's comedies pose as their first question 'How do you reason? If you reason, however, about living in two different places at once as Louise does, you are in danger of losing your mind.

At the end of the 1980s, two key films diametrically opposed in style to Rohmer's neo-Bazinian aesthetic explored even further the ontology of the split female subject. Both combined the comic and the macabre yet were also seen as a gloss on the feminist discourse of the decade. The first was Peter Greenaway's *Drowning by Numbers*, based on a screenplay he had written earlier in the decade, the second *Sweetie*, Jane Campion's first feature, so influential since on the course of Antipodean cinema. While Campion's film is best seen as surreal tragicomedy,

Greenaway's is an ornate yet rationalist, or pseudo-rationalist, fable of the war between the sexes. Hence Greenaway has been placed by many critics close to the forms of narrative fabulation in post-modern fiction. But there is also something very traditional and English in his films which has provoked less comment. The constant juxtaposition of the ornate and the rational is a genuine puzzle, and cannot be understood without confronting Greenaway's Englishness. This is the tradition of the music hall, seaside amusements and the country-house thriller, all elements of which this film contains. The serial and mechanical elimination of bodies is a favourite plot device of Agatha Christie, one variant of which Greenaway uses in the murder at the end of *The Draughtsman's Contract* where 'everybody did it' and a second in *Drowning by Numbers* where one type of murder, the drowning of the husband, repeats itself three times at the hands of three women of three different generations all called Cissey Colpitts. They then join together and plot to kill the lecherous coroner who desires all of them and shares their murderous secrets. Set at the seaside on the east coast of England and shot mainly at night or in the 'magic hour' of twilight, Greenaway creates a kind of outdoor pantomime whose extras on the beach for example have a purely ornamental quality, the human comedy as mere extension of the endless tableaux of cultural objects. There are strong echoes of Fellini's *Amarcord*, but while Fellini had recreated 1930s Rimini on the backlots of Cinecittà, Greenaway uses actual locations for his memory-film of the Suffolk coast. The film is full of schemers, villains and fools which make it resemble a Punch-and-Judy show in reverse, a feminist Judy-and-Punch show which seems to have sprung to life out of the same promenade culture which Greenaway tries nostalgically to evoke. This creates a rather peculiar tinge to the aesthetics of narrative fabulation. Far from being a sophisticate's post-modern charade of ingenious curating, this strikes the spectator as an end-of-the-pier show without an implied audience, let alone a real one.

Three women of three generations (Joan Plowright as mother, Juliet Stevenson as daughter, Joely Richardson as granddaughter) are tripled by the sharing of the same name and the same fate, to kill their husbands who disappoint them and conspire to kill the coroner (Bernard Hill) who tries in vain to displace the dead husband in the bed of each woman in turn. The vaudeville flavour of Greenaway's farce makes it close to the tradition of the Carry-On movies, particularly in the chumminess of the conspiring women and the sexual innuendo (the boy-narrator is called Smut) which is here, of course, more explicit. At the same time Greenaway distances himself from his narrative by techniques of game-playing which act as an pseudo-aesthetic frame for the comic observations of an eccentric English seaside culture. It is the splendid and atmospheric location shooting by which Greenaway clinches his oblique rendering of eccentricity. The numbers game is a red herring as are the 'traditional games' by which Smut the boy-narrator frames each episode, since they are invented by Greenaway himself. It becomes impossible to tell the authentic from the fictional, an obsessive conceit of an auteur who did his time in the ambience of the official documentary. This, if you like, is a Carry-On film straight out of a government office of information. But then Agatha Christie is also in the equation. For it is the oldest of the three Cisseys, the matriarchal Joan Plowright, who sets in motion the ritual of man-drowning, and the plot works as a race against time. The woman all work to kill the men who at each turn are suspicious of the previous killing and then to kill the coroner who suspects all of them. Plowright can be seen here as the matriarchal author of the plot who sets in motion the four murders in such a way that the women will never be discovered. In that respect she actually reinvents Christie for the cinema, where gender domination is a matter of superior plotting in both senses of the word. By plotting within the film, she 'plots' the film itself, and it is she, not the boy-narrator, who orchestrates the film. This means our final split subject for the chapter is Greenaway himself, half naughty-boy narrator reciting rules for non-existent games, half orchestrating matriarch who plays lip service to feminism by feminis-ing his own persona. It is, to say the least, an interesting combination. But its interest is limited for it poses a question that his incessant resort to mannerism never resolves. If he cannot take his narratives seriously, then why should anyone else? We put the same question more cyni-cally. If *Persona* has had such a powerful influence on filmmakers, why has Greenaway had so little?

Chapter 4

THE SCREEN AS SPLIT SUBJECT 2:
Into the 1990s

In the 1990s, film's continuing obsession with the split subject has resulted in the reinvention of film language. Here one thing is striking: the relative absence of invention in the two traditional powerhouses of world cinema, Hollywood bullish and triumphant but also chained to the empire of special effects, and the collective cinemas of the enlarged EU through which Bergman's legacy had echoed down the years. The focus has moved elsewhere and there are three lacunae we must consider, the place of Campion's *Sweetie* in Antipodean cinema, the reworking of subjectivity in the starless, low-budget alternatives to Hollywood and finally the revolutionary film language of the new directors of East Asia. Our continuing theme stresses if nothing else the growing diversity of world cinemas but must surely have as its centrepiece the growing challenge of film in East Asia to our conception of what cinema can be. Here out of an embarrassment of riches I want to concentrate on five specific films: *Raise the Red Lantern* from mainland China, *Days of Being Wild* and *Chungking Express* from Hong Kong; and *The Scent of Green Papaya* and *Cyclo*, one shot in a French studio and the other on location in Vietnam's Saigon (officially Ho Chi Minh City).

Though released in 1989, *Sweetie* seems in retrospect to be one of the key films ushering in the new decade, one early sign of which was its hostile reception at Cannes. Campion's film starts with a naturalistic situation and then deconstructs it by surreal means. Kay (Karen Colston) works in a bank so bleak and faceless it could be any impersonal office

of our age. In a surreal charade of imitation and desire, she impulsive-
ly seduces Lou (Tom Lycos), a workmate's fiancé, in the firm's underground car park to fulfil a fortune teller's prediction. Thereafter she
starts to live with him but her domestic life is turned around by the
unexpected arrival of her obese sister Dawn (Genevieve Lemon), which
freezes her into total inhibition. Campion bravely reverses the narrative
scenario of loving and consummation in traditional romance. Kay goes
down without ceremony on her chosen lover on the concrete floor of
the car park but once living in sin refuses to commit it, performing
abstinence with the same impulsive non-logic with which she had
staged instant sex. Campion then links this narrative reversal with
another flouting of convention. She switches the story's mindscreen
from Kay to the dysfunctional Dawn (Sweetie) and the daily disasters
of Gordon, her drunken dysfunctional lover (Jon Darling).

Something more than household farce is happening here. In the
bleak Southern Australian suburbs, dysfunction becomes a defence
against entropy. The major trope of *Picnic at Hanging Rock*, culture
versus nature, is scaled down to its suburban equivalent, concrete
versus nature. The superb photography of Sally Bongers frames its
characters atmospherically in this unyielding ambience, allowing
Campion to produce a feature exactly opposite to the anodyne TV
soaps that Australia exports around the world. There are no neighbours
in this film but also no viewpoint from which to judge the vicious
circle of eccentricity on display. Seen through the eyes of any one character, the rest are equally impossible. Thus Sweetie is the dysfunctional
daughter-sister of a dysfunctional family where both dysfunctional
daughters choose dysfunctional lovers. Campion makes us laugh here
without drawing the film's tragic sting. The abandonment of Sweetie
by her family and the decimation of her planted backyard tree provoke
a dark regression, the hopeless emulation of an aboriginal identity
complete with absurd warpaint as she strips naked and tries to go
native, holing up in the tree branches of a suburban garden. This
pastiche of the suburban savage ends tragically and Campion keeps
the balance between the comic and the tragic through her refusal of all
sentimentality. Campion's split subject of sisterhood, what we might
call a feminine unsublime, is based less on doubling than on difference. Yet there is a crucial strand of mimesis. As Kay retreats into
chastity, Sweetie echoes Kay's wild seducing power in sexual encounters

of the grotesque kind, while inverting Kay's refusal of self-display with her lurid and viscous flamboyance, her tastelessness in make-up and men. The figure of *Sweetie* is enduring, a darkly comic prophecy of the guiltless grunge of the 1990s which Kay ascetically disdains but which is the future of listless consumerism. The film thus predicates in distinctly female terms one of the central dilemmas of the cultural moment, the choice of excess or of self-denial, both of which can be made to look ridiculous by the other, and often are.

Sweetie's unconventional convention is one which bears comparison with its American contemporary *Edward Scissorhands*. Burton's film is more darkly Gothic and comically invokes the supernatural in its satire on suburban American kitsch. Campion works on a more existential plane in exploring the incongruence of character and setting, and the failure of her subjects to work out obvious relations of cause and effect. The comic idiom which results has been copied and extended in the Australian cinema of the 1990s though largely without *Sweetie*'s tragic power. Films as diverse as *Muriel's Wedding, Dallas Doll, Priscilla, Queen of the Desert, Angel Baby, Mr Reliable* and *Love Serenade* all echo aspects of its deconstruction of cause and effect in different ways. *Muriel* and *Serenade* echo its sibling rivalry, *Angel Baby* its dry-eyed take on wild seducing, *Priscilla* its surreal take on the Aussie outback, *Dallas* its baleful eye upon suburban mores, *Mr Reliable* its surreal take on the siege mentality. None however matches its narrative ambition and none, save *Angel Baby*, matches its power to disturb. Yet it should also be remembered that Campion is a New Zealander and her work stands at the crossroads of the two countries in which she has made all her films up to *Portrait of a Lady*. The dark side of *Sweetie* becomes a key starting point for the development of New Zealand cinema in the 1990s. One can single out here Campion's concern with madness in her version of Janet Frame's *An Angel at My Table*, the bleak solitude and literal darkness of *The Piano* as well as the darkly challenging films of Vincent Ward, Peter Jackson and Lee Tamahori. *Heavenly Creatures* and *Once Were Warriors* have impressed global audiences with their fusion of sharp naturalistic observation and expressionist *mise-en-scène*. This power of observation runs through all of Campion's work so that the Antipodean split which ensues between darkness and light is never absolute. Australian comedies have pivotal tragic moments while New Zealand melodramas have strong comic interludes. But the surreal and the comic fuse more clearly in the former while the dark and the expressionist are more pronounced in the latter, a division which has echoed that split between Southern and Northern Europe in previous decades.

The most powerful input into film form during the 1990s has come from the films of East Asia, notably Mainland China, Taiwan and Hong Kong but also of course Japan and South Korea. Here film connections have spread across troubled political borders. The Hong Kong Film industry with its assembly-line base in commercial action thrillers has been up until 1997 a point of intersection for Mainland China and Taiwan. Mainland pictures which have trying times with the communist authorities have found production and distribution outlets, while Mainland and Taiwanese actors have moved into major features. The early 1990s saw the fruition of Chinese Fifth Generation filmmaking in the work of Zhang Yimou, Chen Kaige and Tian Zhuanzhuan but also the rise of major filmmakers out of Hong Kong genre pictures: John Woo, Stanley Kwan and Wong Kar-Wai; while under financial constraint, Taiwanese cinema has produced key directors in Edward Yang, Hou-Hsaio-Chen, Ang Lee and Tsai Ming-Liang. These are not only landmark cinemas which show us new landscapes, new faces and new names, they are also the key to a vital transformation of film language. With honourable exceptions like the Berlin Film Festival, this achievement is still much undervalued in the West as is the nucleus of actors who are ringing the changes on our conventions of stardom. The great exception of course is the much feted Gong Li, but New Asian cinema has also created the first major cluster of non-Hollywood stars since Western European cinema of the 1960s. Maggie Cheung, Faye Wong, Tony Leung, Taneshi Kaneshiro, Andy Lau, Brigitte Lin, Michele Reis, Tran Nu Yen-Khe and Leslie Cheung have, like Gong Li, all faced the challenge of new acting styles and decisively triumphed. At the same time, the politics of East Asian cinema remain delicate. Changing communist identities in a global capitalist world are prominent equally, for example, in the films of Zhang Yimou and the Vietnamese films of French director Tran Anh Hung, which share in theme and style the New Asian heritage. Overall the political uncertainties of Chinese culture linked to the uneven, Americanised growth of affluence have fed into the new film-making which promises, though nothing is ever certain, to take cinema on a high into the new millennium.

The Mainland directors have largely examined their country's recent history. Outside the Mainland, East Asian cinemas have combined a concern with history with present obsessions. Thus while the Fifth Generation directors possess a formalism comparable in its richness and complexity to that of Ozu and Mizoguchi, elsewhere the troubling concerns of modernity have fed an Asian existentialism on the screen, an existentialism bred out of action genres but then casting them aside. One of the central concerns here has been the focus on sexuality and female identity in which the split subject has been reinvented or given new forms. Here the models of Bergman or Rivette seem inappropriate. There are of course strong echoes of the early Godard, but the difference between continents is crucial. Neither film noir nor New Wave paradigms seem fully appropriate, yet there is still a vein of similarity running through all three paradigms, namely a volatile response to social transformation and political threat. The films of Tran Anh Hung circle around the history of the Vietnam wars, while those of Wong Kar-Wai with their downbeat anxieties of leaving gloss Hong Kong's impending change in 1997 from British colony to Chinese 'zone'.

Zhang Yimou poses a different kind of question about history which actually cuts across culture and continents in the twentieth century by looking at the enduring tension between social constraint and personal intimacy, male authority and female freedom. Here the single and powerful figure of Gong Li has acted as an icon of that tension, a sign of conflict unresolved in the historical *Judou*, uneasily resolved in the contemporary *Story of Qiu Ju*, and entirely tragic in *Raise the Red Lantern*. In his 1920s melodrama Zhang uses Gong Li's sexuality as a sign of China's modernity frozen at the moment of transition. Songlian is the educated nineteen-year-old who takes a step backward by becoming the 'Fourth Mistress' of a rich polygamous lord in a nearby province. Just as Gong Li is confined within the space of the Master's magnificent eighteenth-century palace, so China of the 1920s seems wedded to obsolete tradition, frozen in time. But Songlian's tragedy is also a sign of the upheaval which is to be unleashed, the revolutionary storm after the neo-feudal calm. The incestuous relationship of domestic melodrama and corrupt power is a feature both of this film and also of the powerful Tunisian parable of colonial rule, Moufida Tlati's *The Silence of the Palaces*.[1] Both unpick the household corruptions of patriarchy, but in Zhang's film the relationship to politics is more oblique. The Master's social power is unspecified and he remains a shadowy presence in the mansion. We hear his voice often but rarely see him and then usually in long shot or shadow. There is no close-up, not even a standard eye-level medium shot to show us the face of power. His presence is less important than the response it generates in the household itself.

Here Zhang plays out a domestic intrigue which is narratively conventional, against a sense of resemblance and imitation which is highly uncanny. Songlian's formal title is Fourth Mistress, placing her as an addition to the Master's existing concubines whom she must resemble in order to be different. She is doubled not only by three prior mistresses but also by Yan'er, her illiterate servant of the same age who breaks the rules by secretly hoarding red lanterns in her room and making herself over into a surrogate version of Songlian. Songlian's new-found position has its price. To be privileged is to be watched. Zhang's setting of the recent past, the imposing palace and brittle wealth is linked reflexively through the repeated use of the high-angle roof shot to the idea of surveillance. For Rey Chow the imprisoning palace suggests the double gaze of a Western Orientalism fixated on beauty and ritual and the Chinese security state which relentlessly monitors its subjects.[2] Certainly the wide appeal to Western audiences which Chen Kaige takes much further with the exotic *Farewell, My Concubine* contrasts with the mild interest, to say the least, of Mainland audiences in Fifth Generation cinema. However, Chinese film has a growing audience in the Pacific Rim and 'Western' audiences often include a large Chinese diaspora, many of whom would sense that Zhang is creating a visual landmark in Asian history. To look for purely naturalist landmarks, however, would be misleading. Out of the found reality of the traditional mansion in Shanxi province, Zhang is constructing his own filmic world. The ingenious play upon tradition seen in the film's imaginary rites, the foot-massage, the formal meals and the lighting of the red lanterns, is also cinematic reverie, a re-imagining of the past which matches the beauty of form to the oppressive closure of Songlian's nightmare confinement. Part of that closure is clearly the sense of perpetual surveillance reinforced by high-angle shots of the palace courtyard and long deep-focus shots of the concubines' apartments where all is open to the translucent gaze of the inquiring camera.

It is significant that Zhang uses few mindscreen techniques here. Although this is the story of Songlian, who appears in each sequence, there are few POV shots and a consistency of static framing which is broken only by two key tracking shots towards the end of the picture. This extreme objectivity and formal design makes us part of the surveillance gaze rather than the subjective gaze, for Zhang wants to show us the fatal tactics of divide and rule, which tempt the mistresses into tyrannising their servants and plotting against one another. For Songlian, the palace intrigue involves not so much initiation into sex, to which she remains cold, but power which clearly tempts her and fatally compromises her. This is the duplicity and shifting hierarchy of the luxury prison, mutual betrayals among the privileged who are nonetheless subject to an absolute master. There are echoes here of Coppola's *The Godfather*, and Zhang's film appears at times like a gender inversion of that interior purity of intrigue one finds in the American picture. Yet *Raise the Red Lantern* is about much more than power and corruption. It is about identity, this time not of the rootless but of the subjugated. Of the two, Zhang's cinema always implies that rootlessness is the lesser evil. Filtering subjugation through gender, the heroine is a pivotal figure in Zhang's films and personified to great dramatic effect by Gong Li. Invariably the story is the attempt to break away from subjugation but only in the contemporary *Qiu Ju* is that truly possible. For Zhang, history is a source of doom.

Of all Zhang's films *Lantern* is universal in one key respect. It works through the plotlines of historic patriarchy and ends as a metonym for authoritarian power anywhere in matching the indolence of absolute power to the feverish intrigue of divide and rule. More than all the dark conspiracies of the paranoid Western thriller it gives us the limpid detail of coerced power, diurnal, unyielding, a form of corruption which mixes inertia and cunning in equal measure. Moreover it reinforces this through the displacements of Eros. The ritual foot-massage and the flute-playing of the Master's adult son are Songlian's sources of pleasure where the concubine's bed is clearly not. Power is anything but sexy. It is the negation of Eros. Indeed the pivotal revelations of power in the film are traumatic, forcing a break with the static framing of the form. The film's two key tracking shots are revealing moments which designate discovery of the rotten foundation of power, the malaise which underpins rite, convention, tradition. The first is during the memorable sequence on the snow-covered rooftop where Songlian secretly watches the Master's servants force the unfaithful Third Mistress into a mystery hut to be murdered in secret. This is the power-reversal of the gaze which has until that moment been directed at Songlian. It is her POV we share as she rushes towards the hut, to confront unseen the gruesome fate of female transgressors. The second occurs at the end of winter where the gaze of the camera moves towards her but at the moment of her extreme defiance. She is framed through the open doorway of her apartment as the camera tracks in along the courtyard towards her, her room full of lit lanterns and the voice of the dead Third Mistress (her favourite song on a phonograph) appearing to come out of the room. It is the last gesture of defiance and refusal before she is displaced and substituted the following summer by a younger mistress.

Within the power-frame of intrigue the use of colour is crucial, and controversial. Red, the dominant colour of the Chinese Revolution and its many insignia, becomes something subtly different, the code of dressing which reflects back on Gong Li's fluctuating fortune within the palace of insipid desire. The pigtailed novice is dressed in white, the Fourth Mistress graduates to silver and gold, while her ascent in the palace to Master's favourite concubine is doubly signified through the substitution of black jacket and scarlet dress for white costume. In the delusion of victory where she proclaims herself pregnant and becomes the favoured concubine, she is dressed in a floral red tunic, her face framed by a scarlet headband. If white is the colour of innocence, red is the primary, primary colour, the colour of ripeness, Eros and power. When the Master's physician uncovers her fake pregnancy she strips off the red headband outside her door and throws it away. When she discovers the fate of the Third Mistress, her coat is a pale glacial blue to match the frozen roofscape. The red lanterns which ritually mark the Master's presence in the bedroom of a mistress are empty symbols of Eros which for the women become equally symbols of acceptance and symbols of defiance. Ironically enough Songlian doubles Yan'er, her servant of the same age whom she has betrayed, by also lighting lanterns in her room as a gesture of defiance, thus repeating the earlier gesture by her maid which she has openly condemned. The meaning is clear. Power of the lanterns is marked by their colour, and ironically this melodrama is a 'struggle' narrative which reverses all the rules of socialist realism. Red dominates and decides women's lives in ways which transcend any clear political meaning. While Kieslowski's post-communist *Red*, the 'equality' film in the trilogy set in Geneva, makes over red into the colour of the capitalist commodity, the colour that frames the fashion modelling of Irene Jacob, Zhang sees it as a colour of transient defiance doomed to be overwhelmed by official redefinition. By struggling for it, and against its official definitions, the concubines mark both their resemblance and their rivalry as subordinates in a cruel hierarchy.

A very different kind of historical Chinese cinema can be seen in another film of the early 1990s, Wong Kar-Wai's *Days of Being Wild* (1991). Like *Lantern* it is a historical film made with a daring of which most Western filmmakers are no longer capable. It is set in 1960 at a time when the director was an infant in Shanghai and British colonial rule was being sidelined by US 'Sixth Fleet' culture, and the colony was an economic world apart from the economic disasters of the 'Great Leap Forward' on the Maoist Mainland. It was to be followed in 1992 by Edward Yang's four-hour chronicle of Taiwanese gang culture set in 1960, *A Brighter Summer Day*, which also glosses the impact of new American culture in the same year on Hong Kong's troubled neighbour. Yang's film was in turn to be followed in 1993 by *The Scent of Green Papaya* in which Tran Anh Hung obliquely traces the Americanisation of South Vietnamese culture in the 1960s. While sharing the general concerns of East Asian cinema Wong's films, however, are highly distinctive, for they combine three crucial forms of human experience: the doubling of desire, the imploding of space and the irreversibility of time. In all his films, Hong Kong is a magnet of attraction which is also a point of departure, a finite and fragile colony-city with a fixed time-span and nowhere to expand into. Out of these specific circumstances Wong's films have created a universal cinema for the 1990s, a new cinema of intimacy with themes which in the orbit of the Anglo-American moving image has largely been downloaded into TV soaps or sentimental comedies. He is not only a graduate of the Hong Kong school of action cinema but also a powerful successor to Resnais, Godard and Antonioni. Intimacy here is not so much a battle between love and lust as between availability and denial. The inaccessible is cherished, the available denied. Relationships become transactions, forms of marketable exchange. But in the transfers which take place, nobody wins.

His world of losers is anti-Hollywood not only on account of its razor-sharp ironies of disappointment and disaster, but also because of its spirituality, its downbeat humilities of the striving soul which suffers loss and pain and grief. Thus it would be wrong to see the gangster themes of *Chungking Express* and *Fallen Angel* purely as cute examples of new Asian Cool. They are about lost opportunities in which risks taken by the cop or the gangster echo the risks of intimacy rather than vice versa. Wong works through the faultlines of cops, gangsters and drifters to illuminate a spiritual dimension in daily life which is constantly drowned in the detritus of bars, brothels, seedy hotels or apartments and fast-food joints. His films are about how humans try to distinguish themselves from commodities and very often fail. They crave love, authentic existence, an end to solitude but finish with up with none of these. In this context, *Days of Being Wild* is arguably his most powerful film. Shot in a faded, washed-out colour which verges on monochrome each instant of desire is a snatched moment, measured as in bar-girl Maggie Cheung's initial voice-over, by the power of time. She meets Yuddi (Leslie Cheung) first for a moment, then for a minute and then for an hour a day. But the first shot of their intimacy is also their last, framed by the medium close-up on the touching cheeks of their reverse-angled bodies. They caress, not lying side by side but lying in opposite directions. Consummation is an absence never shown, for Wong is concerned above all with its interruptions and its consequences. Their relationship has gone in real time to the point at which Yuddi wishes to call it off, but in screen time it is a passing moment, expiring after Maggie Cheung voice-overs it into life.

The film shares with *The Passenger* the individual's desire to break the pattern of the normal and become someone else only to find at the end of release the forms of repetition which bind one to the past. Wong bases his cinema on the central paradox of time. It is linear and irreversible, yet like the times of the day and of the seasons it constantly repeats itself so that present encounters always have a past they cannot rescind. Yuddi's search for desire is transient, already trapped into the dilemma resemblance by the power of his foster-mother's displacement of his real family. We find here an existential encounter with the surrogate parent which is treated satirically in Luna's *Jamon, Jamon* and clinically in *La Belle Noiseuse*, the Other who is neither biological parent nor biological lover but could easily be either. Moreover his foster-mother is a courtesan who appears to have taken over the infant of another courtesan and Yuddi's main affair is with Carina Lau, a club 'hostess' who in turn seems to offer her body for money. Yet it is the absent moment of Yuddi's passion for Cheung which defines the film, the passion lost in time which memory can never fully recover. Wong stresses this with the main twist of the plot which sees Hong Kop cop Andy Lau become a seaman who meets up again with Yuddi when he is in the Philippines searching out his real mother.

What links the two men is the rejected woman whose memory engages both of them. The most powerful sequence of the film prior to Yuddi's death occurs earlier when the cop first consoles the spurned lover. Shot in the washed-out seagreen colours of a night-time rainstorm as Cheung leaves Yuddi's apartment, the two figures circle each other like apparitions in a blue light, their faces half-masked, Lau by his peaked cap and its shadow, Cheung by the hair which covers her downturned head. Though they are strangers, Wong always frames them in the same shot though with each cut, the angle and the distance of the camera change. There is affinity, connection but no fusion. The fragmented conversation is about her lost lover. But even though the couple never touch, this elegy for lost space and lost love itself turns into a filmic passion, a love story extraordinarily defined by space, position, look, rain, desolation, the love story which atones for the one which had not been shown earlier. And yet the scene is also defined by something else entirely, the British telephone box, a discreet reminder of colonial rule around which the sequence takes place over a series of nights. Is it just two nights? Or is it more? In the scene's ambiguities of time and space, the moment becomes eternal, a dream reverie of the eternal present. The consolation of love's loss becomes its own love story which in turn is doomed. The phone box at which Cheung promises to phone only rings when the space of the couple around it is now empty, when Lau is a cop no more and in another country and Cheung cooped up in her ticket office at the football stadium.

For Wong the trap of resemblance is framed by the trap of time. The past dictates the present image which attracts as in a reverie. When Yuddi goes to the Philippines and finds his mother who refuses to see him, she is shot in profile under a white light which turns her into a ghostly resemblance of his foster-mother. When he later gets drunk and is robbed by a prostitute, the woman's dress and demeanour resemble those of Carina Lau, who later follows him to the country in vain. When seaman-cop Andy Lau checks in at the same Philippines hotel as Yuddi, the young woman watching him in long-shot briefly resembles Maggie Cheung, but only briefly as she knocks in vain on his door to gain his favours. Yet uncannily we see her resemblance to Cheung more easily than we recognise Lau out of uniform. Shorn of khaki shirt and peaked cap, Lau in that sense is doubled by his own image since the viewer can see into his eyes for the first time. After Yuddi leaves his foster-mother in Hong Kong we see her in a mirror-shot with yet another toyboy lover who resembles both Yuddi and the previous toyboy whom Yuddi has beaten in jealous rage. The film is strewn with body-doubles appearing as naturalistic ghosts of the real in time past. Yet there is autonomy and refusal. Carina Lau refuses Yuddi's sidekick who has taken over his American car and also desires his girl. Maggie Cheung's autonomy lies in overcoming through time both him and the cop who intimates in consolation the love which is never present in desire. Wong doubles the post-mortems both women conduct on Yuddi with other men by the connecting trope of the rain-storm in which their clothes seem to cling to their skin in sorrow. Yet Maggie Cheung is more survivor than victim, the only one who has come out of the other side of love's absence. Their lives in danger, both Yuddi and the ex-cop remember her, so that filmic character comes through the power of memory and the test of time. In the fateful train journey where Yuddi is shot by avenging gangsters, he and Andy Lau share the memory that dare not fully speak its name, the shared subjectivity of the image of the woman who has eluded both of them. Thus the bargirl who is no longer part of the story still dominates it through her absence, through the man who in forsaking her has forsaken love itself and his spiritual brother who, through consoling her, has now fallen in love with her memory even though he admits nothing.

Wong, for sure, equates the spiritual with muted beauty and the raunchy with loud banality. The contrast between Maggie Cheung and Carina Lau is repeated in *Fallen Angels* where sensitive Michele Reis falls for gangster Leon Lai who falls in turn for brassy ginger punkette Karen Mong. The spiritual again resides not in lovers' conversations so much as in the framing of the look, the look which at any angle or distance is an involuntary pose of solitude. This does not need to be in any way metaphysical as the extraordinary wide-angle shots of Reis in glamorous dress masturbating dreamily on her bed show us. The image is immediate, violent, rhythmic, mingling beauty and desolation. Like *Cyclo*, *Fallen Angel* represents a new kind of cinema whose dynamic and fragmented use of the physical poses as if by proxy questions of the spiritual meaning of the world which remain unanswered. Though time is still a constant theme in Wong's recent films – the moving hands of the perennial clock in *Days* are replaced by flicking digital numbers in *Chungking Express* – the poetics of space are intensified by a new sense of enclosure. In *Days* distance both recedes to the horizon and separates characters one from another in deep-focus shots. In *Express* and *Angel* characters increasingly come to occupy the same space but at different times. As resemblance is framed by time through repetition, it is now framed by repeated space. Here the female role is crucial; Faye Wong and Michele Reis appropriate the space of their love-objects in the same way that Maggie Cheung had involuntarily charged the memory of the two men whom by chance she had brought together. The stress on space generates a new dynamic in Wong's filming, time-lapse, freeze-frame photography and step-print editing. His characters may be more settled with their lives, but as 1997 approaches time also seems to be running out.

If in the 1990s time passes more swiftly than in the 1960s, Wong makes his *mise-en-scène* clearly more claustrophobic. The choice of the Chungking shopping mall and apartment complex makes the divide of exterior and interior, a convention of film criticism, seem eerily redundant. We are on the outside and the inside at the same time. The food stalls in the mall never seem to see daylight while the view from cop Tony Leung's apartment is straight out into a busy escalator. The film makes the point in its opening sequence with a long still take of clouds passing across the sky. It is more or less the last we see of them. Thereafter the 'outdoors' returns only briefly when cop Takeshi Kanishiro goes running to evaporate his bodily fluids and thus prevent jilted love from bringing tears to his eyes. The sky is nature's Other which we are doomed not to see except through symbols, the toy airplanes of Leung and his air-steward lover in the flashback sequences before she ditches him, and the boarding pass in her misplaced letter which eventually gets him nowhere. Yet the interior films are less tragic, more affirmative, and as Wong says himself, they are about those who, however crazy, know how to cut their losses and survive within the city limits.[3] Taking loss in your stride is the way to endure. It also allows Wong to create a fine web of comic ironies over love betrayed. When jilted cop Kanishiro vows to fall for the next woman who comes into the bar, in walks drug smuggler Brigitte Lin wearing blonde wig, shades, and cool fawn raincoat, showing us that Wong has turned his famous star into a gangster icon based on Gena Rowlands in *Gloria* but so triumphantly stylised as to rival Bogart and Belmondo. Kaneshiro thus falls in love with a 'made-over' star who shows no interest in him, having just been duped over a heroin deal. In the film's second story, when air steward Valerie Chow walks out on cop Tony Leung, he is desired by waitress Faye Wong who in turn stands him up when offered a date and becomes an air steward instead, returning at the end of the movie in identical Pan-Am uniform to Chow. Not only can roles be transferred and duplicated, however, they can also be reversed. The admiring Cop, a regular she had served at the Midnight Express, is now its manager while she is the potential customer in uniform on the other side of the counter. For Wong role-reversal often has this standard visual sign of comic balancing. For everyone who sheds a uniform, someone else steps into one.

But in the contemporary films what strikes us most in the war of the sexes is, as Gross points out, a new gloss on the intimate sharing of the same space by would-be lovers.[4] It is 'shared' at different times or in different frames, but never in the same shot. The cinema of solitude thus becomes a cinema of time-sharing and space-sharing. Michele Reis assiduously prepares the ground for Leon Lai's hits by scouting the scenes of future crimes, preparing his rented apartment, his food and his booze. They never meet. In Bresson, we may recall, the fetishism of objects exchanging hands is what had linked people in a partial but dehumanised way, through the pilfered wallets of *Pickpocket* or the hot money of *L'Argent*. In Wong would-be lovers come to the same objects twice-over on separate occasions, such as the photos, CDs and goldfish Faye Wong plants in Tony Leung's flat without his knowledge, or the favourite brand of beer which Reis leaves for hit-man Lai. In the former case, Wong is both voyeur and invader, snooping with the help of door keys she has intercepted from Leung's ex-lover, spying on his apartment at the same time that she cleans it and stocks it up with objects which confuse him. In the latter case Wong breaks the linear thrust of his narrative by cross-cutting deliriously between Reis's reconnoitres of target territory and Lai's consequent murders there. The time-reversals thus make the delirium of spatial possession adjacent as well as sequential. These are forms of love by proxy, unrequited and never to be requited, but somehow normalised in the middle of abnormality – Wong's gratuitous flooding of Leung's apartment, Reis's lovesick preludes to mass murder. Wong's comic ironies of spatial doubling are thrown into even greater relief by the exploration of like themes in the Taiwanese *Vive L'Amour*. In the poetic grief which ends Tsai Ming-Liang's film, the mood is stark, tragic, uncompromising, more perhaps than we can bear and, insidiously, enough to make us return for yet another viewing of *Chungking Express*.

Return certainly to the start of the first story in *Express* where Kanishiro and Lin seem to share the same beat, he as cop who bumps into her chasing another villain, she as drugs smuggler setting up a massive export operation with Indian immigrants. Hollywood, no doubt, would have fate blow Lin's cover but Wong's interest is in parallel lives where the ironies of ignorance are somehow outlived by dreams of blissful union which never come to fruition. In *Vertigo* Stewart makes Novak over for the second time into the woman – Madeleine Elster – she is not. But in *Chungking Express* making over is female power on the loose. Crewcut gamine Faye Wong makes herself over into the previous lover in Leung's apartment by first taking her place spatially but not physically, and then following her rival's strategy of flight by leaving Leung for California without having laid him. Finally she returns as Chow has done, taking Chow's place through visual resemblance as a Pan-Am lookalike now sporting long hair and trailing the obligatory suitcase on wheels behind her. If Novak's 'return of the repressed' as Madeleine in the Empire Hotel corridor is haunting melodrama, Faye's return of the repressed in the Chung-King shopping mall is comic irony, while Stewart's deathly obsession is displaced by Leung's stoic resignation. Life goes on, for just as in every Wong Kar-Wai movie as one story ends, another just as surely begins.

The contrast in styles between Wong's recent films and *Days of Being Wild*, ironic present versus the tragic past, is mirrored and reversed in the two feature-films by French-Vietnamese director Tran Anh Hung.

His debut history narrative of 1950s and 1960s Saigon *The Scent of Green Papaya* is historic reverie shot in a studio outside Paris which ends in a dream of heavenly ascent. His second feature set in the Saigon of the present day, officially Ho Chi Minh City, is shot on location as a nightmare of infernal descent. In the films of Tran and Wong, the slow measured pace of the past contrasts with the quick-fire rapidity of the present. The narrative fabulation, though, is reversed. For Tran, the dream of blissful union is in the past, the infernal horrors of human betrayal are in the living present. The contrast between his two films is so extraordinary that on first sight it seems difficult to place them as the work of the same person. On a second viewing they dovetail unnervingly together, not least through the iconography of Tran Nu Yen-Mui who plays Mui as a young woman in *Papaya* and Kien's sister in *Cyclo. Papaya*, for which Tran was refused permission to film in Vietnam, is a trance-like study of a servant girl's childhood which turns, ten years later, into a dreamed idyll of romance with the friend of the family's elder son who has been her childhood sweetheart. The childhood in the 1950s and the romance in the 1960s are filmed with a deceptive formalism, a style indebted to Ozu in its framing but more dynamic in its inception. Though we are in a studio the action within the family house is often shot from outside, partially glimpsed through grilles and screens with sweeping lateral tracks which convey movement but also distance. This visual distancing earlier used by Wong in *Days* through different techniques, extreme deep-focus and the overhead shot, through the intercession of barred gates and surfaces between camera and character, is unerringly similar.

The double equation, past equals distance/present equals closeness, is confirmed by the mobile cameras of *Express, Angel* and *Cyclo*, the multiplicity of sequence shots, all of them complex, and the tight framing, as in *Blue*, of the following hand-held camera. Here the respective camerawork of Chris Doyle for Wong and Benoit Delhomme for Tran is complex and utterly superb. The camera loses its formal distance and becomes *Mitsein* consciousness with a vengeance. Nowhere is this clearer than in the extraordinary rooftop sequence where the Poet brutally knifes the client who has raped Kien's virgin sister during an S&M session gone wrong. This is pure floating camera which moves without a cut from the high-angle of observation above the action to the intimacy of adjacent presence beside killer and victim as they circle round in their dance of death and end perilously on the high rooftop edge overlooking the city streets. It is a measure of the shot's boldness that in such an intense sequence the out-of-field can be as unnerving as the horror we witness, since we see for the first time that this grass-strewn and desolate space of ritual bloodletting is not a field or a wasteland but a roof.[5] The horrific witnessing of slow death choreo-graphed as a perversely poetic ballet is thus capped by the abyss of vertigo where far below traffic circulates as normal, as if nothing had happened. The whole style of filming is a salutary lesson for that bet-ter known 'Vietnam' filmmaker Oliver Stone, whose hand-held camera shots in *Platoon* are often technically ingenious but whose monstrous close-ups lack the aesthetic distance achieved by *Cyclo*, reverting instead to the bottom line of current Hollywood melodrama, gratuitous in-your-face voyeurism.

Kien doubles his purgatorial descent both through kinship and dif-ference. His sister follows him in offering herself to Poet, would-be prostitute to Kien's would-be thief, both of them tested to the limit by Poet's perverse strain of duplicitous caring. The dilemma is a classic one in the neo-realist paradigm, orphaned siblings on the verge of poverty and in danger of going under, and the references clearly self-conscious. The older brother has his livelihood taken from him in the style of *Bicycle Thieves* when his pedicab is stolen; the younger sister shines shoes in the fashion of *Shoeshine* while the older sister's descent echoes more than one of the episodes in *Paisà*. The absence of family becomes here, however, all the more shocking in a world where sen-timentality has become impossible. For Trang, the split subject is part of Vietnam's post-war world where the cross-over is between the real family which has gone and the surrogate family of the Boss Lady and Poet, the young hoodlum who runs her operations like an adopted son. Trang's 'Godmother' undermines the family ethos of Coppola's 'Godfather' through its lack of residual sentimentality and the conspir-atorial ethos of its family plotting. Kien cannot see that his pedicab has been stolen by his boss in order to make him over as a gangster and turn his sister into a prostitute. We share the confusions of his mind-screen, the jagged fragments of his daily life. The camera witnesses his events, his resolute daily forms of being-in-the-world but never shows plotting or conspiracy in the grand manner of gangster melodrama. Unknown to Kien, his sister comes to Poet to be pimped without his knowledge and without our knowledge of motive, of that explicit but elusive 'why?'

Yet Saigon's past is equally there, to hand, in its present, the absent presence of war which was conspicuously missing from *Papaya*. Twenty years later the posthumous images of war remain, the helicopter which topples off its transporter in the main street outside Poet's apartment, the gangster veteran who sells his AK47, the airplane monument at the swish restaurant where Poet pimps Kien's sister, the visible exit wound in the neck of Mr Lullaby the professional killer who recalls his closeness to death then croons to his victims before slitting their throats. In Tran's imagistic *mise-en-scène* the lyric has now become a crucial battleground in the war between good and evil. At the airplane restaurant a woman sings a nostalgic ballad of old Hanoi while the vet compares the sound of his automatic weapon to the singing of a song and Mr Lullaby both in name and action links the balm of the soothing lyric to violent death. The lyrical fragments of the natural world in Poet's versified voice-over, his 'poetry', are balanced by the harsh disco rendition of 'Creep' in the night-club where he fatefully pimps Kien's sister to the client who will beat and rape her, and his action is defined by the bald English lyrics of the song. After the horror of Poet's rooftop revenge, Tran cuts elliptically to a chorus of uniformed infant schoolkids sitting at their desks and triumphantly chanting a rhyming verse as the Tet festival approaches. In *Cyclo* lyric-verse is both source of future redemption and flower of evil which prefaces a season in hell.

This evocation of Baudelaire and Rimbaud is not arbitrary, for Tran matches the poetic intensity of their obsessions with a visual style which matches the poetic density of their verse. The film's apocalypse, where Poet sets fire to self and apartment while Kien paints himself blue and shoots himself unconscious, are fed by the polarities of red and blue, fire and ice. But this is also the Tet New Year Festival, the Year of the Pig, and Tran's apocalypse obliquely mirrors that other Tet apocalypse of Saigon thirty years earlier in the midst of civil war. In his para-suicide war paint with its nod to Belmondo at the end of *Pierrot le fou*, Kien becomes a double of the Boss Lady's mad son who had earlier confronted him as a ghost double painted in yellow. After the mad son's death, Kien in deathpaint becomes the cradled surrogate song of the ruined Boss Lady. But he also survives for a last breathtaking long-shot where Delhomme's camera pans from seedy wasteland across the vast expanse of a new luxury hotel complete with tennis court and swimming pool to the street where Kien's pedicab is emerging with sisters and grandfather into the traffic of Saigon. Outliving the nightmare. Eternal return. Nothing resolved.

In the US the split subject had long been a feature of Hitchcock and film noir. In the 1990s it remains without Hitchcock as the minor pursuit of a few independents and noirs, some of them straight-to-video movies. The noir connection is underwritten, as we shall see, in low-budget films like *Kill Me Again* and *One False Move*. As far as serious money goes, a screen marriage of Hitchcock and Bergman would not be seen as bankable. One looks instead to the action thriller. Here *The Crying Game* remains a rare box-office success of the form as does *The Usual Suspects* where ingenious Kevin Spacey under police interrogation either confesses or invents the existence of his gangster double, Keysar Soze, who may or may not exist but has, for sure, the same initials as the actor who brings him to life. Both these powerful thrillers are more likely to have been seen by readers of this book than the four I shall now discuss: I wish to place them against *Suture* (1994) and *Liebestraum* (1991) which did no business at all and have practically passed into oblivion, against the modest success of Atom Egoyan's *Exotica*, which critics praised at Cannes in 1993, and Lynch's self-styled and much decried'prequel' to *Twin Peaks*, produced by the French company Ciby 2000, *Fire Walk with Me* (1992). After Lynch's TV smash hit shot on video in 1989 came the box-office and critical flop of one of his key 35mm pictures in 1992. The Hollywood domination of film culture is such that films on the fringes can be minor gems, and still lack audiences or critical recognition.[6] It leaves our four films to be rescued occasionally by retrospectives, cult viewings or the video circuit. *Exotica*'s modest success derives, moreover, from the fact that it was Canadian and not made in the US where producers searching for like themes end up with big-budget turkeys like *Showgirls* and *Striptease*.

In *Twin Peaks*, Lynch had doubled Laura Palmer in a token homage to Hitchcock by getting Sheryl Lee to play her look-alike cousin, Madeleine Ferguson.[7] In *Fire Walk with Me* the shading is more subtle and more shocking. The alternating mindscreens of daughter and father, Laura and Leland, balance each other out in their hallucinatory madness. The drug-addicted daughter imagines her incestuous father as hippie Ben, an insane vagrant who comes through her bedroom window at night. The obsessive father sees in the affection of Laura and best friend Donna (Moira Kelly replacing Lara Flynn Boyle) an earlier semi-naked pose of Laura and S&M partner Ronette as they sell their flesh by night in his lover's seedy motel. The demented doubling of Donna and Ronette is induced in Lelend's deranged mind by a scene, echoing *Cries and Whispers*, where Laura and Donna seem about to kiss as he walks into the living-room. His sexuality under threat, he cannot dissociate his daughter from his lover, the first doubling, or Laura's doubled partners, Donna and Ronette as the second doubling, from the pose of lesbian passion which both attracts and repels him. His secret lover, waitress Theresa Banks (Pamela Gidley) is in turn a look-alike for his daughter so that his brutal murder of Laura is both a compulsion to repeat the murder of Theresa and to annihilate the echoes of lesbian passion they evoke in his schizoid imagination. One feels this is Lynch's first major acknowledgement of Hitchcock in work which fuses the murder repetition of *Psycho* to the passion repetition of *Vertigo*. Yet there are other lineages too. Incest, one of the great thematic horrors of the small-town South in the novels of William Faulkner, is taken by Lynch into the filmic territory of the small-town North-West where he transforms it in a reflexive Gothic fable. Reflexive, that is, in the sense of that other source of Lynch's inspiration which we shall explore in the next chapter. For Lynch's aesthetics are moulded as strongly here by *Persona* as by any other American film-maker of his period.

The tragic clash of generations is a theme echoed not only in *Fire* but more strongly in Mike Figgis's noir thriller of the previous year, *Liebestraum*. At least one clue suggests it played a role in Lynch's pre-quel to *Twin Peaks*. In both films Pamela Gidley is the beautiful victim of illicit passion and her death is a spanning of generations, something new for Lynch that was not in *Twin Peaks*. Yet the early sequences of *Liebestraum* also have a clear Lynchian flavour to them, in which case we have a plausible scenario of Lynch influencing Figgis influencing Lynch. Though close to Lynch, however, the film is much closer to Hitchcock, so much so that it comes across as one of the greatest explorations of the male gaze since *Vertigo*. As English directors in America both men were able, one feels, to nurture the imagination necessary to such original vision because they were not filming in their own country. The historic link here is Kim Novak. Thirty years on, *Vertigo*'s object of desire becomes *Liebestraum*'s avenging mother. The plot too is like an inverted sequel to Hitchcock's movie, as if Novak were the real Madeleine Elster taking revenge upon her deceitful husband and the woman imposter he had seduced into murder and imitation. A reverie film like *Spider's Strategem*, which links past and present through resemblance, *Liebestraum* deals with a similar theme, the sins of one generation visited upon the next. Thus Kevin Anderson and Gidley who are the film's present-day lovers, Nick and Jane, double the adulterous 1940s lovers murdered in the department store of the Ralston building in the opening flashback where Figgis uses a jazz rendering of Liszt's powerful refrain to give the film its defining title. At the end the lovers re-enact the scene of the crime, Gidley as adulterous spouse reborn in a clear echo of noir melodrama, Anderson as the lover who mimics his father in the nightmare of repetition. But the ending is open. We do not know whether murder has been repeated down the generations, whether the jealous husband (Bill Pullman) has shot them both or whether the last shot of them lying as still embracing lovers on the dusty floor of the ruined department store strewn with ancient mannequins is one of post-coital sleep.

The use of déjà vu and the refusal to separate flashback and dream are reminiscent of Bertolucci. Nick Kaminsky's search echoes that of Athos Magnini in *The Spider's Stratagem* – substitute the train to Elderstown for the train to Tara in the opening sequence, the town of the old and the dying. Visiting his dying mother Nick becomes involved in the search for his absent father, not having the legend of a heroic father to contend with like Athos, but never as an adopted child knowing his father at all. He only discovers the truth of his father's identity by finding the image of identical likeness. In the police archives he tracks down the murder photographs of the Ralston killing which show him to be the spitting image of his father. The dead weight of the past upon the present highlights the film's constant struggle as in *Vertigo* between Eros and Death. Here Figgis often places a lighting scheme of blazing scarlet against a frame-within-the-frame of cool purplish blue, as in the brothel sequence, and the two colours are constantly fighting for domination on a screen which often fades to black or frames its characters tightly squeezed in the dark vertical silhouettes of door frames. The door ajar is the favourite domain of the reverse angle close-up and the intimate conversation, compressing its subjects, slicing their bodies in half, in a novel gloss on claustrophobic noir.

The poetics of resemblance are ubiquitous, both expressive and surreal. The ruby-lipped brothel hookers whom Nick visits with the insane sheriff after his drunken foray to Paul's party become in the sequence of the following day the pale-lipped nurses who attend his mother's sick-bed. This perhaps is the film's closest point of affinity to the shock tactics of Lynch, but Figgis uses the *mise-en-scène* of sex-for-sale even more effectively. The slinky dresses are replaced by severe uniforms, their faces scoured of make-up. From the chilling sequence where Nick licks vaginal fluid from the fingers of a blonde hooker springs the absurd irony of his mother's claim to smell 'cunt on his fingers', since the fluid of the smell comes from the actress who is playing the role of the nurse attending to her daily hygiene. Yet resemblance becomes curiouser and curiouser. In one sequence – is it Nick's dream? – we see him visit the Dalton mansion where he finds Jane in a huge room with an empty wheelchair with the surviving son of the dynasty. There is a gaping wound – a bullet wound? – from which blood runs out of her forehead. Later in the hospital, waiting in the corridor as Nick visits his mother, Jane finds in an identical wheelchair an old sick woman with an identical wound. Ralston comes in and calls her 'mother'. The chance of fearful symmetry now emerges. Just as Nick has seen his genetic likeness in the murder photograph, Jane sees the identical likeness in Ralston's mother. The alert spectator, or even the lazy one using the rewind VCR button since this movie has had little theatrical distribution, would make the image association from the discrete sequences. The brain-dead patient is the maimed Mrs Ralston shot by the killer of Nick's father, and now in the adjacent ward of the same hospital as her jealous rival, Nick's mother, sharing the propinquities of death where once they shared the propinquities of desire.

In matters of resemblance the film effectively matches the open mystery of Bergman to the finite suspense of Hitchcock. While it blurs the boundaries of dream and reality until we cannot tell at times which is which, it delays crucial knowledge with the promise that true discoveries are to be made, the discovery of Nick's father, the plausible discovery of Jane's mother, the true identity of the killer. The parallel cross-cutting between Nick and his mother which defines the film, also defines its climactic ending where Eros and Death cut across one another. As Novak convulses in her death throes, Nick and Jane finally consummate their love in the doomed building in a simulation of the primal scene of copulation which may define them as possessing the same father. In the parallel cutting Figgis juxtaposes the death cries of Novak to the love cries of Gidley. But he triangulates the parallel, inserting monochrome flashbacks of the original killing in a reprise of the opening sequence. This time we can place the faces which are missing from the long shots and body close-ups the first time around. It is Anderson and Gidley as the original lovers and we see this time the lower body of a pregnant woman holding the fatal gun. A cut to frontal close-up enables us to see from the earlier evidence of Nick's photograph that this is the young Novak with child, reflexively the young *dark-haired* Novak before the age of *Vertigo*. Thus Nick would in a macabre twist be 'witnessing' the death of his father from the womb.

Yet a further option presents itself in the poetics of mindscreen, the same option posed by homage to Hitchcock, in Peter Weir's *Fearless*. For this could be the hallucinating mindscreen at the moment of death. Indeed this could be the mindscreen film of a woman on the edge of death willing the repetition of the original sin which ruined her, like father like son, in her demented and despairing mind. We will never know. Yet there is here an enduring sense of an Oedipal struggle over mindscreen, mother against son. Do we attribute the oneiric sequences which puzzle us to the inquiring gaze of the son or the dreamscape of the mother? There is no clear answer. In *Lone Star*, a memory film with similar theme in the relation of son and father and the implications of incest, John Sayles gives us a naturalistic solution and the mystery is resolved. Here we remain in the wake of Hitchcock, Bergman and Buñuel, hauling our imagination back over the perilous route of dreams within dreams within dreams. *Liebestraum* derealises the contours of its recognisable world and they cannot be re-formed.

The off-beat pastiche thriller, *Suture*, was shot by debut directors Scott MacGehee and David Siegel in downtown Phoenix in black and white Cinemascope.[8] Just as *Liebestraum* pays homage to *Vertigo* but has a life of its own, *Suture* pays its own tongue-in-cheek homage to the amnesia and talking cure of *Spellbound*. But there is an even closer

connection. *Liebestraum* and *Suture* are both effective in their visual
sculpting of the small American city. While Figgis reworks the noir tradition, MacGehee and Siegel self-consciously move away from it in
their use of 1960s architecture and abstract modernist design. In their
filming, they use overexposure, the space of the wide-angle and the
sculpted elegance of depth of field to match the found locations of
their setting. Yet to the cinema's history of mimetic desire they add
another crucial transfer to those of class, gender and generation, that
of race. Their two brothers are of different races, black and white, one
dark in pigmentation the other pale so that common parentage is difficult to imagine, and their meeting at their father's funeral strikes an
unlikely note. But this unsettling incongruity is precisely what sets the
tone for the film. Its characters take for granted what its spectators
clearly cannot. This alienation-effect is a vital thread in the drama of
role-reversal which in turn spoofs the studio Hollywood melodrama
out of which it is born.

There is also a new gloss on mimesis and desire in the film's challenge to modern identity. Clay, the black working-class brother takes
on the identity of Vincent, the white middle-class brother, because
Vincent has ordained it, plotting to kill him and swap identities in
order to avoid arrest for the murder of their father. His phone call
triggers the car bomb which Clay survives, but only just, with a wrecked
face and a lost memory. Melodrama demands that plastic surgery
dramatically changes the faces of its characters as in Frankenheimer's
Seconds or earlier still the post-war thriller *Dark Passage* with Humphrey
Bogart, also called Vincent. In the latter, Vincent's POV dominates the
first ten minutes of the movie, not for aesthetic reasons but because he
cannot at any cost be seen until after his car accident and the surgery
which changes his face. He thus emerges from his hospital bandages
as screen icon Humphrey Bogart and while the voice remains the same
we are led to believe that the face used to be entirely different! *Suture*
stands this cliché on its head. After surgery and the removal of his face
mask Clay looks exactly the same as he did before, but in a case of the
Emperor's new clothes, everyone thinks he now looks like Vincent, and
for the most part treat him accordingly. Of course his psychoanalyst
has doubts because he is not the deceitful sleazeball that his brother
clearly was. Here the film plays deliciously upon colour metaphors.
White in soul, Clay is now treated as white in skin whereas Vincent,

always dark in soul, remains pale. The racial question of invisibility is broached but in a different way from its obvious forerunners, Ralph Ellison's classic *Invisible Man* and Wendell Davies's independent feature of the 1980s, *Chameleon Man*.

The parodic line of the film comes, instead, through its deadpan sensibility. It is pastiche which so drains its psychobabble of all meaning that the huge Rorschach blots on the wall of Dr Chinada's office frame the reductive surfeit of his talking non-cure where he finds significance in absolutely anything, while Dr Renée Descartes, falling in love with her patient like all good female doctors in Hollywood films, babbles on about the Greco-Roman characteristics of a face which is clearly African. While the bland couple are sublimely colour-blind, the audience cannot fail to notice the colour contrast because it is built in to the look of the film, in the over-exposed high-contrast photography, or in the abstract design of Vincent's apartment. Here the brothers are shot even in the same frame against a backdrop which either tones with their skin colour, or contrasts with it, as in the final shoot-out. In fact the shoot-out sequence which begins the film as flash-forward also ends the film and contains its most mesmerising shot. This is the overhead shot of Vincent returning to kill the brother who has taken on his persona and now stands to inherit their father's fortune. Vincent, aficionado of the white suit, now returns gun in hand in a sleek black suit while Clay takes refuge with his shotgun in the white-tiled circular shower.

Clay is literally forced by his carers to copy his white brother, to become him in his absence and in the absence of his own memory. There are memory traces, of himself as a crane operator living in a small town on the wrong side of the tracks. But the pull of social expectation is too strong. If society has made him what he was, it now remakes him into what he is: someone else, the well-behaved 'white' brother, the lover of his wise doctor and elegant socialite almost standing in her shadow, and in the final twist to the colour metaphor, the black sheep of the family now reformed – the new 'Vincent'. The film-makers self-consciously do two things in their play upon the title. The suture is the wound surgically stitched, the gap closed, and in film theory – Lacanian of course – it is the gap closed between the spectator and the drama by a montage of reverse-angle absorption. While the 'gap' is closed for Clay, both literally and metaphorically where he is stitched up in both senses of the word to be a full member of society, the gap widens for the spectator since there is no attempt at the suspension of disbelief in a narrative genre which has always demanded it. There is no suture in *Suture*. Yet things are even more complex. For Clay-as-Vincent also fills up the gap which the original Vincent left, the bad white heir and possible murderer become polite, charming, wealthy and part of the social scenery.

In *Exotica* we find a similar dialectic at work. Its male doubles, the gay pet-shop owner and the straight tax-inspector are of alternate sexuality, not colour, but they swap roles in a similar way. In the strip palace Exotica they too are voyeuristically monitored by MC Elias Kotias and manager Arsinée Khanjian as they pay for official congress with Exotica lap-dancer Christina (Mia Kirschner) by whom one is obsessed and the other, as his coerced double, pretends to be. Not since *Vertigo* has any film director redirected the gaze upon its desiring subject with such clinical precision. But all its males are desiring subjects of different sensibilities who share an ambiguous field of perception, an unconscious sharing of failed sexualities, a collective male gaze disintegrating under the weight of its own obsessions. The intersecting lives of pet-shop smuggler Thomas, obsessed taxman, Francis and sleazy DJ Eric, are based on unbounded modes of substitution and desire. Like Hitchcock, Egoyan uses substitution both as a dramatic triggering device and as a sign of the dissolving male persona. Through elliptical cutting, flashback and flashforward, he stripteases narrative into enigmatic revelation. But film is also a battleground and his male subjects are casualties of war. All three have a relationship of sorts with Christina, who performs a 'bad schoolgirl' club routine choreographed to Leonard Cohen's 'Everybody Knows', and knowingly cut by Egoyan each time it threatens to become voyeuristic. Moreover the object of the male gaze is always doubled and therefore undermined. Christina's former lover Eric has also been the lover of the club's owner, Zoë (Arsenée Khanjian) who is pregnant with his child. The obsessive Francis, we eventually discover, has known Christina in a previous life as a good schoolgirl who used to babysit his daughter. He now uses his teenage niece to take on a similar role but this time to babysit his empty house and repeat his daughter's piano performances. The gay, introverted Thomas, blackmailed to take on the role of Francis after the latter has been kicked out of the club for touching Christina, has slept with a very different bureaucrat, a black customs officer who confiscates the illegal Mackaw Hyacinth eggs he has imported into the country.

All three men are locked for very different reasons into a culture of disappointment to which desire is intrinsic only as that male striving which is never satisfied. Exotica, club emporium of the hyperreal where pleasure is promised yet touch forbidden, is disappointment's true home. For Egoyan the selling of desire of which pornography is just one instance, becomes the antithesis of desire which in a consumer world goes well and truly beyond the pleasure principle. As Eric never stops telling his clients, the price of a lap-dancer is five dollars, and for that they reveal 'the mysteries of their world'. There is, however, no mystery, only addiction to the promise which endlessly conceals its emptiness. Exotica, like Genet's brothel, is a house of illusions where desire has no essence but is founded purely on the obsession with a copy which displaces the original object. The lover whom Thomas picks up outside the opera house is thus a copy of the two pick-ups he has rejected on previous visits. Christina in turn is a female copy of each of them, while as a lap-dancer she is a double copy, first of the original woman whom Eric once loved and before that the original girl to whom Francis had been compassionate. She is a copy of herself in two earlier stages of her life now reinvented and transformed through erotic masquerade, the copy as simulation of different originals through endless performance.

Like *The Adjuster*, this is a film which interrogates the inability to mourn but also like *Vertigo* a film which explores the compulsion to repeat. Egoyan locates the negation of pleasure within the pleasures of the consumer world where what is consumed is never consummated. While his film shares erotic denial with *Sweetie*, Claude Sautet's *Un Coeur en hiver*, *Fallen Angel*, *Cyclo* and *Beyond the Clouds*, it differs in one crucial aspect. Its rivalries of desire are lost in a boundless infinity of doubling personas in which everyone is themself only by standing in for someone else. The mirroring of doubles in which everything is displaced is an ironic counterpoint to the lyrics of Cohen's song, repeated in Christina's double performance, first at the start where she is watched by Francis and then towards the end where she is watched by Thomas, his bemused stand-in. The song, which ironises transparency and is echoed in Eric's candid assessment of Francis's fixation, 'How do you know?' 'Everybody knows', is a prelude to an exploration of the limits of the gaze, the point of the imaginary at which it stops dead. Yet in Egoyan there is more. For the watching eye the horizon is both in front and behind at the same time since it is always seen through an infinity of mirrors.

The film's sharp parallel cutting not only links the male mindscreens as equidistant points on a triangle whose symmetry is uncanny, it also conveys a shared haunting which is a distancing device to efface the lure of any one 'exotic' *mise-en-scène*. Christina's first Cohen routine is intercut with Thomas's adventures at the Opera House where he offers a pick-up a free ticket, and to make the point, Egoyan runs the music over the cut. Thomas, seated inside and listening attentively, a model of decorum, glances casually down to see if his pick-up has an erection. The interweaving of parallel experiences is stressed spatially in the iconography of the raised platform, distinctly echoing that of the film censor in *The Adjuster*, which all three men occupy at some point. The office space at the back of Thomas's store has a desk at a raised vantage point of surveillance, yet Thomas is the one being 'watched' by the authorities for smuggling and tax evasion. Thus Francis is the double of the customs man who watches Thomas at the airport through a one-way mirror in the film's opening sequence and later becomes his lover for a night. Francis, in working through the store owner's files, displaces him at his desk as if metaphorically to iterate his role of watching. The raised desk at the store is doubled by the DJ's raised dias at the club, where the film's visual design again stresses identity and difference. The downward look of both echoes the high-angle of the surveillance videocamera, but as the film progresses we find the occupiers of the vantage point are themselves being watched by others. Like *The Adjuster*'s viewing auditorium, club and store are pastiche panopticons in which the gaze is returned. Elevation is conspicuous. The dominant colour tones of the store are a cool aquamarine, colours of the sea captured in the stacked rows of fish tanks, whose thermostatically controlled waters are themselves another metaphor of transparency while that of the club is a dark and overheated indigo blue which tinges into deep purple. Each seems a colour facsimile of sea and sky respectively, a consumerist pastiche of the colours of nature which of course join at the horizon. It is the horizon beyond which the gaze cannot, by definition, see. The link between different shades of blue with differing emotive hues is captured by Eric's garish turquoise jacket worn over black vest and jeans, and by the stuffed paraqueet on a perch in front of him. Both are displacements from exotic pet shop to exotic strip club. Both places are versions of exotica, the rare creatures, exotic birds and fish as rare creatures transported to the cooler climate of Canada; and in the Armenian-Canadian club rare creatures who are not so rare, pale Anglo-Canadian women attuned to the male desires of a Northern culture, stifled desires reheated by the hyperreality of 'exotica'. Here, a surfeit of plants and palm trees – real or artificial? – is a sensual surround for a surfeit of dancers whose excessive flesh is distinctly pale.

The film's puzzling flashbacks feed into shared mindscreen. The pastoral motif of the search in the countryside shared by Eric and Christina is triggered not only by their look, but by the gaze of Francis who was not there. Egoyan's time-images here are closer to Hitchcock than they are to Resnais. The mystery of what they show is gradually revealed and their ellipses are part of narrative suspense. But like Pinter's *Betrayal*, the infidelity drama by one of Egoyan's favourite playwrights, receding into the past is also a form of suspense. Egoyan matches mystery and past tense uncannily in the look of Mia Kirschner as she recedes through four different personas: the exotic dancer, the jaded fashion Goth, the fresh-faced hippie and finally the spotty teenager who used to babysit the murdered daughter of the fixated Francis. The mystery which remains unrevealed is more than just the question of shared mindscreen. How, for example, can the present gaze of Francis lead onto the past event at which he was not present? It is also a question of shared resemblance. How can people who are so dif-ferent come to resemble each other so closely in such unlikely ways? The answer lies in something we have more than hinted at in dis-cussing this picture, the relation of resemblance to the power of the gaze. Here the boundless matching of the split subject returns to that other vital dimension of Pasolini's aesthetic. The vertigo of the split subject in *Exotica*, where in some respect everyone resembles everyone else, is inseparable from the camera's double vision, its inimitable gloss upon the mysteries of looking, mysteries to which there is no answer.

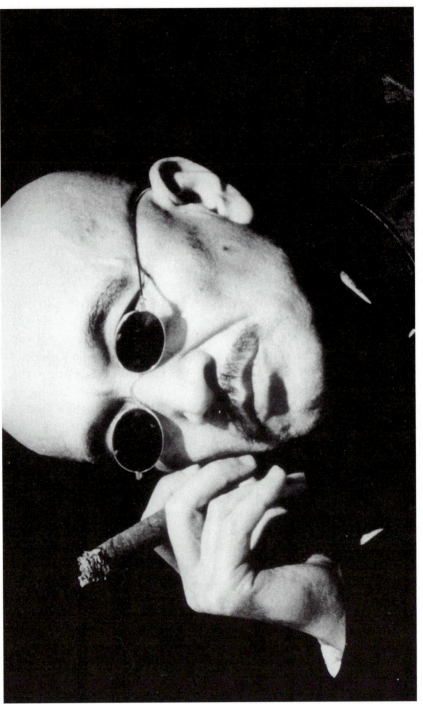

Shanghai Triad: see no evil, hear no evil. Li Baotian

Vagabond: trekking in the wrong direction. Sandrine Bonnaire

Stalker: flatcar special, Zone travel only. Aleksandr Kaidonovsky

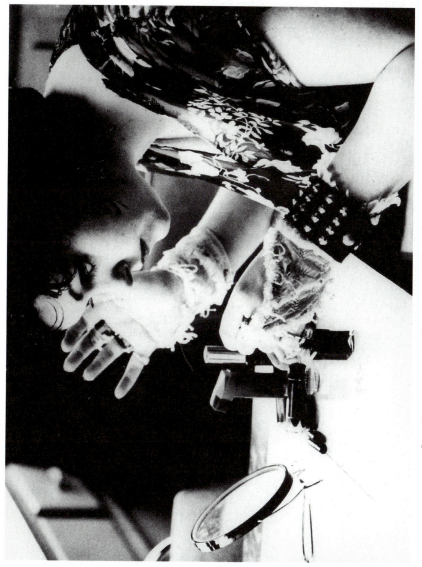

Sweetie: was beauty always this sublime? Genevieve Lemon

The Adjuster: exposing the gaze, torching the world. Elias Kotias

Raise the Red Lantern: innocence fades, resemblance begins. Gong Li

Chungking Express: cop chases disappearing spaces. Takeshi Kaneshiro

Exotica: surveillance equals desire. Don McKellar, Calvin Green

Beyond the Clouds: manipulating the endgame. Peter Weller, Fanny Ardant

La Belle Noiseuse: imagining the substitute. Jane Birkin, Emmanuelle Béart

Chapter 5

THE CAMERA AS DOUBLE VISION:
Blow-Up to *La Belle Noiseuse*

To speak of the double vision of the camera is to explore a cinema of poetry founded on the presence of the camera. It may also seem another excuse for the endless playbacks of the film vision in the age of the VCR. Criticism now is so fixated on the filmic gaze and its role in the electronic media that at times it is little more than a baleful act of voyeurism. It is a tactic which can end up as bad faith, but that is also true for filmmakers since films about filmmaking often have attached to them a seal of knowing approval. It is equally true for audiences. What tempts us to be lazy is the sheer multiplication of moving images which have increased so dramatically over the last thirty years and which, against the best of intentions, we can use as a good excuse to be couch potatoes. It is often said we live in a culture saturated with electronic images. This assumes that saturation point has already been reached. Future invention promises more not less, different kinds of images on different kinds of screens, many of them as yet unknown. In one sense, the double vision of the camera is a plausible, and some would argue necessary response to the ubiquities of image-saturation. Since moving images are produced all around us, then film must surely film some vital aspect of the perpetual assembly-line. On the other hand, the very complexity of those images could make the double vision of the camera harder to sustain.

We have already had the defining films about filmmaking, we could assert, by pointing to the unmatched accomplishments of *Eight and a Half* and *Le Mépris*. The form now works best not when film films

130

filming but when it films other forms of representing. At the very least the camera works best as double vision when narration observes some form of Pasolini's double-register either *within* the medium of film or *between* film and the representing medium it films. The former works best in the double-register of director and filmmaking subject who is *unlike* the director, not just a veiled impersonation. This has been seen to great effect in the Polish cinema, in Wajda's *Man of Marble* and Kieślowski's *Camera Buff*. More importantly, it also works through the double-register of filmmaker and film process, a register which runs through contemporary cinema from *Persona* to *Dreams*. The other dimension of the reflexive is equally important. It registers dramatically the difference between film and its representing other, be it drawing, photography, architecture, painting, video, television, sound recording, or even, as in Kieślowski's *Short Film about Love*, the simple prying telescope. Not only that. It must also register dramatically the perennial tension between the means of representing and the object represented. One thing is for sure. The other form cannot be a simple mirror of filmmaking since both forms contribute to the finished image. Each form must have its partial autonomy, its special world and its special way of representing that world, or of failing to do so. Thus *The Draughtsman's Contract* is a film about the power and limits of the architectural drawing in an age before film was invented. In *Caravaggio* and *La Belle Noiseuse* the exploration of painting is also an exploration of cinema. For above all else the camera as double vision has been about the unexpected limitation of vision.

Both forms of double-register are not formal devices, therefore, but take filmmaking outside of itself by engaging the social, the political, the historical. The power of the camera comes from what it chooses to examine and equally, at times, from what it fails to examine. It can only interrogate the limits of perception by interrogating what is perceived and why. Here the ontology of film is problematic in one vital area. The limits of the camera which the film explores are limits of time and place, of history and culture, but at the same time universal limits. They *are* because of X, Y, and Z but in addition *they just are*. At its best, the self-examination of representing ends up as universal mystery. In such a scenario, the boundary between the cultural and the universal often becomes invisible and we do not know when it is being crossed. The film 'passes' from one to the other at different junctures on different

viewings. Here film interrogates representations of the world by investigating their sounds and images, even though some of these may
well be its own. In this case it can become an object to itself. From this
perspective, its central subject is usually an investigator-who-creates-
images, images which the film interrogates and who is therefore a
figure objectified. Across the board this ontological condition, objectified
subjectivity, is identified isolation. For the film subject feels isolated not
only from persona and objects but also from the technologies by which
he or she represents them. Using the chosen medium of communication
which is the film's topic, a brush, a tape, a camera, intensifies solitude
rather than alleviates it. This relationship between representation and
solitude goes beyond the grand isolation of previous archetypes, say
the private eye or the Westerner, or the romantic figure of the lone
genius, since it finds the nub of solitude in the technical means which
are meant to end that very condition, in media which are meant to
provide connection with others. How should we read this paradox?
The mean streets down which a man must go have now become lonely
streets for men and women alike, and the disconnection runs deeper.
It is solitude at the heart of the electronic network and is a function of
an urban mindset which is the complete antithesis of the grandiose
Nietzsche at Sils Maria or of Rousseau's late pastoral solitude. In short,
there is no standing apart. For the inquiring mind, there are the usual
suspects – confidants, cops, agents, lovers, carnal encounters – but
uncannily the creative investigator steps back from all this, a creature
apart, not as a sign of Bogartian toughness but of an unacknowledged
fragility. To investigate is to represent, to represent is to go out on a
limb. It is to make the world, however banal, in one's own trivial
image.

Two key films of the 1960s which inaugurate the aesthetics of double-
seeing in the city are as alike on first sight as chalk and cheese. In
Blow-Up (1966) the young photographer in London (David Hemmings)
is the investigator of a possible murder, while in *Le Samourai* (1967)
the young contract killer in Paris (Alain Delon) is the investigated, the
object of the surveillance gaze, the suspect who has committed a
night-club murder. In Antonioni's picture, Hemmings is subjective
subject and we see London largely through his selective eyes. In Jean-
Pierre Melville's film, Delon is objective subject. We see Paris largely
through his eyes and, simultaneously, see him through the manifold

watching eyes of Paris. As subject and object respectively both men are isolates of the process of investigation. The further it proceeds, the more they feel separated from their daily world. If investigation brings them closer to others, it makes them feel further away. While Hemmings has been taken mythically as a predator-photographer of the swinging sixties, a holistic archetype whose brittle arrogance defines a decade, we find on close scrutiny that he has more in common with the split subject of the modern screen. He is two kinds of photographer and two kinds of social being. His work combines the photorealism of Don McCullin in the pictures of the South London hostel – the photos are in fact McCullin's – with fashion photography in the style of Terence Donovan or David Bailey in his mews studio. In the former instance we see the photographs but not the process of Hemmings taking them. In the latter we see the process, Hemmings in the studio with female models, but not the photos resulting. As working-class lad made good, his persona is that of a contemptuous philanderer driving a Rolls Royce around the fashionable areas of London. As working-lad made bad, his persona is that of one of the vagrant homeless on the streets with whom he seems surprisingly at home in the opening sequence of the movie.

The sudden switch can be read as a fantasy scenario. We presume that Hemmings is a successful photographer, brash and loaded, faking vagrancy to get secret pictures of destitution. Mindscreen inversion, however, invites the opposite reading. The 'swinging' life of the photographer is the wishful mindscreen of the young vagrant down on his luck. At dawn, as he leaves his fellow dossers and disappears under the railway bridge, the Rolls emerges as if by magic on the other side, a utopian fancy transporting him into a new world of sex, glamour and money. On the face of it the two readings – the reality of slumming or the fantasy of ascent – are mutually exclusive, but Hemmings' mindscreen integrates them smoothly into the narrative. The theme of split subject is echoed in the opposition of park and studio, a binary opposition of nature and culture, the artifice of the fashion studio where unreal images are manufactured versus the natural light and tranquillity of the park with its verdant grass and trees. But this too is deceptive. The grass in the park had been painted greener, tree trunks and branches painted grey, shopfronts on the streets through which Hemmings cruises in his Rolls painted a deep red. The park itself is a built environment, so its photographic images are not copies of nature but copies of copies of nature. Images too change with time and light. The park looks different at night from during the day and different yet again when Hemmings goes back at dawn. The pictures themselves look different according to their size. The blow-ups which might prove the existence of a man in the shrubbery with a gun, look less like photographs and more like his neighbour's abstract paintings. At the point where the photographer's evidence blurs into dots, the painter's desire for an inner reality of shape takes over. The evidence too depends on sequence so that Hemmings hangs the photographs from beams in the studio in some semblance of sequence, tracing his finger from one to the other as if the movement might give the life of a pro-jected film. While the still frame, however, captures the mystery of the moment by freezing it, it cannot capture the meaning of the movement to make it go beyond a lover's tryst to a planned murder.

In its look and its appeal, *Blow-Up* is designed as a topical film. Its puzzles of representing are later taken in two different directions by two films of the same year, 1982, which owe much to its style of bemused investigation, *The Draughtsman's Contract* and *Blade Runner*. Greenaway's film reprises *Blow-Up*'s external puzzle of the park, the act of representing. *Blade Runner* echoes the post-production of the studio, the transformation and manipulation of the image. Eighteenth-century draughtsman Anthony Higgins undertakes twelve drawings for Janet Suzman of her stately country home in which her adultery with him is part of the contract. His perspective frame is a frame-within-the-frame of Greenaway's camera given formal style by the director's static shots.[1] Here detection concerns what intrudes into the draughtsman's frame when it should not. The drawings by their nature are intended to de-dramatise, to capture the shape and the look of the house alone. But action intrudes with intimations of murder most foul which the drawing by its remit cannot hope to capture. Formal repre-sentation fatally omits the substance of intrigue which rebounds at the end on the draughtsman's own head. Greenaway embellishes his point with the comic device of the moving statue which freezes at the right moment to capture resemblance. But the resemblance is false. The limits of the draughtsman's vision then become the limits of his life which ends so brutally.

Blade Runner moves forward in time to the future where Harrison

Ford's search for replicants uses two powerful variants of the electronic image, the futuristic lie-detector called the Voigt-Kampff (or V-K) analyser used against replicant Leon by a Tyrell employee and later on Rachael by Deckard, and the Esper machine on which Deckard runs a digital scan of a replicant photograph. The V-K's main measure of detection is involuntary dilation or retraction of the pupil, a sign of pressure to queries about emotional response which Leon and Rachael find difficulty in answering. In looking at the eye through a viewfinder the interrogator looks at the blow-up of the eye of the suspect, creating a bizarre mirror-image effect, the telephoto eye which scrutinises almost touching the eye which reveals. This is a virtual reality effect which short-circuits material space. By electronic means the eye which is a window opening onto the world is watching the eye which is a window opening into the soul. Its flickering changes reveal when the soul lies and the human has become inhuman. But the gaze of the investigator itself is dehumanised by the V-K and the film's message comes across: the human and the non-human are relative concepts.

In the case of the Esper, Scott's design team created a simulation of computerised images in the decade before they became standard by videotaping a montage of still photographs of Leon's room shot through with special effects.[2] But the illusion is of a purely computerised image subject to voice-command in which Deckard can demand different photographic copies of the room from different angles and length. He is thus able to make two discoveries: a blonde-haired man sitting at a table and the figure of a woman reflected in a mirror at the back of the room. A further blow-up shows a snake-tattoo at the back of the woman's neck. This is the hi-tech evidence for Deckard to link the replicant Leon with replicants Zhora and Roy Batty. The authority of Harrison Ford's voice and the power of the visual technology imprint upon the audience the aura of revelation at hand. But as in Greenaway's film, we have to ask what is being revealed. The answer is nothing that is obvious at all. While *Blow-Up's* photographs affirm and then go beyond what Thomas thinks he has seen in the park, there is no external check on Deckard's certainty. Short-circuiting the photographer's craft, Deckard has discovered the truth, or so we are led to believe. Against Antonioni's cultural scepticism we have the positivist illusion of certainty which is a very American trait. But it is still an illusion. What we see in the image are not Rutger Hauer and Joanna Cassidy who act the part of the replicants but two unknown doubles who stand in for them on a post-production reshoot by Scott in London. Batty is not Batty, Zhora is not Zhora and the audience cannot know at this point in the narrative why Deckard is so fired up. On the film's rerun in 1992 they could accept more clearly a new convention which has come into film as a result of *Blade Runner*. The aura of hi-tech certainty has formed the mythical acceptance, in Barthes's sense, of the new convention. Similarly on the V-K the images of the eyes are not those of the actors either but standard eye-images taken from stock archive footage. Scientific certainty equals the V-K and the Esper plus Harrison Ford. Just as the strange movements in and out of the draughtsman's perspective frame are non-clues which lead us nowhere in particular, so the V-K and the Esper are 'scientific' guarantors that something is being solved even though we have no idea what it is.

Here we need to take a complete change of tack by returning to *Le Samourai*. Here the represented image is matched in its power by represented sound and both are unique. Henri Decae's photography with its steely greys and blues gives us a largely nocturnal film shot in low-level lighting which soon became familiar in the revamping of American *Noir*. The Samurai look of Delon himself, the recurrent profile shot of the fedora hat and trenchcoat fuse the image of Bogart with the still repose of Japanese cinema, a hybrid icon which improbably crosses Ozu with Kurosawa and the French New Wave. As such it has been taken up, among others, by Walter Hill, Tarantino in *Reservoir Dogs*, and in the Hong Kong films of John Woo and Wong Kar-Wai. Its paranoid structure of feeling resurfaces in the 1970s films of Pakula, Coppola and de Palma, and its cat-and-mouse Metro chase has been a model for the street-action flourishes of *The French Connection, Diva* and *Subway*. The intertextual fuse of this much-neglected film cannot be explained solely in terms of its distinctive look. It is Delon's stillness in motion, his paranoia as stoic repose which fills in the iconic look and his neurasthenic sensitivity to sound which make the film so uncanny. Never has so much depended on the sound of a canary in a cage. It is the sound which confronts the abyss we feel is the silence that the 'samurai' must live through in his desolate apartment, and where any external noise is an intrusion. Thus the bugging of his apartment for one who seems to live under a code of silence is a surreal non-sequitur. His concern for the source of the bug planted in his flat is an obvious precedent for the deranged desperation of Harry Caul in Coppola's *The Conversation*. Caul ransacks his apartment in the hope of finding the elusive weapon which he thinks has been turned against him, the wire-tapper tapped, the surveillance expert under surveillance. But in Delon's Jef Costello there is no sense of desperation, rather one of destiny where capture or survival seem a matter of chance.

Le Samourai and *Blow-Up* contribute in equal measure to the American cinema of paranoia which succeeded them. Yet here the paranoid structure of feeling seems a quality of the film itself, not purely its subject, so that it is something indefinable in the air. The objective chain of connections which eventually causes Delon's downfall is there, ascertainable, ineluctable. Yet there is also the perfect fantasy scenario of paranoid delusion. The beautiful black jazz pianist who sees him commit the murder is the woman who has actually ordered the killing through the middleman who then tries to kill Delon after the killing. She in turn contacts the police to kill Delon when he finally returns to kill her. Objectified delusion is based on visual repetition with a symmetry as compelling as any film of the decade. What matches that symmetry is the relationship between hunter and hunted, the investigator and the investigated. For Delon is both at the same time. As the police investigate him, he investigates the source of the attempt on his life which merely leads him round in circles, back to the scene of his own crime. It is Delon's look which is so crucial here, the sharp angular take on the hat and trench raincoat, but also the poise, the stillness in movement which means that in flight and pursuit there is a visual glide through space and time. This repose within nightmare is far removed, for example, from the different tangle with authority and pursuit through the streets of Paris in Polanski's *Frantic* which, as its title suggests, is much more desperate. Melville by contrast matches the Parisian look to the solitude of the warrior which the Bushido specifies. This is a film whose title clearly lives up to its name.

Back in the USA paranoia of course becomes melodramatic. Though both ingenious, *The Conversation* and *Blow-Out* are at key moments of the frantic variety. If the focus in the films seems aural, then let us not forget that as spectators we also *see* what is imperfectly heard, the conversation in Union Square at the start of Coppola's movie, the fatal car crash in *Blow-Out* which reminds us of John Kennedy's assassination in Dallas and with the fall of the car into the river, also of Edward

Kennedy's Chappaquiddick.[3] Therein lies that film's difference with *JFK* whose re-enactment of Kennedy's assassination in Dallas reminds us not so much of American history as of the obsessions of Oliver Stone. To those who have always insisted that the CIA did it, we can now retort that Oliver Stone did it and at much greater expense than the paltry six million dollars shelled out by the House Select Committee in 1979 for its exhaustive investigations into the assassination. There are many fascinating facets of Stone's epic re-enactment of recent history.[4] Here are some of them. He uses more extensive newsreel footage, his eulogy to Kennedy recalling the eulogy to Charles Foster Kane in the 'News on the March' sequence of Orson Welles's debut film. Not only are the two films linked by the seamless interweaving of fact and fiction, actual newsreel and fictive replay, but Stone also has the ambition to emulate the sheer spectacularity of *Citizen Kane*, and has many more technical weapons at his disposal. There is more newsreel and with it the novelty of television, witness Walter Cronkite's terse and grieving announcement of Kennedy's death. Also at Stone's disposal was the most dramatic piece of *cinéma vérité* in American history, the Abraham Zapruder 8mm film of the assassination on Elm Street.

What Welles filmed as Kane's obituary – the News on the March sequence as a parody of movie newsreels of the time – Stone does straight, with no satire, as dramatic re-enactment of JFK's day of death, generating swiftfire images to fill out the accusing words of Jim Garrison the New Orleans DA, played by Kevin Costner, on whose book the film is partly based. This is not then a biopic of just one politician but of two who, in the course of the film, never meet. While Garrison is always Costner (even though Garrison guests briefly as a pro-Warren judge), Kennedy is nearly always Kennedy. Nearly but not quite. A few Elm Street motorcade shots appear where the faces of the famous belong to body doubles turned away from the camera as the film speedily flashes over its images, MTV-style, as part of the countdown to destiny. This is the dubious spicing up of fact which Stone employs generously elsewhere and which leads to a generic hypocrisy. If the Establishment is accused of faking evidence in denying conspiracy, then Stone can be accused of faking evidence in alleging it. Witness the famous photograph of Oswald holding his Mannlicher-Carcano rifle where conspiracy theorists claim fakery because of the lack of shadow. Stone recreates the photo with similar lack of shadow, though now Oldman is replacing Oswald, as he does again in the key jail-murder sequence when he is shot by Jack Ruby. Stone's fakery is on a par with that of which Costner-Garrison accuses his enemies, the pot surely calling the kettle black. As document, sadly, the film cannot be taken seriously. In terms of form, however, there are compensations. The restless mix of colour and monochrome is never less than intriguing. Because the Zapruder film is projected in colour, most of the motorcade shots follow suit. Yet elsewhere the past tense is in black-and-white since in current convention black-and-white usually is the past. Hence the flashbacks of Oswald, mainly in the form of Costner's speculations, are given the flavour of truth by the switch from colour, a switch which also disguises the time-differences within the narrative. Costner's flashbacks come mainly in the period of the Garrison investigation between 1967 and 1969 when Clay Shaw was put on trial, a short time-difference which nonethless makes Costner colour-coded. The voice of authority is in colour, his vision in black-and-white. It is the perfect mythic mix. He does not speak to us. He speaks for us. In this, his voice is aided by the electrifying camera of Robert Richardson and by the elliptical staccato editing. Both imprint the image upon a 1990s audience with maximum, Oscar-winning force.

This then is a quest narrative which proclaims conspiracy but actually discovers none. There are instead multiple fragments of various conspiracies, some implicating A or B, others implicating X and Y, so that Costner-Garrison becomes Stone's mouthpiece for a breathless compendium of insinuations which flashback makes flesh in murky, low-lit interiors where unusual suspects exchange knowing glances and soundless words. The flip side of Costner's sanctimonious verbal attack is a line-up of unreliable witnesses who in Garrison's time might have had some ring of truth but by Stone's time had been largely discredited. True to form Stone has his own Deep Throat in the shape of Donald Sutherland, but this is the opposite of *All the President's Men* where Redford and Hoffman generally find what their informant tells them to look for. The fictional and nameless Deep Throat of Sutherland puts forward a universal conspiracy theory whereby the whole American establishment wants Kennedy out of the way. As a result Costner-Garrison does not know where to start and goes insanely local. He spends the rest of the film persecuting Clay Shaw (Tommy Lee Jones), a gay right-wing extremist with possible CIA connections in New

Orleans. Neither Garrison in his original prosecution nor Stone in his movie version nor any other conspiracy buff for that matter has ever provided hard evidence that he had anything to do with Oswald.

The centrepiece of Costner-Garrison's paranoid persecution of Jones-Shaw is not the florid fantasy scenario of fascist conspiracies fusing with gay orgies. These are done through the lurid mindscreens of Garrison's unreliable suspects who fail to testify in court. It is the Zapruder film itself which, metaphorically speaking, takes the witness stand. Costner interrogates the film and like all good Hollywood witnesses, the film provides the right answer. But what answer? It is one of the most momentous and horrifying documents in the history of film and its impact cannot be denied. But it shows at best how Kennedy was shot, not who shot him. Undeterred, Stone slides from the former to the latter and slides further again from 'those' who shot him, unnamed and faceless in Costner's fantasy flashbacks, to those who wanted him dead. The picture's court finale masquerades as prosecutor interrogating defendant. In fact, it is film interrogating film. Stone's mega-budget picture interrogates Zapruder's home movie. But at various times it also simulates it, dovetails with it, tops and tails it with its fantasy flourishes. Yet save for the home movie, the attorney's display-case is empty. There is the promise of names but no actual names. There is a brilliantly shot and edited reconstruction of the assassination which matches aesthetic boldness to moral conviction. But none of it bears any relationship to the truth. It aspires to like Eisenstein's unforgettable images in *Oktober* of the storming of the Winter Palace which was never actually stormed, a fake image of a real event destined to be etched in the cinematic imagination. Unfortunately it is Zapruder's film not Stone's which will remain etched in the memory and the least we can do is thank Stone for having shown it again to an audience of millions.

Here we need to go back to the power of *Citizen Kane* and note that what JFK fails to achieve in its reprise of *Kane* at the start of the 1990s had already been achieved fifteen years earlier in Wajda's remarkable *Man of Marble*. This was also a film in which politics and self-referentiality, in communist Poland rather than capitalist America, had become an explosive mix. It is the one film to date which has convincingly taken the sensibility of *Citizen Kane* forward into the age of electronic media without sacrificing history to myth. Like *Citizen Kane* it investigates a figure of history, but one who in his time was elusive, buried, forgotten. This is precisely what Stone's movie lacks, the intent focus on either Oswald or Kennedy as historical figures. Kennedy is merely the great 'radical' leader – no evidence given – whose aura demands submission before the legend. Unlike Don de Lillo's docufiction *Libra* where Oswald is the key player, here his background is merely one element in the never-ending plot. Stone's concern with absent conspirators means the central figure of the film is the investigator himself. His greatest achievement in the film is not to unmask falsehood, however, but to convey the turmoil of the 1960s in which the liberal American consciousness was traumatised by the quickfire assassination of its three leading icons, the Kennedys and Martin Luther King. Conspiracy theory is nourished by genuine bewilderment and radical scepticism, but the scepticism which rightly greeted official versions of all three killings is sadly not retained for Costner's wild yet pious alternatives.

In his film Wajda had struck a crucial balance between investigating subject and historical object which Stone lacks. Agniezska (Krystyna Janda) the driven student making her diploma film seeks out the story of Birkut, a forgotten hero of socialist labour. While our composite image of Birkut comes from multiple mindscreens similar to those used in *Citizen Kane*, Janda is as much the object of Wajda's narrative and gaze as Birkut (Jerzy Radziwilowicz) since the film intently watches her intently watching him. The filmmaker is duly filmed, the investigator duly investigated. While Stone sanctifies the dead Kennedy and celebrates his failed avenger, Wajda confronts the vulnerabilities of both female subject and male object. The richer the reflexivity of his film, moreover, the more powerful a gloss it provides on Poland's communist history. While Stone's Garrison is also Stone's mouthpiece, Wajda provides us with two filmmakers, Burski, a successful Wajda-clone of his own generation, and Agnieszka a determined novice of the younger generation. There is thus a double-take on the life of the mysterious Birkut since Burski has filmed him in the early 1950s and his film becomes a source which Agnieszka uses for the 1970s, a reflexive layering, an elusive spiral in the space of duplicated images. Like *Citizen Kane* and *JFK*, *Man of Marble* weaves Wajda's monochrome images in and out of documentary footage, in this case official newsreel of Stalinist party rule and of its popular overthrow in 1956. If the student's film doubles the celebrity's early film, then censorship is also doubled in the treatment of both of them. Agnieszka sees out-takes of Burski's film never previously shown and suffers in turn when her project is judged too controversial. Money and backing for the unfinished piece are withdrawn by her film school. The fragility of film is stressed by a dark repetition. Then and now the state intervenes to doctor or suppress, and indeed Wajda himself was prevented from filming his original ending which made it clear that Birkut has died during the Gdansk shipyard riots of 1970. Equally the frail nature of film as a document of the past which can easily be censored or destroyed is mirrored in Janda's own response to her subject. She falls in love with Birkut's image and finally Birkut's son (also played by Radziwilowicz) who is his spitting image, the uncanny look of the mysterious hero updated for the 1970s by blue denims. The lost son stands in for the lost father and spans the generation between image and flesh.

The doubling of images also reveals that side of Wajda which is so important, his Polish romanticism. The composite image of Birkut is not so much a romanticised socialism as critics of Wajda might allege, but the opposite, the romantic figure made socialist. Thus while it could be seen as an anti-Party film it was not an anti-socialist film and the figure of Birkut remains the outstanding socialist figure in any cinema of Eastern Europe. The construction of Birkut's image depends upon the peasant's naive but enduring idealism. Called to the task of the socialist industrial sublime, he fulfils his duty to excess but in doing so questions its premises. This is not idealism corrupted as with Kane, but the horror of disillusion. Here another Wellesian lacuna suggests itself. Birkut's iconography obeys the same logic as the image of Rita Hayworth in *The Lady from Shanghai*. The more it is knowingly deconstructed by its director, the more powerful it becomes. Since we never see Birkut in the filmic present but only on film or the past, Wajda supplements his partial presence by two other representations which top and tail the narrative. Finding a marble stature of Birkut by chance in a museum storage vault, Janda sits astride the sculpted image with her 16mm camera and films the toppled hero with a satisfied sigh. It is a gender inversion of the Hemmings/Verushka photoplay in *Blow-Up* but also a doubling of images, the film image of the sculpted image which stresses the starting distance between Janda and the subject intriguing her. The rest of the film is the eating up of that distance, the clawing back of space and time. So it is that when she finally returns from Gdansk with Birkut's son, Maciek, down the endless film-school corridor, she has completed her metaphorical journey. The plastic image is made flesh, by her side, arm-in-arm, and Birkut has come back from the dead. Surrogate sex with the toppled statue is replaced by romance with the living descendant.

Maciek, deadpan in spectacles, has the resemblance of Birkut but not the look. Yet it is the look by which Janda and the audience have been seduced in the course of the film. The son is the facsimile, expressionless where his father has been expressive, anonymous where his father had been a transient cult. Yet the image of Janda for the audience is equally seductive. In his framing of his central actors, Wajda seems to split in two the visual legacy of Welles. Janda is spidery, impatient, hyperactive and shot from low-angles which along with her tight flared denims, knee-length scarf and platform heels, all exaggerate height and power. Radziwilowicz is square and compact, shot naturalistically at eye-level and in close-up where his exalted smile seems gently to mock not only communist documentary but the whole construction of the expressionist gaze. Janda is existential, chain-smoking, impulsive, her body flying at all angles, her style a visual embodiment of the ruthless quest of the triumphant director she wishes to be. For her, you feel, history zig-zags and turns around upon itself. Birkut by contrast is either still and solemn in moments of crisis or in moments of exaltation striding in a straight line which mimics the official course of history he represents. Comrade Birkut as Commodity Birkut.

History is also a difference of film styles. Janda who berates her film crew for their old-fashioned methods is edgily shot in the fractured style which is self-consciously New Wave. The Birkut in all of the different reminiscences is shot naturalistically and here Wajda is more consistent than Stone. Film and newsreel are in monochrome but flashback is in colour. Other contrasts are conspicuous. Janda's journey takes place in blazing midsummer light but her informants are framed either in dark interiors or at confusing speed in car or helicopter. Each has their own music track for their own age, the man of marble the rousing lyrics of socialist patriots, Janda a pulsing electronic beat with choral backing which places her in the 1970s rock generation. As Agnieszka and Birkut *fils* walk arm in arm down the film-school corridor at the end, Wajda overlaps them, creating a comic but uneasy dissonance of effect which is very knowing. He has after all created a 1970s motif for his 1970s investigator to match the rousing chorus of the previous generation. We believe in Janda as star female subject in the same way that Burski had make of Birkut a star male subject. The difference lies in the politics. The 1970s model is iconoclastic, the 1950s model an official version. But Wajda makes clear what Stone fails to recognise. Film cannot escape from its own presuppositions. The sublime of one generation may mirror or destroy the sublime of its predecessor but it has no claim to absolute truth, and celluloid can give it none.

   Wajda's ending is unashamedly and triumphantly romantic. Janda may have lost her unfinished film but she gained a lover in the image of her film's star. The solitude of the maverick investigator is ended and she comes in from the cold. Yet the ending has a sting in its tale. We still know the film has not been made and never will be, just as we know at the end of *Blow-Up* that Thomas will never resolve the mystery of the corpse in the park. Two other Polish films provide different sequels, as it were, to this lingering ambiguity. The first is Wajda's own *Man of Iron*, which simply destroys ambiguity in a fit of didacticism which moves Wajda further away from Welles and brings him closer to Stone. The second is *Camera Buff*, Kieślowski's low-budget 16mm feature made during the period of martial law, which articulates more fully the invidious pressures of the Polish censor. In *Man of Iron* Wajda's almost instant coverage of the Solidarity occupation of the Gdansk shipyard has a great sense of daring, filming history as narrative as history makes itself. Yet the film's uncritical adulation of Lech Walesa resembles Stone's eulogy to Kennedy and the brief appearance of Janda as a jailed, pregnant and subdued Agnieszka makes nonsense of her previous iconography. For that reason *Camera Buff* is *Man of Marble's* true successor. Again the double register is electric. In place of Wajda's female film student we have the textile worker Filip (Jerzy Stuhr) as amateur film buff who stumbles into making pictures.[4] Stuhr is an obsessive who starts by making a home movie of his newly-born daughter but then ignores the pressing needs of his family to make a film of his factory which wins first prize in an amateur contest and means he later gets to meet Krysztof Zanussi. Soon however he runs into trouble with the factory director by highlighting the role of a disabled worker and is forced into the trap of doctoring his films. As his wife leaves him in protest at gross neglect, he makes his own protest by opening the cans containing his footage and exposing the film. While Janda's film is never made because it is deemed too subversive, Stuhr's is made to be doctored to suit official purposes, a gloomy scenario which points the way forward to the constraints under martial law.

Here Kieślowski is on record as saying that martial law, unwanted by nearly everyone of his generation, ended up in bringing that generation down. He deals with this dilemma thematically in the 1984 *No End* where Radziwilowicz is cast as an updated Birkut, a ghost from the past who haunts the present lives of those his death has left behind. Here Birkut the absent worker-militant becomes Zyro the absent lawyer, the one whose talent is over-looked in the mire of martial law. Kieślowski's film was in trouble with the authorities for its contentious nature. It was, alas, also in trouble artistically by trying to merge three different stories without notable success. However it provides a clue to the reflexive treatment of the martial law period in another film which simply has no mention of politics, *Short Film About Love*. Along with *Killing*, this became one of two key episodes in the *Dekalog* to be filmed in a double version, one for television, one for cinema. The television ending is a closed ending, in the form of moral fables, which defines the *Dekalog* as a whole. The film ending is open, powerful and unresolved. The difference is the difference between television and cinema and despite its high praise in the West, the *Dekalog* is good television but not great cinema. The similarity with Lynch and *Twin Peaks* is readily apparent. That too is good television drama. But *Fire Walk with Me*, whatever its outrageous weaknesses, is both more ambitious and cinematic as an art form.

Short Film about Love works as an integral part of Kieślowski's cinema of solitude, the very opposite of the feel in his earlier documentaries, especially since the film version was edited down to minimise extraneous, documentary elements in its *mise-en-scène*. It has the intimacy of Bergman's middle period and its intense claustrophobia. Magda the single promiscuous woman who is the object of Tomek's obsessive gaze is played at times by Grazyna Szapolowska as an extension of the widowed Urzula of *No End*. But the later film has a concentrated purity of focus which the earlier one lacked, as absent presence is transformed from a metaphysical onto a material plane. In

No End the absent presence of a dead husband, in *Love* the absent presence of the young suicidal admirer. Here Kieślowski opts for an abrupt mindscreen reversal two-thirds of the way through the picture, as stark as that in Ray's classic noir *In a Lonely Place* but even more focused around the obsessive point of view of its two subjects. For most of the film we see Magda purely though Tomek's eyes. When Tomek disappears we experience his absence through Magda's eyes until in desperation she usurps not only his prying telescope but also his gaze through it into her apartment. The last shot is of Magda hallucinating through the telescope an image of herself talking with Tomek in her room, in a shot which repeats and alters an earlier one where she is upset and literally crying over spilt milk. In seeing him so inscribed into the memory of her grief, she also sees herself as he then saw her. They have literally changed places but she has always stayed as she was. To look through (the telescope) is to look back (at her past).

There seem to be two visual texts running parallel which blend and interweave. The first and more immediate is that of obsession. Nineteen-year-old Tomek is an apartment voyeur like photographer James Stewart in Hitchcock's classic thriller *Rear Window*, an obsessive who has spent a whole year scrutinising the nocturnal love-life of Magda in the flat of a neighbouring tenement block. The film begins with Tomek's theft of a powerful telescope to replace the opera-glasses he had previously used. Kieślowski replicates the telescopic view with extreme long-lens shots so that we adopt head-on Jacek's sightings. The difference in age – the striking and beautiful Magda could be nearly twice as old – cues in the polarity of innocence and experience, his tortuous virginity set against her cynicism and endless stream of lovers. It is also regularity versus uncertainty. Tomek always sets his alarm for eight-thirty to begin his evening watch but has no idea in advance which lover he will be watching in the company of his beloved. For him to watch is also to love, up until that point where jealousy strikes and he must avert his gaze or become the substitute, the auto-erotic lover. For Magda, however, to make love is not to love at all but rather to negate love altogether. Obsession gives us the film's central paradox. To believe in love is never to consummate it. To consummate it endlessly is no longer to believe in it.

Beyond this love which strives and fails to speak its name is a sub-text which connects, quite obliquely, with Kieślowski's earlier concerns.

In the practical grind of daily life Tomek makes of himself an obstacle to Magda's easy living. As a postal worker he sends her forged money orders, as stand-in milkman he messes up her daily supply. As mischievous voyeur he calls in the gas board to look for leaks in her apartment when she is involved in a steamy love-session. The niggling obstructions seem incidental yet somehow they are integral. The voyeuristic intrusion is matched by petty bureaucratic obstacle. Without doubt this is the director's glancing blow at the miseries of daily life in 1980s Poland. Yet it is more. Combined with Tomek's scopic obsession it suggests an allegorical reading. Tomek's perverse passion also mirrors a perverse politics, a trope in Kieślowski which bears comparison to that of Neil Jordan in *Angel* or *The Crying Game*. The link for Kieślowski is surveillance. Yet the prying gaze means powerlessness, not omnipotence. Tomek cannot stop Magda living the life that she does, and his quiet desperation exposes his own weakness. Here a different dialectic of the decade of martial law seems to implode in the film and suggests an additional reading. The Party attempts to regulate the life of a depoliticised and cynical civil society by keeping a zealous eye upon it but in the end its surveillance has altered little at all, exposing instead its ideological bankruptcy. Both sides in Poland, Kieślowski has suggested of the 1980s, helped to grind each other down. The allegory echoes the tragic course which the intimacy runs. Tomek tries to use his secret knowledge to gain some advantage but in the end the telescope represents no kind of power. Its only power lies in its secrecy and when he confesses to his victim, the roles are reversed and he in turn is put on the line. He ends up humiliated at the hands of a knowing older woman and tries to kill himself. Surveillance here suggests not the Foucauldian panopticon or the Orwellian nightmare of total control but the futile gesture. Lest the analogy seem too far-fetched we should also remember the primal rationale of communist politics, its ideological sublime. The Party devotes itself to the working people, a devotion which in the age of communism's terminal crisis had become again a kind of impossible love.

In the cinema's last decade, the images of watching in this film are only rivalled in their intimate intensity by *Raise the Red Lantern*, another masterpiece to come out of a communist country. Both play upon and deconstruct the mechanics of surveillance. Both use outstanding film actresses in Szapolowska and Gong Li to reflect and deflect the

intensity of the gaze. In one case the gaze is singular, focused and technological, a product of telescope and telephone. In the other it is that
of hieratic tradition, the generalised gaze within the landlord's palace
which Gong Li defies but from which she can find no resting place. But
there are crucial differences. Gong Li is a kept woman whose place is
fixed within a patriarchal hierarchy at a time of social transformation.
Magda is a modern independent woman whose 'place' is fixed by the
naive gaze of a solitary obsessive. In *Love* there is a terse and compelling play upon the therapeutic cure which makes Hitchcock seem
by comparison very euphemistic. The affliction of the virgin gaze is
cured by the reality of touch, but the touch is cruel. Magda deflowers
Tomek by placing his hands on her thighs and bringing him to involuntary climax. Humiliated in the flesh, he cannot bring himself to spy
any longer on the image. He breaks his addiction by cutting his wrists.
Yet the addiction remains, transferred onto Magda herself who feels
the absence of the gaze more palpably than its presence. It is she who
takes up the compulsion to repeat. Tomek's absence is a reminder of
his constancy, of which love and surveillance are alternate forms, the
opposite of each other but also of the structures of feeling which have
governed Magda's life – lust, transience, cynicism, loneliness.
Perversity is thus registered as the lesser of two evils, the choice
between a life in which nothing matters and one in which the wrong
thing matters. That, indeed, is the darkness of Kieślowski's vision
which does not convincingly change until the final sequence of *Blue*.

The covert politics of Kieślowski provides a contrast with a number
of films banned by the authorities during martial law which resurfaced
at the end of the decade. Most notable of these was Ryszard Bugajski's
Interrogation where Krystyna Janda plays Tonia, a cabaret singer arrested
and tortured in Stalinist Poland for refusing to make false confessions
about political 'wrongdoing'. On its release in 1990 after the fall of
communism and eight years after it was made, Janda rightly received
the Best Actress award at Cannes for a virtuoso performance as an
innocent and persecuted woman. With its use of hand-held camera,
jarring close-up and volatile mindscreen, *Interrogation* at times matches
Raging Bull in defining its post-war history through the explosive
mindscreen of its historical subject. Though *Interrogation*'s Tonia is a
composite of two women victims of the post-war terror (unlike
Scorsese's Jake La Motta), both films fuse biography and emotional

violence, the extremes of cinematic realism and expressionism in equal measure. As Janda herself notes, Bugajski's film explores the detail of the world of Stalinist Poland that Wajda had opened in broader terms to cinema. In *Man of Marble* Janda plays a young woman of the 1970s moving back into that history, in Bugajski's *Interrogation* she plays a woman already there; with these two performances she has staked her claim in film history.[5] The doubled casting, where one role seems to lead into the next is also interesting as we have seen in the cases of Szapolowska – *No End* and *Love* – and that of Radziwilowicz – *Man of Marble* and *No End*. But Radziwilowicz was also cast by Godard on the basis of *Man of Marble* for his 1982 film, *Passion*, about a film by a Polish filmmaker that never gets made. This was an altogether different world.

Godard's film was symptomatic of a reflexivity crisis in the cinema of the cinema from the start of the 1980s. *Stardust Memories, Identification of a Woman, The State of Things, Passion*, and later *The Player* and *Calendar* all add to our understanding of film as medium, but in a marginal way. Woody Allen's comedy, *Stardust Memories*, is one of his weakest and most self-indulgent, the films by Wenders and Antonioni are their least imaginative, narratives in which the fictional subject is too obviously close to the director. Recently Atom Egoyan in his low-budget *Calendar* is daringly reflexive but contrives, very badly, to play himself. *Passion* is an inspired failure, stranded between Godard's desire to film lyrically a series of tableaux of classical paintings (which he does brilliantly) and to make a film about a Polish filmmaker being exploited by a ruthless French producer (Michel Piccoli). The exploitation theme is a frantic imitation of something done with greater subtlety in *Le Mépris* twenty years earlier, and here Godard at times repeats himself to the point of self-parody. Movie directors as characters in films are also notorious red herrings. Bertolucci's use of Jean-Pierre Léaud as a frantic New Wave director in *Last Tango in Paris*, a clear composite of Godard and Truffaut whose favourite actor he was at the time, becomes a laboured in-joke. In *Wings of Desire* Wenders's casting of Peter Falk of *Columbo* fame as an American filmmaker in Berlin, just seems tedious.

Films about the industry fare little better. Altman's attempt to send up Hollywood in *The Player* in which half of Hollywood clamoured to have a part in the movie, very quickly defeats its own purpose. At the point where the ruthless young producer (Tim Robbins) accidentally kills an errant screenwriter (Vincent D'Onofrio) and gets away with his sly cover-up, young Hollywood executives were reputed to have cheered – and no wonder. Like *Pulp Fiction* Altman's film ends up condoning the amorality it claims to parody and Altman who had suffered so much from the kind of people his film affectionately mocks comes back into the fold by inadvertently giving them good publicity. This cute version of the reflexive ends up as a form of dead-end irony, epitomised by Altman's opening eleven-minute take outside the studio offices of his villainous producer. It is done for no reason other than self-display, the vacuous virtuosity of a director showing his skill for no good reason, which is an apt summary of the qualities of the film itself. That same vacuous virtuosity is shown by Wenders in his portentous *Until the End of the World* where wimpish traveller William Hurt and the inept Solveig Dommartin flap and fluster their way around the globe to Australia trying to invent a machine to register hi-tech computer images for the blind. This listless dirge about the horrific power of the recorded image is itself a waste of the recorded image, reflexivity at the point of complete exhaustion. The dead-end ironies of the reflexive fix in *The Player* are followed up in the USA by the enjoyable slapstick of *Ed Wood* and *Living in Oblivion*, while in France *Irma Vep* is a great vehicle for Maggie Cheung's charm but little else.

One thing is clear. The power of Hollywood is too great and too formidable to suffer frontal attack from within the medium it largely controls through the world. Reflexivity renews itself by moving outward to other media, in particular video and television. Crucial to this is the renaissance of Canadian cinema as a response in part to the audio-visual power of its larger neighbour. First, though, we can return to Lynch's strange, flawed reckoning with *Videodrome, Persona* and *Fire Walk with Me*. The reflexive fix of going back to the scene of the crime and making a 1992 prequel to the 1989 *Twin Peaks* is not just Lynch's stated motive of wanting to prolong the fictional duration of the dead Laura Palmer. It is to reverse the normal process of visual technology. Most people now see most features not in cinemas but on television or video. Having shot a cult serial on video for television, Lynch goes in the opposite direction by exposing the dark side of Laura Palmer more directly to his audience on 35mm film. But critics were hostile to the movie and accused Lynch of showing contempt for his audience, which is one reason why only a fraction of his television audience watched the prequel. We could of course reverse this by saying that anyone sitting through the tedium of *Twin Peaks* deserves contempt, and Lynch may unconsciously be supplying it. But his considered risk is nonetheless fascinating. Usual processes of film-to-video and film-to-TV are reversed and challenge our cultural expectancies. The Twin Peaks familiar (i.e. the TV version) deemed by fans to be surreal and excitingly unfamiliar, really is made unfamiliar. Here the sporadic breakdown of the TV screen, a recurrent trope, echoes the breakdown of the projector in *Persona* as if this more visceral narrative of Laura is one with which the box in the corner cannot cope. Just as the projector goes haywire with Bergman's efforts to give birth to new images, the television cannot cope with Lynch's frontal attack on Laura's tragic life which at the same time is a resurrection of a previous fiction, self-consciously hyperreal, the copy which burns more brightly than the original at the very moment when the latter is just a fading memory for 1990s audiences whose jaded appetites have 'moved on' to *Cape Fear, Reservoir Dogs* and *Pulp Fiction*.

Just as Lynch is more direct in the movie he is also more oblique. Reflexive framing fuels mega-psychodrama as the cute coffee-shop idioms of Agent Cooper are junked in favour of hallucinatory incest, and the start of Cooper's investigation is seen to repeat the inept investigation by a disappearing agent of Leland's previous victim, whose murder that of Laura also repeats. Another kind of repetition is also at hand. Just as Lynch had cast Laura Dern in *Wild at Heart* after *Blue Velvet* in a very different part, so he remoulds the fictional Laura once more for the movie of the soap. The similarity of the name is, one assumes, more than just coincidence in this frenzied bout of cinematic quadrophenia. But the auteurist hand is visible in more immediate ways. Lynch appears as partially deaf Gordon Cole – a dreadful cameo – the FBI boss of Agent Cooper, an oblique statement of auteurist lineage in which Cooper's investigation in a way is an execution of his narrative master-plan. We find equally in the case of the disappearing David Bowie (Phantom Agent Jeffries) another Lynchian gloss on the uncanny. Was Bowie really there? Did *Twin Peaks* really happen? Agent Cooper replays the videotape of the monitor in the corridor to prove that Bowie did pass through. The electronic image proved him to be more than just a ghost. But does it? At the end the infamous Red Room doubles as celestial antechamber and director's editing room.[6] An uncanny reading of the Dwarf and the Agent side by side in the Red Room suggests the doubling of Lynch's auteurist persona – half investigator, half dwarf. But there is a further dimension to Judgement Day. Together they look at the doubled persona of Laura's murderer, hippie Bob and daddy Leland who is strung up beside him, a hanging man on invisible rope. We can read this as the idealised auteur and his deformed double passing judgement on his monstrous creation and *his* deformed double, the Red Room as sublime editing room in which the doubled auteur passes judgement on his doubled self-projection as through an invisible mirror. This is Lynch lingering through repetition over Laura's death the second time around by authorising his fictive double to show what *Twin Peaks* has withheld, the moment of killing.

The filmic nature of the process is evoked by the closing montage of images which echoes the opening montage of images in *Persona*, Bergman bringing his film into life, Lynch making his final cut the second time around. But this is also an antechamber in which Lynch as God and the FBI combined also passes judgement on his characters. Leland is despatched to hell while Laura ascends into heaven. Bergman's emotional terrors of intimacy are placed by Lynch's kitsch metaphysical horror, yet both are reflexively framed. Far from being surreal, a word whose popular usage now threatens to empty it of all meaning, Lynch repeats Bergman's fusion of the expressive and the reflexive, but in an all-American way which trades subtlety for excess and intimacy for the ineffable. While Laura goes to heaven to the accompaniment of a celestial chorus, one might be tempted to say the Good David and his weird double condemn the Bad David and his even weirder double to head in the opposite direction.

Apart from Lynch's flawed and fascinating gestures towards the reflexive which tend to unravel through their own complexity, American cinema has largely ducked the serious challenge of the presence of the camera, a presence which by now has come out of the cinema and into every aspect of daily life. That challenge has been taken up instead by America's immediate neighbour and plays an integral part in the renaissance of Canadian cinema. The Canadian subversion has a direct link in turn to its most eminent critic of modern culture, Marshall McLuhan, whose speculations upon the totality of electronic media in the 1960s were so prophetic. Yet the filmmakers who respond in part to his vision do not share his optimism about the thriving community of the global village. The electronic is a source, for them, not so much of communication as distortion, not empathy but dislocation. We have already noted the McLuhanite subtexts in *The Adjuster* and *Jesus of Montreal*. We can point, for example, to the latter's finale as a strong instance. In the subway station as the dying Lothaire Bluteau is taken to hospital, we see the actor whom he succeeded in the Passion Play as a blow-up look-alike on a billboard, the centrepiece of a perfume ad captioned 'L'homme sauvage'. This is Jesus transformed for visual display, the acceptable face of idolatry. The merchants whom Jesus ejects from the temple have, metaphorically speaking, now taken over his image. The image as a frozen duplication of the 'other' dying Jesus is indeed a form of living death. What preserves the image here is the blow-up photograph. But death lives on under other forms too, the preserving balm of videotape, for example, which is the centrepiece of Cronenberg's *Videodrome*.

In Arcand's Brechtian fable Jesus was human and crucified by the culture industry, where along the way his feting by the same people allows Arcand some fun at the expense of the Montreal media. By contrast, Cronenberg uses the format of melodrama, and his film edges over into the American paranoia thrillers of the 1970s such as *The Parallax View* where similarly weird disturbing events are orchestrated by a right-wing conspiracy. The difference here is in the nature of the medium. The evil of conspiracy lies in preserving through the Videodrome Show the images of the dead and the dying, the murdered and the tortured, a prophetic glimpse of an evil by now deeply rooted in the criminal underworld of rape and snuff videos which use kidnapped women and children as their victims. But *Videodrome* is prophetic in a more complex way, in its visionary take on electronic reproduction. Cronenberg breaks with the Hollywood code of melodrama by showing us a world which is amoral from the start. Max Renn (James Woods) is happily into the new technologies of sleaze before he realises the image not only seduces but can also kill. Here Cronenberg's visionary take on the reflexive is one which channels into the mainstream cultural unconscious. It is the horror genre reinvented, with the curse of the video monitor replacing the curse of the mummy's tomb. The dead spring to life not out of the tomb or through the mad robot inventor, but out of the moving video images in which they have been preserved by technology. Long before interactive video became a buzz word Cronenberg had given it an ominous meaning. Thus his chilling portrait of McLuhan as Brian O'Blivion, the murdered expert whose image has been preserved on tape, suggests the working out of the live expert's theories on his undead persona. O'Blivion, now dead as his name suggests, has been programmed to answer onscreen the queries of the bemused Woods as they are being put to him years after his death. The screen image is thus a form of living death while the difference between the materiality of the flesh and the ideality of the image disappear in the S&M routine between Woods and Debbie Harry. While the incited Woods whips his TV monitor the videotaped Harry sighs onscreen with pleasure as if feeling the blows. We are thus party to the mindscreen confusions of a flaky TV programmer looking for new sources but totally bewildered by the power of the Videodrome since he no longer knows the relationship between reality and the imagination, cause and effect, life and death.

At times the power of film is vitiated by its dated and somewhat tacky special effects. On its modest budget there is no way it could hope to rival, for example, the Voight-Kampff or the Esper of *Blade Runner* which appeared in the same year. Cronenberg's habitual confusions of body and brain are also damaging, so that the hollow stomach cavity which acts as VCR orifice on Woods's body, drowns the promising idea of visual sensation in the more familiar obsession the director has with blood and entrails. But there is a specific agenda behind this mismatch of body and brain. Cronenberg combines William Burroughs's paranoid belief in the image as infecting virus with the gospel according to Baudrillard where the image is pure simulation. The servant of two masters, his film fails at crucial moments to find the right equivalents for its visceral power. As a Canadian heir to McLuhan he is fully stretched in matching American visceral-Burroughs to French cerebral-Baudrillard. At key moments in the film, the polarities fly apart. But the film still has visceral power, a power which almost certainly had an impact on the young Atom Egoyan. But while *Videodrome* is a visceral horror movie, Egoyan's films are more reflective. Out go the blood and entrails, but there is no excessive tilting of the balance on the side of the cerebral. Egoyan takes from *Videodrome* the enduring image of the electronic undead and promptly rewrites Bazin's ontology of the photographic image as an ontology of the video image. From *Family Viewing* onwards the double-register resides in that elusive relationship of film and video, the film as the medium the film-maker uses, the video as the image by which his subjects do two things, watch each other at which they are usually successful, and communicate with each other at which they often are not.

There are other electronic forms, notably the telephone sex of *Family Viewing*, *Speaking Parts* and *Calendar*, all woven into the texture of narrative and form. The telephone act, communicating sexual noise, connotes immense and hopeless solitude. The framing of it, a solitary and intense spotlight often arcing out of the darkness which surrounds speaker or listener, suggests the physical isolation which the voice momentarily overcomes. But the phonic image is integrated into the screen image as its natural accomplice, its born supplement. Watching and being watched, filming and being filmed are other media forms of communicating which isolate. The mainstream cliché of video pornography – the lovers who video themselves in the act of loving with a preset camcorder and then playback or simultaneously watch the tape for further excitement – is the ruse which Glen's father forces on Sandra, his reluctant lover. But he over-complicates it by supple-menting it with telephone sex courtesy of Arsinée Khanjian. Thus Sandra is forced to enact the whispered commands of a surrogate third party who, being at the other end of the phone line, has no knowledge of her effect. In this way Egoyan not only links sex to its new media technologies but also points out its isolating consequences. The three-way split may turn the father on but in effect it dissolves his sexual identity. The two women in this strange threesome by proxy are secondary to the process itself, commodities of a low-tech sexual commerce of which one is ignorant and the other contemptuous. This is literally the patriarch at the end of the line.

The difference between film and video is established not only by the look – rich contrasting colour interiors versus uniform bluish haze – but by the angle and the cut. As Van forces his lover to obey the voice on the phone, Egoyan cuts back and forth between two shots of the horizontal couple, the movie camera eye-level frontal, the videocamera high-angle diagonal. In the age of simultaneous playback it is not after all a mannerism. First we see them through the camera and then we see them on the screen, but in such a way that in the audience's imagination screen and camera eventually merge. In *Family Viewing* both wall-screens and cameras are shot on the high diagonal.

It is not only sexual identity which is threatened. The other source of attack concerns that icon of classical liberalism, the division of the public and the private. *Family Viewing* and *The Adjuster* give us very similar intrusions into the domestic world, the former from the telephone sexpert and the latter from the amateur filmmaker. Both are technological violations of intimacy, but also mirror the official intrusions of voice and image which the television screen brings indiscriminately into rooms in homes and institutions such as the nursing-home where Armen, Glen's grandmother, is dying. In this delirious ubiquity of screening where surveillance monitors sit alongside entertainment screens, everybody is either watching or being watched, or both. Egoyan stresses this through a recurrent trope, the high-diagonal wall-shot from the position of a screen which could be either for surveillance or for entertainment, and the plot confirms it when Van hires a private eye to check on his son and Arsinée Khanjian, and video is the chosen mode of surveillance. The challenge to the spectator becomes clear. Not only do we watch his characters on screens and see his characters watching screens, we also watch at times from the standpoint of the screen, as if the screen itself, no longer a medium, defiantly watches back. As in *Persona* the reverse-angle seals it, so that one of the opening shots at the hospital features a TV screen with a programme about animals which Glen's grandmother is watching. The film then shoots from the angle of the screen because Glen eventually looks straight at the camera, walks up to it and puts his hand in front of it before the image flashes off. The implication is clear. By turning off the set, he has also turned off the camera. But he does so out of the fear that engenders substitution. It is as if the screen as a source of receiving images has become a camera which is a means of making images. The triumph of the image suggests not only the ubiquity of the screen but also the philosophical dissolution of cause and effect by visual means.

If Egoyan is always aware of the screen he is equally aware of the camera. *The Adjuster* reprises Liv Ullman's unnerving camera-awareness in *Persona* in the 'High School Confidential' sequence of *The Adjuster*, the cheerleader scene where Bubba and Mimi visit the ball park and Mimi 'performs' with the football team. As cheerleader Mimi wraps her thighs around the shoulders of the nearest muscular player, Bubba stands in front of the camera blocking our view of what is, anyway, a very indistinct long-shot. Knowing our attention is on what is occurring in the far distance, Bubba performs the filmic equivalent of a defensive block, and the audience is grounded. Moreover as an unlikely cross between Liv Ullman, in mode of audience-defiant gaze, and a defensive end now fat and gone to seed, he defiantly eyeballs the camera, daring us to look past him at that to which the camera tempts our gaze, a bored woman imitating a teenage cheerleader simulating oral sex.

Finally we come to the vexed subject of painting. So often, films about famous painters have been an excuse for little more than a glossy biopic ringing kitsch changes on the creative agony. Of the recent biopics, Altman's *Vincent and Theo* is perhaps the best because it breaks the rules by dealing with Van Gogh's brother as much as with Van Gogh himself and by engaging the vexed theme of art as serious money. In the last ten years we have seen three distinctive films in which a film director creates a painter after his own image. In Scorsese's *Life Lessons*, the short episode he made for *New York Stories* with Richard Price's sharp and effervescent screenplay, a middle-aged action painter in SoHo, Nick Nolte, loses his young lover Rosanne Arquette to a mime artist. Scorsese sees in the American tradition of action painting a mirror of his own dynamic and hyperactive camera. The zoom and tracking shots of Nolte at work in his loft studio with a dynamic rock score on the soundtrack give us this sense of restless and limitless energy which seems, simultaneously, to be a feature of brush, figure and camera. Nolte's moving physical bulk makes the act of representing an intensely physical act, the creator as flying body and facsimile of raging bull. Scorsese thus adds the New York painter to the iconography of New York boxer, New York gangster, New York cabby and New York computer operator, his studied cross-section of Big Apple hyperactive. After the worlds of crime and commerce, this is really not that much of a change and the joins in his cinematic opus remain seamless.

Caravaggio is another studied self-image of filmmaker as painter, with Derek Jarman finding in the historical subject of his picture an icon bearing his own sexuality and also his own visuality, for Jarman clearly saw his hero as the originator of cinematic light. This, then, is a genealogical version of the Renaissance Creation which attempts to bind homoeroticism to the visual image for Jarman's own loosely defined epoch, with its trains and typewriters, which Jarman injects back into his narrative. In archaeology the past presents the present with its relics, but in Jarman's cinema it is the opposite. The present presents its relics to the past, cigarettes, lorries, bicycles, coloured light bulbs, even exhibition brochures, for the subject of his film. There is an even stronger sense of inversion achieved through the paintings. They are the inspiration for Jarman's *mise-en-scène*, and serve as *tableaux vivants* which thread the narrative together. Jarman's film, in that sense, is a cinematic meta-narrative of painterly narratives. In fiction-alising the compositional process of the paintings which inspired the look of his film, Jarman shows them in the process of being born by bathing them in a cinematic light indebted to the painterly light of the canvasses themselves. Caravaggio's paintings thus give birth to the cinematic process by which they are brought into creation. In the painting of St John the camera's reverse-angle track behind the figure of Sean Bean also opens up the three-dimensional space of the cinema, indebted to the paintings which of course have no reverse-angle in their fixity. Here Jarman takes up and improves the *Tableaux Vivant* conception of *Passion* by giving it a context which is clearly indebted to Pasolini by breathing narrative life into the figures on the canvas and giving the most intense rendering of the sacrificial unconscious in his uneven career.

The mindscreen of the dying painter, played by Nigel Terry, transports us back into an invented life which sacralises crime and prostitution, the hustler, the pimp and the hooker in the manner of *Accatone*, while at times Jarman gives his painter-hero the limpid sacredness of Pasolini's Christ in *The Gospel according to St Matthew*. His reinvented creation myth thus renders Terry as an art-Christ with pimp Sean Bean painted as St John and hooker Tilda Swinton portrayed as the Virgin and as Mary Magdalene. The film's bisexual triangle thus becomes a Holy Trinity and the act of painting becomes eroticised by reciprocal desire. It is here that the sacrificial unconscious becomes supremely self-conscious for analogy is never far from the surface. The presence of the camera, incorporating cinema itself, turns the latent into the reflexive. For Jarman is also playing on the perilous traditions of gay artistry filmmaking which had ended in early deaths for Marlowe, Murnau, Fassbinder, Pasolini and, nearer home, Joe Orton. Jarman himself was soon to die a premature death through AIDS and *Caravaggio*, as a film about the past, seems now to have also been a prophetic statement of his immediate future. This reflexive and sacrificial use of painting depended not only on Jarman's mastery of cinematic light but on the superb paintings and production design of Christopher Hobbs which create under studio conditions the illusion of the originals *in nascendi*. The collaboration of Hobbs and Jarman makes this the most powerful English studio film since *The Red Shoes* while its tight and claustrophobic bisexuality is surely indebted to that great studio movie of the 1960s, *The Servant*. The colloquial Yorkshire accents of Bean and Swinton, recalling those of Bogarde and Sarah Miles, as they 'service' both Caravaggio's bed and canvas are a surefire giveaway.

Jarman also takes mindscreen into new dimensions, foreshadowing the use of voice-over in the 1990s by giving it a poetic resonance in Terry's dying reminiscence to counterpoint the tensions of painting and fighting 'oil and pigment', as the screenplay has it, 'versus flesh and blood'. At times the director triumphantly combines the later sensibility of *Life Lessons* and the earlier sensibility of *Raging Bull* in the erotic knife fight between Bean and Terry. The voice-over convention is also one that is used later to great effect by Tran Anh Hung with his poet-gangster in *Cyclo*. Finally we have the sense of an almost magical illusion in watching this picture. It is as if Caravaggio is himself bathed in the unique painterly light which he created, as if it had travelled out of his canvasses and wrapped him round like a mystical shroud. While Jarman's painterly rival Greenaway had used the designs of architecture and drawing as facsimiles of the film process as a whole, Jarman's concentration on the canvas bespeaks a concentration on the camera. While the Japanese tourist in Kurosawa's *Dreams* steps into the picture of Van Gogh hanging on the wall, thus penetrating the canvas, the figures of Jarman move out from the canvas back into the studio from which they originated after being immortalised by his painter-hero in their stillness.

La Belle Noiseuse has a totally different strategy, and sensibility. It does not work at all on the raw datum of genius and the use of very ordinary sketches to represent the work-in-progress of Frenhofer, its imaginary artist, seems a clear attempt to demythologise the myth of the genius. It lacks the painterly imagination of *Caravaggio* but at the same time deromanticises the process of painting which is so often idolised in biopics. Indeed, the film dissects the very process whereby the myth of genius is often created. The power of Rivette's film lies in its unique match of the intimate and the reflexive. This has recently been echoed though not rivalled in Antonioni's *Beyond the Clouds*. It also contains what *Blow-Up* assigned to anonymity, the symbiotic relationship of observer to the observed. As opposed to Egoyan where the reflexivity of the moving image ends up a moving hall of mirrors, the painter's gaze has a fixed and finite quality, a knowledge of limits. Uncannily, Frenhofer's studio reminds us of Thomas's *Blow-Up* studio, not least in its interior depth of field and labyrinthine quality, and gives the sense that although we spend so much time there, as viewers it is never truly familiar. Whereas the photographer's studio is populated by women 'passing through' and leaving little trace, Béart's nude body defines the identity of the space it occupies. It returns Piccoli's studio to life after years of neglect, a literal resurrection of the flesh. Thus for the viewer what matters is not the figure on the canvas so much as the figure in the studio. The moving representation of the figure is more important than the still representation of the moving image, yet at the same time the absence of the painterly, Piccoli's painting of Béart which we never see, haunts us by its absence. The process of transcribing the image remains a mystery even though we see the painstaking sketches and the repeated brush strokes of the forearm in real time, and hear the grating scratch of charcoal upon paper like some arcane ritual which has to be repeated daily.

In Jarman it is the painter who is sacralised as an aesthetic Christ. In Rivette it is the life-model who spends time on the cross, time on the cross, that is to say, in real time. She it is, who is the 'crucified'. Rivette's narrative interest here is in the *durée* of process, in the time-image conveyed over and over again in the single space of the studio whose angles and perspectives, however, change kaleidoscopically during the space of the four-hour movie. It is a time-space image punctuated by the other dramas which intersect elsewhere, painter and wife, painter and agent, model and lover, lover and lover's sister. Béart's split identity is conferred through these largely nocturnal configurings. She resembles wife Jane Birkin, the original model over whose portrait her body is painted. She is superseded too by the woman who preceded her, the attractive sister of Nicolas, her painter-lover whose sister is clearly still attracted to her brother. Her substitution of two other women is made worse by the absence of the presented image which might define her and which Piccoli has buried in the studio wall. Instead she is on canvas a headless rear-view body, effaced, decapitated, non-existent. The image cannot atone for the sufferings of a fractured identity but fractures them further. In the studios Béart is either a double twice-over or a nonentity. It is only in the moving image as viewed by the audience that she is whole. Rivette's superb irony here is to create Marianne's substance by default, in the cinematic durability she displays through the circumstances in which her life is fractured. In the end we do not care what the painting is like, we pass through curiosity to the other side, because the film has brought Marianne to life on screen. To us, that is, but not to her. At the end, the film's anonymous voice-over identifies itself as Marianne at the very moment when she no longer knows who she is at all.

This is during the spatial *la ronde* sequence after the ritual unveiling of the 'wrong' painting in the studio. The camera pans incessantly through the chateau's entrance-hall and garden, catching dual encounters of all six characters as they fake celebration of the botched event. The snatched conversations, polite, downbeat, concerned, are all barbed post-mortems on the event which has misfired and character assassinations within a group whose ties no longer bind, whose cohesion has dispersed with the wind. This is an update perhaps of Renoir's *Règle du jeu*. But the pace is more measured, and less frantic. It captures the aftermath of any viewing, preview, special view of a visual spectacle gone wrong, which is not what its exclusive audience desired, the culture of disappointment still trying to masquerade as the appreciation of high art. Rivette's classical severity of judgement here is tempered by our knowledge of Frenhofer's duplicity, his secret burial of the original portrait. What starts off, however, prior to the painting with the convivial dinner party in the garden ends with a series of isolated brief encounters, as if the characters were all garden statues who had come to life and exchanged words in passing as they exchanged positions outside the chateau. Rivette films them as singular images, spatially separated, in the pastiche of the process which has taken place in the studio for the duration of his narrative. These are 'his' portraits and he proves himself as wilful, as determined and as knowing as all his characters whom he freezes momentarily before time and space take over again. The cinema of representation becomes a theatre of illusion in which both the author and his subjects are playing endless masquerades. Meanwhile the split between 'true' painting and 'fake' painting, between original and substitute, itself mirrors Rivette's ironic project, the representation of representation and its final impossibility.

Chapter 6

AMERICAN REVERIES:
Altman, Lynch, Malick, Scorsese

——⊃⊂——

Pasolini's poetics can seen as the core of post-modern cinema or its absolute denial, depending on one's point of view. One thing is for sure. Pasolini's vision is antithetical to current discourse, though closer to Lyotard's fragmented world of competing language-games than it is to Jameson's 'post-modern' cinema as a place of pastiche, nostalgia and the triumph of surface over depth. But it goes beyond the concern with 'the heterogeneity of culture' which Dudley Andrew has opposed to 'the organicism and moralism of a cinema of quality'.[1] Its free indirect vision means different things in different cultures but is not amenable to any of the sea-changes of ism and prefix which seem to occur for some critics on a regular basis as realism lurches into modernism into late-modernism into post-modernism and no one really knows which films belong to which.[2] Here, sadly, criticism is colonised by petrified taxonomies which scarcely function yet masquerade as cultural teleologies, taking us towards the millennium. Perhaps then, Baudrillard should have the last word over definition. In 1991 he said: 'It's not even a concept. It's nothing at all ... It's because there is nothing to express that an empty term has been chosen to designate what is empty. So in a sense there is no such thing as post-modernism.'[3] Moreover, Baudrillard has described much popular cinema as kitsch and has claimed that the films of Antonioni and Wenders among others have spurred his most recent reflections on 'the desert of significations'. Thus *The Red Desert* and *The Passenger* are where, he asserts, Antonioni proves himself the European precursor of 'the hyperreality of landscapes and of passions'.[4] In the same vein his close collaborator Paul Virilio has claimed that twentieth-century war and cinema interact to create a profound derealisation in the everyday logistics of perception. Not surprisingly Virilio has sought out a kindred spirit in Atom Egoyan.[5] Though we may question Baudrillard's hyperreality even when it has had a clear influence on cinema itself, notably in the work of Cronenberg and Egoyan, its complexities still cannot be reduced to the standard clichés it sometimes inspires.

The hyperreal, it could be argued, is one particular and local instance of a wider change in the cultures of the West and the Pacific Rim which are now becoming global. If any generic term captures this process it might be that used by Marc Augé who has argued that we now live in a *supermodern* age defined by the spatial experience of non-places, places of transit with no fixed identities. This is not the whole story, for the simple reason that there is no whole. The 'supermodern' is also specific, like Eco's spatial rendering of the hyperreal. Its spatial phenomenology posits an individual subject whose experience of non-place is an unprecedented form of solitude.[6] We have already seen the dissolution of identity in the filmic ontology of the split subject. But the road movie too is a key cinematic imaginary of the supermodern, a spatial narrative of travel through non-places, travel as flight, search, adventure, quest mirrored through indeterminacy.[7] Derealisation means above all disjunction, disjunction between identities of self and place, persona and non-place. Films like *Zabriskie Point, Paris, Texas, Sans toi ni loi* and *Red Rock West* highlight disjunction in their very titles. Their heroes are in a state of existential drift through non-places, ontological moments *en route* which possess a found reality based on a play of images or signs. Paris, Texas is important because Travis's brother catches up with him at that point on the map. From the narrative viewpoint, it is a non-place through which Travis strides in his red baseball cap and comes to a halt, whereupon it is duly named. As Auge stresses, Baudrillard's view of images as pure illusion (taken up by his disciples as a cryptic and surrogate theory of alienation) does no justice to realities rooted in culture, time and history.[8]

While Baudrillard possesses partial insight, Jameson's cult of the post-modern often means the return of modernism with a special prefix helped by dubious borrowings such as the lifting of pastiche from Adorno's critique of Stravinsky's modernism as reactionary pastiche of the primitive, or his later use of Baudrillard's account of the modernist Beauborg as a blueprint for post-modern American architecture.⁹ The dehistoricised use of pastiche and nostalgia also fails, however, to register a crucial turn in American cinema. This comprises a transformation not only in the poetics of space but in the poetics of time. Even on the level of pure Americana things get sticky for the post-modern fixation on nostalgia. Jameson takes *Blue Velvet* and Jonathan Demme's *Something Wild* as key American 'postmodern' movies since they play with pastiche and nostalgia to such an extent that their psychopathic villains cannot be taken seriously by their audience.¹⁰ He thus dismisses Dennis Hopper and Ray Liotta out of hand as cardboard demons who are no serious threat to post-modern blandness. Yet this ignores the existential horror the presence of Hopper and Liotta created for their young audiences, a horror not merely Gothic in its convention but situated in suburb and small-town, representing disturbing normality in daily American life. For sure, in Demme's 'yuppie nightmare' movie the element of pastiche is clear in the motel seduction of Jeff Daniels by vamp Melanie Griffith, made-up with the look of Louise Brooks and the style of an S&M dominatrix. Yet pastiche or no pastiche, Griffith projects the erotic threat of female power as a register of change in the American metropolis while Liotta embodies the darker side of the male response, that veil of charm cloaking the murderous psychopath.

In *Blue Velvet* Hopper's performance as the unpredictable Frank Booth, with his narcotic mood-swings, narcissistic rage, mock camaraderie, infantile regressions, closet homosexuality and predilection for rape and cruelty, is an even more convincing facsimile of the new psychotic male on the fringes of consumer culture, even in the all-American small town which Lumberton represents. Hopper is too immense here to be simply pastiche or window-dressing. For sure, elements of 1950s pastiche echo the small town of Hollywood iconography. But Lynch goes even further back. Hopper's performance draws heavily, not to say excessively, on the look of silent Expressionism. This, however, does not draw the sting of terror. It merely helps to launch it. The truth may be unpalatable to some, but Hopper is both real villain and cardboard demon, a veritable monster and a sophisticated joke. With Lynch the monstrous masculine is clinched by striking detail and Hopper's oxygen mask has become an enduring image in film history. We do not know what drugs within his system it stimulates, nor do we know when he will next put it to his face. Here the 'post-modern' refusal of depth also excludes a narrative reading that has attracted other critics. Mulvey, for example, argues that the terrifying rite of passage of Jeffrey (Kyle McLachlan) is also a journey into the Oedipal unconscious. His voyeuristic witnessing of Hopper's brutal rape of Dorothy Vallens (Isabella Rossellini) after she has threatened to rape him, is a Gothic version of the primal scene.[11] It is also, as she rightly points out, self-consciously Freudian. For Lynch, like Welles and Hitchcock, is knowingly attuned to the movie possibilities of 'dollar-book' Freud, and more so than most of his critics.

The defining feature of *Blue Velvet* and *Something Wild* is this: they both aim at a poetic narrative of pure oscillation, oscillation between depth and surface, the unconscious and the self-conscious, profundity and banality, paranoia and pastiche. Sadly, though, it is not quite as effective as many think. Lynch's self-conscious reworking of the expressionist gesture, of the ordinary turn of phase as melodramatic half-truth, are forms of risk-taking which do not always come off. Two things in particular detract from its impact; the laboured plotting of Jeffrey's voyeurism and the sentimentality of the young lovers who lack the raw freshness of their earlier models in *Rebel without a Cause*. *Blue Velvet* is also shackled by a prurience with uneven poetic texture, especially in the rape scene with its sadistic victimisation of Rossellini. It is this prurience which Hitchcock at his best transcended in his poetics of the male gaze, and the dream-quality of *Vertigo*'s narrative is echoed more closely in *Wild at Heart*. Here Lynch is liberated from the constrictions of small-town pieties by the euphoric rush of the road, the 'bal(l)ade' Deleuze saw as integral to modern cinema. He is no longer shackled by prurience or saccharine sentimentality. While Kyle Mc-Lachlan and Laura Dern are cloying sweethearts, Laura Dern and Nicholas Cage are natural-born lovers. Though both directors might deny intertextuality, a comparison of Lynch and Godard is instructive. With good reason, Lynch deemed his road movie 'a cine-symphony', just as Godard had declared *Pierrot le fou* part of a poetic opening of film based on the simplicity of the silent cinema.[12] Both start with complicity in murder and with elaborate bourgeois parties which go horribly wrong. Both use bracketing devices. Belmondo voice-overs an image of the Champs-Elysées; 'Chapter Two. A Surprise-party.' And in English: 'at the home of Monsieur and Madame Expresso, whose

daughter is my wife'. Lynch runs captions over his opening shot telling
his audience they are 'Somewhere near Cape Fear, North Carolina'. For
both couples, Karina and Belmondo, Dern and Cage, the road is a form
of flight with overlapping topographies. Ferdinand and Marianne head
south to the Côte d'Azur, Lulu and Sailor head south to New Orleans.
Both couples are implicated in murder and are on the run.

As derealised flight, both films are imaginary instances of the supermodern in their phenomenology of non-places, and both are key
variants of Pasolini's poetics. Godard's lacuna is what Pasolini called
his temptation in the midst of one film to make another, a 'second
film', the deviation from the planned route, the improvised, the collage
of quotations which characterise so much of his work. For Lynch it is
something equally knowing but very different, the power of pastiche to
show the past as that something else and somewhere else which is
uncannily present in the immediate image. Let us take Godard first.
In the surprise-party which Belmondo spoils, there is first a banal conversation shot fully in red, mimicking TV commercials, then Sam Fuller
by contrast declaring emotion as the basis of cinema, then Belmondo
shot in bright yellow strolling past Karina as she kisses another guest,
then another commercial soundbite with a talking couple shot in full
blue. The sequence ends when Pierrot throws handfuls of iced cake at
a guest and leaves. For Godard, the alternations of colour, theme and
mood are typical forms of poetic dissonance. In Lynch, by contrast,
there is a double pastiche instead of multiple dissonance. The initial
illusion is of being in the lush 1940s Hollywood studio interior of a
large Southern mansion for a special occasion, with guests in evening
dress and Glenn Miller on the sound track. This is set alongside the
sense that when violence erupts it is in the kind of action which
Hollywood sees as the attention-clinching mode of all bankable
movies. Lynch is calling attention to this cliché by compressing the first
five minutes of an action movie into the first thirty seconds. Sailor, with
Lulu, is threatened by a black man with a knife who crudely accuses
him of wanting to rape Lulu's mother in the toilets. As Lulu's profile is
caught, Münch-like, in expressive scream the guests scatter and to the
accompaniment of Angelo Badalimenti's heavy jarring riffs, Sailor
leaves his attacker lying in a pool of blood. In a matter of seconds, not
minutes, Lynch defines his movie but does so only by vacating the false
scenario he has set up in the first place. Instead of dissonance within

the sequence, of a Godardian alienation technique, we have a sudden rush out of lilting pastiche into full-blooded paranoia. Godard includes in the diegesis extraneous details filmed in brief vignettes. Lynch constantly incorporates the past into the present, diegetically through the flashbacks showing the sexual abuse Lula suffered as a girl, and reflexively through the look of the recent American past itself filtered through Hollywood and television. While Godard parodies the bourgeois pretensions of the guests by having them talk like advertisements, Lynch raises the question of Hollywood's tactical political correctness by confronting us with something the studios would not touch, a black villain in a 'white' setting who gets brutally assaulted by the film's white hero for no obvious reason. Then as if to reassure us, Lynch knowingly clinches the convention of audience recognition with a flashback shot of what actually transpired between Sailor and Marietta, Lula's mother, in the toilets. Sailor's action is thus 'vindicated'. Or is it?

In both films it is through flight that non-place is established, dissolved and derealised by the transience of moving through. Both directors use a register of poetic counterpoint, the growing sense of non-place offsetting the growing sense of shared nightmare for their romantic couples. The recurrence of the Matisse red, the colour of Marianne's dress and the danger sign in *Pierrot*, work against the radiant landscapes of the Mediterranean summer, the sea as the final limit of romance in nature itself. In *Wild at Heart* the landscapes of the American South-West with its harsher light define the journey from the lushness of the old south into ochre desert landscapes. The photography of Frederick Elmes with its saturated reds and yellows stresses pitiless heat and luminous summer light, offset by the deep blacks of the nightscapes in New Orleans and the open road during the crashed car sequence. In the motel scene where Bobby Peru (Willem Dafoe) threatens to rape Lula the burnt gold feel of the interiors is a match to the exterior hues of a parched landscape. The local feel of the American South-West means we are patently somewhere, but we also feel we could be anywhere. The place has a name but no nature. It is a non-place on the road to unknown destiny. For Godard romance narcissistically falters at the sea edge in the mirror of nature. In Lynch it survives the harshness of hyperreal encounter in climatic extremes of semi-desert heat. Each film provides here a different gloss on romance to match its different poetic variants, a unique way of distancing itself from the romance integral to its conception. Godard tries to exorcise romance through misunderstanding, quotation, distraction and pastiche gags out of silent comedy. But he fails because romance in his films is usually inseparable from despair, which intensifies as intimacy falters. Lynch, the conservative optimist, pretends that true love is really true lust when his picture in fact proves the opposite, or rather he edits the film so that pastiche and true lust symphonically intersect. Cage, out of jail and dressed in his snakeskin jacket, is Elvis the undead, his singing voice a more than passable imitation. Dern's true lust is underscored by adulation of the Elvis effigy, as Cage displaces Heavy Metal in the club scene with a rendition of His Master's Voice and girls in leather swoon on cue to Southern rockabilly crooning. The film is a 1990s version of 'Love Me Tender', where tenderness is the restful aftermath of lust, not its sentimental prelude. Yet though Lynch is symphonic, his narrative rests as much as Godard's on disconnection. Flashback, ellipsis, continuity cuts and parallel montage offer the audience the chance to go with the metaphor of the road, a rapid gear-changing scenario to contrast with the actuality of the smooth convertible in which they drive.

The connecting link of the disconnected is again specifically American. For Godard it had been a European obsession, the continuous dislocation of life and ideal through the passage of an idealised flight, the triumph of the non-place, the breakdown in the gap between the ideas which drive Ferdinand and the feelings which drive Marianne. For Lynch it is conspiracy and paranoia. His film shows that while Jameson's 'post-modern' is misplaced, his view of American conspiracy as the quest for an unreachable totality is unerringly right.[13] The poetic openness of flight is always undermined by a key motif of modern Americana, the will-to-connection as the New World form of the will-to-power. In Lynch's movie the picaresque nightmare of meeting different threatening faces on the journey West is made worse by the silver dollar passage of transference which connects them all. The dangers Sailor and Lulu face are not unrelated nightmares. They are the different staging posts of Marietta's plot to kill her daughter's lover, which pass through Harry Dean Stanton, Crispin Glover, voodoo ritual, the blonde-haired femme fatale Isabella Rosellini, and psychotic war vet Willem Dafoe. After pastiche and romance, paranoia is the third point on the triangle. The American sensibility constructs meaning out of chaos through the premise of conspiracy as the Great Chain of Being. Though Lynch follows in the footsteps of the new cinema which began with M.A.S.H. and *Easy Rider*, he goes much further. He parodies the paranoia which nourishes him.

Mention of M.A.S.H., Altman's brilliant spoof on the classic war genre brings us to the start of the movement of which Lynch is still a part. As a dark comedy of the Korean war made at the time when the Vietnam war has entered its darkest phase, it brings us onto a central feature of the American cinema of poetry. The films which explored the new freedoms most fully were knowing contemplations of the American past, a past which genre had always shrouded in the myth of the founding of modern America as a form of Manifest Destiny. This is the cinema of Latent Destiny, for its contemplation of the past tries to replace myth not through document but through reverie, the phantasmagoria of the poetic image rooted in historical knowledge. It thus fashions an imagined history out of verisimilitude during a time when the American present was experiencing a civil turbulence possibly as great as anything since the Civil War. But the cinema of Latent Destiny offers no mythic consolation. The new American cinema of reverie is not a cinema of pastiche but something more vital and more immediate. Pasolini had, as noted, suggested that the cinema as form is always in the present tense. The paradox of the past as immediate present is the paradox of the film projected as film. The action takes place on screen. Only in a written review does it enter a text as literary past tense. The classic epic of Ford or Griffiths in which the past is another country is duly transformed. The past as reverie is a living dream of the visual imagination, an existential past, not the mythic past recreated by Leone's American epics which willingly enter the realm of the hyperreal, never to escape.

If Lynch explores the poetics of space for the living present, it is because Altman, Malick and Scorsese had already reinvented the poetics of time for the cinema of poetry. After M.A.S.H., where Korea is an allegorical stand-in for Vietnam, Altman produced an even more ambitious picture which recreated the American West as an immediate past, a living dream. *McCabe and Mrs Miller* was an anti-heroic, antimythic Western which evoked the newly settled Northwest of the 1890s. It had a studied naturalistic look but one fashioned for non-mimetic purposes. In it Altman created poetic narrative out of a community *in nascendi,* a mining settlement, 'Protestant Church', a visual non-place in the forests north of Seattle. The film is shot largely in autumn and winter, an antidote to desert heat and the epic look of Ford's Monument Valley. The 'flashing' technique used by Vilmos Zsigmond of deliberately exposing the film, so desaturates the colours that the harsh transparent light of the American West gives way to the muddied colours of woodland, hillside and shrub in winter and to the burnt ochre of lantern light in darkened saloons, where the wide-screen image appears fudged around the edges.[14] Many images shot in this vein stand out. The prostitutes of Constance Miller (Julie Christie) arrive from Seattle by struggling up the muddy hillside on foot after their wagon has broken down, drenched by incessant rain. Later John McCabe (Warren Beatty) strides to his fatal end from a porch framed by icicles and conducts his disoriented, desultory shoot-out with the Company's hired guns in a fierce snowstorm. His dying body is made to disappear in the raging blizzard as he slumps, fatally wounded, into a snowdrift. As the townspeople celebrate their triumph over a fire threatening their unfinished church, drifting snow effaces his corpse.

McCabe's death-journey in the snow lends to the image a brightness missing from the desaturated images of the ragged settlement and its smoky interiors, where sunlight never seems to penetrate. But it is, like *Odd Man Out,* a brightness in death. The white blanket of the deepening blizzard dazzles the eye, its colour a backdrop for a derealisation which works in truly American fashion, that is to say through an oscillation between pastiche and paranoia, farce and tragedy. Just as McCabe cannot set up a brothel on his own, neither can he do business on his own. His bungling attempt to do a deal with the company which tries to buy him over misfires and the fear of retribution sets in, where any stranger is a potential enemy. The figure of Keith Carradine fuses paranoia and pastiche, contrary to current orthodoxy, by incorporating parody. The distant silhouette of the Stranger on horseback complete with low-slung holster and wide-brimmed hat suggests retribution is at hand. But Carradine is merely looking for the town brothel and a closer shot reveals a ten-gallon hat pulled down to his ears. The deadly echo of Jack Palance in *Shane* dissolves into the image of the amateur dude. This parodic standby is a trademark of Altman and here specifically a pastiche of the rodeo cowboy. Of the three gunman, the 'Kid', the young Aryan who guns Carradine down on the bridge, is closer with his peaked cap and tight-waisted suit to the style of a German student fraternity than to the iconography of Palance, Eastwood or Lee van Cleef. The other two gunman are dressed in the style of mountain men, trappers, one half-Indian, the leader sporting a plummy English accent. The motley trio contrasts with the uniform look of traditional gunmen. Not only do they go against the stereotype of the trio from *High Noon* whom they echo, they are reconstructed from the photographs of the frontier men of the period. Keysaar has pointed out the function of free indirect subjectivity in the sequences where we see the men from Beatty's point-of-view as he gropes towards understanding a plot against him which is never confirmed.[15] His enemies are not outlaws but assassins who never admit to their profession, instruments of the Harrison-Shaughnessy Mining Company.

Carradine and Beatty become doubles, the fool as dude cowboy mirroring the fool as dud entrepreneur. Both meet a bloody end from the same killers. Altman gives us a picture of the small-time capitalist of the Frontier as a Holy Fool who tries to live out the myth of individualism, only to see it destroyed by corporate power. This was the obsession of American radicals during the Vietnam era and was soon to be made worse by the Watergate cover-up which seemed to confirm all the darkest suspicions of many Americans. There is a sharp contrast here with the paranoia films of Alan Pakula during the same period. Unlike Woodward and Bernstein, alias Redford and Hoffman, whose uncertainty and paranoia are absolved by their hard-nosed investigation, and of Bree Daniels in *Klute*, whose fear of male persecution is vindicated, the individualism of McCabe entails separation from the vital knowledge that is power. On a mythic level, Pakula's contemporary films absolve the fear which Altman's history film turns into a poetic reverie of dissonance. As cinema of poetry Altman's film rests on the margins of genre where it can play with myth and allegory more freely than *The Conversation, Blow-Out* or *The Parallax View*, with their highly melodramatic plots. The visual image of the dying Beatty's effacement in the blizzard gives us a poetics of obliteration which is echoed by his assassination on the darkened catwalk above the Convention hall in *The Parallax View*. But Altman's *mise-en-scène* and montage in this final sequence are much more powerful. The intricate subtlety in his switch from pastiche to paranoia is repeated at the end of *Nashville* with the shooting of Barbara Jean which, though coming completely of the blue, uncannily evokes the assassinations of King and the Kennedys in the previous decade. It echoes, in particular, the traumatic events of Dallas through the sudden eruption of the shots at the rally and the public reaction to them, the unexpected followed by panic and fear. Ironically, the echo works through the death of someone who is neither male nor political, but who tenuously shares the dubious status of celebrity to which singers and politicians both aspire. Altman's focus on the powerless grief of those present, those who have witnessed but failed to prevent the killing, strikes a chord with us all. It also echoes the powerlessness of McCabe in the face of corporate conspiracy.

We have a similar instance of political helplessness in Polanski's *Chinatown*. J. J. Gittes has the anti-heroic posture of McCabe, but the cute persona of Beatty is displaced by the more endearing persona of his close friend Jack Nicholson. Here the parody-pastiche of the hard-boiled private eye extends from his tasteless jokes to his foppish sense of fashion and finally to the bandaged nose which turns him into a damaged icon. The material detail of Altman's movies is matched here by Robert Towne's screenplay, with its close attention to the politics of LA corruption over that precious commodity of a desert city, the water-supply. It is also matched by the actual lifestyle of the new private investigators of the period, self-made narcissists with their own office staff, dabbling professionally in matrimonial affairs. Polanski adds to this the visual look of Southern California which had long been buried in the functional backlots of studio movies. In its effective use of the latest camera technology to capture the past, *Chinatown* rivals *McCabe and Mrs Miller*. But its visual look is almost the exact opposite. John Alonzo, Polanski's cinematographer, used a Panavision anamorphic lens to produce the closest analogy which camera technology had to human perception with a lens range of 43–45mm.[16] Moreover, Polanski insisted on using no diffusion, thus getting a clarity in the colour image which ran against the grain of the noir tradition. Yet he retained noir intimacy through the proximity of the camera to its characters, often achieved through the use of a hand-held Panaflex. Thus *Chinatown* uses mimetic images of transparency in a world where truth lies still concealed, creating a visual and diagetic counterpoint which it turns into poetic narrative. It remains indebted to the private-eye genre, to its place within a familiar form, but it also transcends that form through the free indirect discourse of Nicholson's quest, in which he finally discovers terrible truths he is powerless to prevent. This paradox of transparent darkness belies the false assumptions of post-modern critics about the surface qualities of pastiche, and is echoed in Altman's demythicising of the private-eye genre, his remake of *The Long Goodbye* with its architectural transparencies, its glass Malibu beach house and its minimal use of artificial lighting, a visual look again photographed by Zsigmond appropriate to the confused misadventures of Elliott Gould's anti-heroic Marlowe. Seeing through things can make them often blank, but for Altman blankness is always a source of parody and beyond the blankness there is always the stuff of paranoia.

The Red Desert and *Stalker* made a wasteland of the senses because their materialities are toxic and dangerous in ways that are abstract and invisible. The American cinema of poetry has been equally material, but also crucially different since it is inseparable from the mythologies of the American Dream. In Altman's North-West he recreates a world of rough and piecemeal settlement driven by the ambition of ultimate success. Terrence Malick's cinema is similarly driven by the world of work, by the garbage Martin Sheen collects in *Badlands* and by the physical force he later exerts on the cattle in the feed-lot. In *Days of Heaven* it is driven by the furnace which Richard Gere stokes at the Chicago steelworks before his flight to Texas and by the harvest he and Brooke Adams help to bring in as sackers in the wheatfields of Alberta, standing in here for the fields of Texas panhandle. Work as doubled – for in each case Sheen and Gere default then resume at something else no less physical – is the driving motif of Malick's episodic chronicles, though not in any pastoral or idyllic sense. The world of work remains smalltime in the mythic spaces of the American Dream. The intense striving to supersede it, which both films treat seriously, drives them daringly away from the dictates of Hollywood genre. Malick is extraordinary in his separation of the sublime from the mythical. The poetics of flight and the growing fear of discovery are set off against the repetitions of the seasons and the banalities of everyday life.

The stress on a material history contains elements of pastiche in the evocation of the past and elements of paranoia in the evocation of flight. Yet his flair for transcending both structures of feeling makes Malick unique among the American filmmakers of his generation. He is just as challenging as Altman or Scorsese but more enigmatic. This makes his work easy to imitate, as in Quentin Tarantino's screenplays for *True Romance* and *Natural-Born Killers*, but difficult to rival in the intensities of poetic vision so that both these films fall acutely short of the power of *Badlands*. Equally *Days of Heaven* echoes passages of American films by European directors who seem to read the American landscape through his lens. *Paris, Texas*, Kusterica's *Arizona Dream*, Philip Ridley's *The Reflecting Skin* all spring to mind. But none possesses the white light of the original. In *Days of Heaven* dream and reality fuse in visual narrative as poetic reverie of time past as Malick meets head on the historic challenge of Manifest Destiny.

Here Malick radically alters the conventions of the sublime in the filmic rendering of the West. It is not merely the ineffable grandeur of landscape so powerful in the classic Westerns of Ford, Hawks and Anthony Mann. The majesty and power of creek and canyon, desert plain and snow-capped mountaintop had after all been a feature of the landscape paintings of Bierstadt and Remington which sold a mythical West to an entranced American audience back east and helped to generate the movie Western of the next century.[17] Malick is interested in the rather different crossover between landscape and the machine. Thus one of the first images of his film, a steam train crossing an immense viaduct in the mountains, was a striking image of early American photography and painting. It is the tense co-existence of natural and industrial sublime which gives his picture such generative power. The image of the Chicago steel furnace leads onto the image of the Western train which takes the lovers to the Texan prairies, then in turn to the steam-driven harvesting machines of the farm and finally to an image fitting to the new technologies of the twentieth century, those of the motor car and the aeroplane. Gere's ascent in the world is also a changing relationship to the machine, where he moves from being its servant to its master as a new automobile driver. Malick doubles two forms of tension, the world of work and the world of nature, that of the natural and the machine-age sublime. But the film's oneiric continuity, its free, partly improvised, narrative also bind the ascent. Malick thus captures the ambivalence which Marx has suggested was in the culture itself, the machine as source of speed and progress and the machine as dangerous and monstrous. Malick goes beyond the classic Western by taking his story into the second decade of the twentieth century and showing the match of contrary forms in the American sublime. Significantly, the film's opening in 1978 came at a time when the New Left pastoral of the American counter-culture was on the wane.[18]

Malick's visual imagination also reinvents the sublime photographically through the work of Nestor Almendros. By doing so, he invokes both Emerson's transcendentalist philosophy and the Luminist painting which in many ways was its visual equivalent. As opposed to the faded, filtered look of *McCabe and Mrs Miller* inspired by the pastel colours of Andrew Wyeth, the virgin Alberta landscape with traditional Hutterite wheatfields is largely filmed in the 'magic' or twilight hour, the twenty minutes after sunset before darkness falls.[19] The eerie magic of the northern prairie light, its lingering softness, is a major bequest to contemporary cinema, since it alters by natural means our whole cinematic way of seeing. The film's context partly justifies this since, as Malick well knew, farmworkers did start at dawn and finish at dusk. But it also enables Malick to go further and do several contrary things at once. The light simultaneously conveys the sense of effort expended by the end of the day, the nostalgia of a lost age, the serenity of place and the forbidding darkness to come in which the fortunes of all the film's characters would inexorably change. This multiple signifying is astounding, creating a layered narrative in which the sounds of the farm-engines, the voices of the sackers and the music of Ennio Morricone combine lyrically with the editing of Bruce Weber to produce a narrative tone-poem of great expressive power. History and the dream of history fuse to give a new meaning to montage. Strictly speaking the film departs from the free indirect vision of Pasolini but uses the voice-over of the young sister (Linda Manz) to invent its own. Manz is naive witness to adult events she only half understands, a participant like Sissy Spacek in *Badlands*, but also an onlooker who lives through the destruction of the fatal triangle of Gere, Brooke Adam and farmer Sam Shepard. For her the flight to Texas, life on the farm and then in the farmer's house are a poetic adventure, 'days of heaven', a lyrical journey, a form of childhood poetry without the pain which afflicts the adult love triangle. She thus shares our objective position as spectators with the subjective experience of the tragic lovers. Their tragedy is within her reach but also beyond it. This allows Malick to circumvent the pitfalls of melodrama and use film as poetic chronicle, fragmented, existential, incomplete. At the same time he can chart the vagaries of social fortune, the lucky escape from Chicago after Gere has murdered the foreman at the steel mill, the unrelenting toil as sackers in the wheatfield at harvest-time, the ascent into the big house on the prairie when Adam marries Shepard and they no longer have to work from dawn to dusk to survive.

The big house on the Banff prairie is a built facsimile of Edward Hopper's *House by the Railroad*, and the film is set in the same period (1917–18) as Hopper's painting (1925), based on his earlier etching *American Landscape* of a solitary railroad house framed by passing cattle. In the painting the animals disappear and the house stands alone by the prairie railroad, framed from a low-angle and devoid of secondary elements. The Victorian house with mansard roof was ingeniously recreated by Jack Fisk, Malick's production designer, almost exactly from Hopper's painting and is often shot by Malick from an identical angle, a frontal diagonal. The crucial difference with the painting lies in the disappearance of the railroad, which is removed from the sight of the camera lens, literally in out-of-field space. The house stands sublimely rootless on the prairie, separated not only from the railroad but also from the sackers' makeshift quarters. Hierarchy is thus symbolised not only by size and style but also by spatial solitude, with Shepard as the lonely *patron* whose marriage to Adam trades social status for companionship and love. The house then becomes a major character as it changes from Shepard's lone majestic abode to the shared household of farmer, wife, 'brother' and 'younger sister'. The duplicity of the outsiders where Adam pretends to be Gere's sister echoes the power-struggle in the Knightsbridge flat of *The Servant*, where the position of James Fox is challenged by servant Dirk Bogarde and his 'sister-lover' Sarah Miles. As opposed to the studio claustrophobia of Losey's urban drama, *Days of Heaven* plays powerfully on the dialectic of intersecting exterior and interior space. This power comes from using the interiors of the constructed house for the actual filming, and makes for comparison with the Chekhovian summer-house in *The Sacrifice* where the vast space of studio construction makes possible the film's intricate long-takes. With his quick-cutting variations on montage Malick is not confronted by the same difficulty and creates a visual match which is also a painterly match between Hopper and Vermeer.

The interiors of Fisk's house were mainly lit by rays of natural light falling through the windows in the style of Vermeer to bathe the faces of the characters. As Shepard's suspicion about his wife's continuing relationship with Gere grows, the house comes to have that symbiotic transparency which Barthes thought defines the essence of the Eiffel Tower, another grandly isolated edifice, as a central cipher of modernity. It is a place to be looked at and simultaneously a vantage-point for looking. This is illustrated by the high-angle long-shot from the roof where Shepard witnesses the show of too-intense affection between his wife and her 'brother' as Gere reluctantly accepts the marriage and leaves to seek his fortune. The tensions of jealousy are thus conveyed spatially and visually, Shepard's on the inside looking out, Gere's in a variety of sequences on the outside looking 'in'. These unspoken jealousies also relocate the females at the centre of the household to which they only just gained entry. Here they are framed like figures out of Vermeer. They share an unspoken knowledge whose tensions create the absent presence implied in his letter paintings and in the prototypical gaze towards the painter, the slightly anxious turn of the woman who knows more than she conveys. With the figure of Manz, Malick invokes the portraits of *The Milkmaid* and the *Girl with Pearl Earring* and also the famous profiled look of the face in front of the window, bathed in natural light.

This female centring echoes that of *McCabe and Mrs Miller*, where Julie Christie takes over Beatty's brothel as her own. It becomes her establishment with her girls, an assertion of the autonomy of female space. In both instances the advent of the woman into the domestic interior prefigures the downfall of the males in the external world – Beatty shot and dying in the snow, the jealous gun-toting Shepard speared through the heart with a screwdriver by the resisting Gere. The images of nemesis are images of contrast, Beatty effaced in the worst elements of winter, Shepard dying amidst the embers of the fire which has destroyed his crop, already devastated by locusts, both sacrificial offerings to Manifest Destiny. Malick's fire and locusts have strong biblical echoes but their filming is another cameo of superb mimetic drama. Almendros abandoned the Hollywood practice of backlighting fires to film the prairie flames naturalistically, using only the farm-workers' lanterns as sources of additional light. The visual effect was made possible by a newly invented technique for naturalising the moving point-of-view. The Panaglide camera, prototype of Steadicam, gave us heady onrushing shots of farmworkers rushing forward with blankets to douse the fire. Like Altman, Malick had transposed nature's extremes onto a new mimetic plane.

In *McCabe*, Altman's parallel cross-cutting displaced Beatty from

Christie and the townspeople as he reluctantly sought a showdown with the hired guns. But they in turn are separated, the townspeople trying to douse the fire, Christie taking refuge indoors in a Chinese opium den from sure knowledge of McCabe's fate. This triadic separation breaks with the Western romance, but Malick renews it by transforming it, by making love and death inseparable, by seeing in romance not linear resolution, but tragic repetition. As the seasons repeat themselves, so does Gere's murder of his superior and so, consequently, does flight. This metonymic repetition incorporates the four elements. The fire of the steel furnace is echoed in the fire of the wheatfields while the river, idyllic place of play between Gere and Adam, now offers escape from the farm's scorched earth. Thus Manz and Adam, who faithfully join Gere after his first murder, faithfully join him again after his second. Yet like Christie, the two females outlive the man to whom they are attached and go on to lead their own precarious lives. Malick invokes romance only to part company with it.

The anachronism in both films is striking. The songs of Cohen, the drugs of Christie, the brothel's unglamourised sexuality, suggest the presence of the new American counter-culture which marked the turn of the decade. The reveries of Altman and Malick thus contain involuntary echoes of their time, its desire to rediscover the pioneering roots of the country as the basis of a new freedom through the commune, through rural retreat, through a makeshift existence on the land. Just as Altman and Malick gloss the photorealism at the beginning of the century so the images handed down to us of the counter-culture of the early 1970s possess the feel of a makeshift settler idealism, the look and style of the clothes evoking through unconscious pastiche the world of the Indian or the wilderness pioneer. The outlaw motif, the flight from the law, the ubiquitous grip of corporate power, all were counter-cultural obsessions and help to explain the re-imaging of the American West in both pictures, bringing history forward more vividly into the present while retrojecting current obsession into the filmic imagining of the past. The same can be said for *Badlands*, with its pastiche feel for the films of James Dean, whose look Kit (Martin Sheen) self-consciously tries to imitate in his deranged quest for notoriety. This *is* the age of James Dean, but devoid of Dean's sensibility, for Malick's movie signified anachronistically the absent presence of Vietnam in the forest scene after the getaway where Kit lays traps for the law and plays at being the ultimate desperado. It was as if his journey upriver for Coppola as Willard in *Apocalypse Now* was a more complex reprise of the outlaw journey Malick had already given him.

Malick's disappearance from the cinema after two major films was a hard blow for American art. It followed the disappearance of Rafelson and prefaced the failure of Altman in the 1980s to match the standard of his great movies of the 1970s. The contradictions between art and money were making themselves felt in *Apocalypse Now* as it ran way over budget and the poetic inspiration of its early epiphanies gave way to chaos and narcotic excess which made a travesty of its depiction of the 'heart of darkness' in the Cambodian jungle. United Artists, obsessed with the problems of bankrolling Coppola, were driven into nightmare by the debacle of Michael Cimino's *Heaven's Gate* which finally forced them into merger with MGM after an inventive decade.[22] Cimino, like Coppola, wanted to deal critically in American myth and history with his portrait of the Wyoming cattle wars as naked class struggle between ranchers and poor settlers. Both Coppola and Cimino had researched assiduously, Coppola using a screenplay by Michael Herr, author of *Dispatches*, the best American chronicle of the war, while Cimino wanted to bring to light a forgotten chapter in the savage history of the West. Yet this material foundation was undermined by the lure of genre and the power of money. Cimino's inclination to mix modernistic technique with melodramatic excess, naturalism with the Western sublime, drove his budget further into debt.[20] The cinematography of Zsigmond has higher production values in *Heaven's Gate* than in *McCabe and Mrs Miller* but less visual impact because Cimino wanted to mix the visual poetry of Malick with the epic narrative like Ford and overlay it with allegories of class war on the range.

The five-hour forty-million-dollar hybrid which the studio cut to three hours for general release was a disaster and also a turning point. At the same time as *Heaven's Gate* another film project which troubled United Artists was underway, a boxing picture with a screenplay by Paul Schrader, directed by Martin Scorsese. In the course of negotiations with the studio Scorsese agreed to have the screenplay (first draft Michael Mardik, second draft Paul Schrader) rewritten to tone down its violence and obscenity. The revamped script done by Scorsese and De Niro and unattributed in the credits lessened the violence but toughened the tone, making it more uncompromising.[21] The film was a watershed in Scorsese's career as well as a watershed in American cinema history. It marked the end of the freest, most critical and more fruitful decades of American film which had started with *Easy Rider* and ended now with the declining fortunes of independent producers like Burt Schneider and Edward Pressman and the demise of United Artists. It was to signal the return of the power of the major studios, the emergence of a new age of special effects and multi-millionaire stars. After the failure of *New York, New York* it looked as if the despairing Scorsese could have gone the way of Malick and Rafelson but instead *Raging Bull*, released through UA, became his magnificent lacerating answer. It is perhaps the jewel in the crown of the American cinema of poetry which tried to mirror its contemporary world through that world's previous generation.

It contains that same oscillation between paranoia and pastiche which we find in *Chinatown*, *The Long Goodbye* or *Apocalypse Now*, but images it even more powerfully. While Coppola had created an idealised pastiche of 1940s New York, Scorsese follows Malick and Altman in aiming for the historical look of the period. The black-and-white cinematography echoes the earlier boxing movies of the period, *Body and Soul* and *Somebody up There Likes Me*. It also gives the boxing ring the look, quite deliberately, of Weegee's black and white photographs for *Life* magazine, while the clothes of the blonde-haired Cathy Moriarty echo women's fashion of the period as well as Hollywood's previous blondes of the period – Lana Turner, Rita Hayworth, Kim Novak and Eve-Marie Saint. Moriarty speaks and looks like a New York girl dressing up in the style of her favourite stars, but then that is probably what many New York girls did. Pastiche may be an integral feature of modern film but it is also an integral part of modern culture. La Motta's story is topped and tailed by his obese middle-age where he does night-club turns which trade on his waning celebrity. Hence the famous rehearsal shot in front of the dressing-room mirror where he imitates Brando's 'I could have been a contender' speech from *On the Waterfront*. The irony is self-conscious but not gratuitous. La Motta was a contender and a successful one, but his life had fallen apart. Terry Molloy had lost his chance of the title but is redeemed by his courage and in the happiest of endings by the love of a good woman. La Motta has lost two wives who have both walked out on him. Yet the primary elements of the film outweigh these forms of pastiche. The black-and-white look of Scorsese's Bronx, actually shot in Little Italy, has the luminous and gritty feel of the Italian neo-realists, not the chiaroscuro of film noir. This is a story of working-class New York which, as Scorsese knew, had only been partly told in 1940s thrillers like *Kiss of Death* and *The Naked City*. It is closer in its look to these movies than it is to Rossen's 1947 boxing movie *Body and Soul* but at the same time has the attention to light and *mise-en-scène* we associate with *Citizen Kane* and the mobile camera of *Touch of Evil*. If Stern is right in suggesting the choreographed and balletic effects of the fight scenes owe much to *The Red Shoes*, the lyrical panning and tracking of the domestic interiors, often done in deep-focus long-takes, are indebted to Renoir.[24] The parallel editing of the film integrates its realist and expressionist phases through a very intricate form of montage. In addition Scorsese absorbs the cinema of psychodynamic space from the European directors of the 1960s, Godard, Antonioni and Bertolucci. This takes his concern with paranoia and erotic obsession to new and challenging dimensions which 1940s Hollywood movies never had.

Contrary to those who view the film as being exclusively about boxing and the plight of masculinity, male paranoia overlaps the dimensions of the public and private because it oscillates in La Motta's mindscreen between two obsessions, that of the ring and that of Cathy Moriarty, between violence and eroticism, masochism and paranoia. The poetics of the narrative thus lie in a form of stark juxtaposition which is fast, severe, elliptical. Its poetic rhythms thus disorient the viewer through their speed, which makes Scorsese closer to Fellini than to Altman or Antonioni, but also shows a continuity with the earlier aesthetics of Renoir. The viewer is given the choice of being an interested onlooker who must nonetheless keep pace not only with the rush of events, but adjust to sudden and dynamic shifts in space and time which are always determined by La Motta's own mindscreen. To these are added the forms of editing in which Scorsese frequently varies the speed, the angle, the duration and the length of shot.

Scorsese turns La Motta's divided obsession of boxing and desire into a delirium of form and then clinically charts the growing paranoia after his marriage. Bouts of sexual abstinence fuel his delusion that his oblique control by the Mob is mirrored in Vickie's erotic attachment to the Muscle. Here paranoia is also an externalisation and projection of the guilt felt at violent transgression. He has persecuted Taddie, his first wife and, *in extremis*, resolves the guilt he cannot redeem by feeling himself persecuted. The persecutor thus imagines himself, in Freud's classical formula, as victim. The first appearance of the Mob Muscle, never overt, the trio always talking closely in low voices just out of earshot, gives rise to Jake's immediate suspicion of being manipulated, but comes just after his vicious treatment of Taddie. Here Scorsese's use of sound is crucial. We share Jake's failure to hear fully the conversations just out of earshot and we share too the highly disorienting ambient sound, a mindscreen of subjective sound which recalls the Greenwich Village courtyard in *Rear Window*. The sounds of traffic, kids in the street, dogs barking, jazz on the radio, arias and love songs on the gramophone all off-screen, sound whose sources are never pinpointed but whose volume is in excess of the natural neighbourhood noises which they mimic. This wall of sound, coupled with the snatches of unheard conversation which run through the narrative, forms a key dimension to the unbalancing of Jake's mindscreen. For at times the sound of the outside blots out the sound of the inside. Public noise obliterates private intimacy. The wall of sound is not gratuitous. It is a continuation by other means of the wall of sound which La Motta faces from the crowd who pay to see his contests.

Jake's sightings of Vickie begin with the first swimming-pool sequence. The slow angled zoom on the face of the sunbathing teen-ager echoes the downward zoom on Rita Hayworth sunbathing on the yacht in *Lady from Shanghai*. In the club sequence which follows, the male gaze is *Vertigo* transfigured. The slow forward track through dining-tables to the distant girl recall Ernie's Restaurant where James Stewart first sees Kim Novak. Stewart's eyes are averted, but De Niro's gaze is intense. The slow-motion fight shots of Jake's victims on the ropes or falling down, are echoed in the slow-motion exit shot of Vickie surrounded by the Muscle, a mindscreen shot of obsession, producing expressive rhythms out of natural context. It is a visual motif repeated through the film, the slowed shot on the face of La Motta's opponent in medium close-up juxtaposed with the slowed long-shot of Vickie in the club scenes in fleeting contact with the Muscle, a mindscreen of the persecutor transformed into a mindscreen of the persecuted.

One early cut from the club returns us to a daytime shot of the swimming pool where Joey hails Vickie, in bathing costume, from the street through the wire mesh and asks her if she wants to meet his brother. This master-shot has a single pan first through the wire towards Vickie then back to the roadside where Jake is waiting in his new roadster. After Jake goes up to the pool, Scorsese cuts to a medium two-shot, the wire-mesh tightly framed between their faces. A few words of small talk and then the sequence cuts elliptically to an interior shot of the roadster with Vickie beside Jake in summer outfit, finally moving close to him as he drives along open parkway. A further cut takes us to a miniature golf-course where Vickie tries, perhaps symbolically, to play her ball into the entrance of a miniature church. As they kneel and squat and look for the lost ball, Scorsese combines angles of looking with sparse dialogue which stress through bodily posture both awkwardness and growing attraction. The camera cuts as they change positions. The game has forced them down on hands and knees, postures akin to love-making and Vickie's backward glance, while facing the tiny church entrance, signifies this knowingly. The courtship sequence ends in a tight low-angle, over the shoulder, with Vickie looking up at Jake. The spatial tension is renewed when they return to Jake's apartment but is enhanced by the dramatic tension of Taddie's unexpected absence. She has left the apartment and also the film, and Jake is already making Vickie over as her replacement. A long profile shot frames them sitting at opposite ends of the table against a wall, and the space between them is palpable, recalling for example the similar apartment shots between Brialy and Karina in Godard's *Une Femme est une Femme*. For Godard the separation is that of bored spouses. For Scorsese, however, it is a gulf about to be bridged.

Taddie's unexplained leaving echoes the disappearance of Anna in *L'avventura*, just as the spatial dynamics of Jake and Vickie recall Sandro and Claudia searching on the island. Scorsese's approach is faster, more claustrophobic than Antonioni yet somehow he conveys the same bleakness as Antonioni's exteriors in the interior of the Bronx apartment. Vickie is coaxed into moving to a closer chair, then to sitting on De Niro's knee so as to annihilate space. Yet the long-shot simultaneously suggests a space between the couple and the camera which can never be conquered. As Jake coaxes her into the bedroom and onto the bed, sitting, they are framed again in long-shot against a bare wall marked by a solitary crucifix. The framing is anti-erotic, the room almost Bergmanesque in its spareness. The bedroom is not the place of love and in the film we are never to see any love-making there. Sitting under the cross Vickie moves quickly out of his embrace to a framed photo of Jake and brother Joey on the dresser, again all in a continuous shot. There they are viewed in profile, bisected by the photograph which they look at and discuss. As Jake's lips move across the photo towards hers again the movement is one of annihilating space, this time intimately. As first Vickie and then Jake move away from the dresser, the camera rests on the photo their faces had momentarily blocked from our view. The relationship of brothers has the greater durability but only perhaps in the mindscreen of the paranoid beholder.

Scorsese then cuts to the captioned Sugar Ray Robinson fight with its multiple variation of shots from the camera inside the ring – the tracking and panning which follow the fighters, a static wide-angle to give distance juxtaposed against medium close-ups of Jake and Ray trading punches. The sudden cut back to the lovers leads into an intimacy which appears to be private, but shows how the boundary between public spectacle and private ritual is now porous. The aborted love-making we see is explicable only as a prelude to his next fight. It opens with a long-shot which is almost a reverse-angle of the first bedroom shot. Since it is shot from beside the bed, we cannot see the wall crucifix which defined the first bedroom scene. Instead the long deep-focus shot of Vickie by the bathroom contains Jake's reclining feet on the bed in the bottom of the frame before it moves into medium-shot and tracks to meet her coming towards him. A fluent pan catches a mirror-reflection of her embracing Jake as he lies on the bed. They start love-making as an operatic aria wafts in through the window. Romance turns into the perverse erotica of the boxer arousing himself for his next fight. The bedroom mirror gives a doubled reverse image of Vickie straddling Jake, then kissing his cuts and bruises in angled and profiled close-ups. Vickie's lips go down on Jake's face and body in sensuous intimacy which recreates in its own fashion the washing of Christ's wounds as a sexual rite. Jake's perverse denial of coitus rests on the recharging of hormones for the cruelty of the impending fight. The camera pans back to the bathroom where he rushes to douse his erection in iced water, an image repeated after his fight, when he uses an ice bucket to heal his damaged fist. But the scene is not complete. Vickie follows him into the bathroom and in a second mirror scene with its doubled reverse image we see a close-up of their lips brushing each other's faces. As Vickie returns to the bedroom, leaving Jake by the door, the sequence ends by inverting its opening. As Vickie has opened the door to Jake's call, Jake closes the same door behind her, excluding her. The sequence confirms the lack of division between public and private. The love-games are rites about fights, and for both the erotic buzz comes from the part they play, the risk, the uncertainty. Surprisingly it is the game of loving more than the game of fighting at which Scorsese's camera excels.

La Motta's ascent to world champion is a descent into endless suspicion. It is one thing to suspect your spouse of being too intimate with friends, another to see her as the sexual link in the Sordid Chain of Being which connects his brother to the Muscle and the local-made man of the Mob. Travis Bickle's defiant 'You lookin' at me?' becomes the deranged 'You lookin' at my wife?', but the question remains unuttered and perversely turns its psychology around. Coveting Vickie is a form of persecuting Jake. Evidence for cuckoldry is actually ambiguous and the ambiguity of the image echoes *Shanghai* where Rita Hayworth is the centre of the male gaze but the audience cannot decipher, any more than Welles, her exact relations with any one of her onlookers. The reference is made knowingly in the scene where Joey catches her at the club with Salvy and the Muscle. As she denies intent and claims her right to free association – 'I'm tired of havin' both of yous up my ass every night' – Scorsese frames her in the multiple mirror images which echo the duplicity of Hayworth in *Shanghai*'s hall of mirrors. He refrains, though, from the positive fix of providing an obvious solution and builds into the look of Moriarty the looks of Turner, Hayworth and Novak which constitute her film prehistory. But the look is also uniquely naturalised as that of a working-class woman who finally divorces the man who has failed her.

Suspicion of Vickie is linked to the fear of manipulation, Jake feeling that he is the Mob's commodity, their sacrificial offering to the power of money. Against the heroic individualism which marks the classic mythos of the American Dream as male, Scorsese places his disturbed subject as commodified demon, the sacrificial 'raging bull' whose masculinity is bred and controlled for the contest in hand but who is merely punished so that he lives to fight another day. At points Scorsese's love of excess flaws this, his most powerful movie. The fights are the most logistically complicated sequences in the film but not always the most aesthetic. There is too much blood, too much slowing down of the frame, the stretching of a bold technique beyond saturation. Yet the film's free indirect subjectivity never violates its story and this in itself is an extraordinary achievement. Scorsese's later move into the gangster biopic, seen in *Goodfellas* and *Casino*, lacks that same libertarian urge as the telling of the story becomes uppermost and the narratives are fragmented. True, the bold use of multiple voice-over provides him with a new auditory lyricism to match the movements of his camera, and while the existential feel of his narratives are preserved, especially in the stormy marriage of Ray Liotta and Lorraine Bracco, the gangster story predominates. These narratives in a sense are an unconventional return to convention, to ready genres, using a new style in order to undermine the melodramatic line of the *Godfather* narratives by their documentary detail. Improvisation, unpredictability, chaos. They are all there, but perhaps a little less open and in terms of subject matter a little more predictable, while De Niro and Peschi show again their dependence on Scorsese to elicit great performances and Scorsese in turn proves his reliance on them to bring his gangster narratives to life.

While Lynch by setting *Wild at Heart* in the present, integrates the past into the present as living myth – thus Cage's rendition, clad in snakeskin jacket, of Elvis – Altman, Malick and Scorsese do something roughly analogous but very different. They set their films in the past with the poetic immediacy of the present, matching naturalistic setting and idiom of period to subjectivities which are largely contemporary and to narratives which often seem to be created as they go along. Thus they highlight the paradox that improvisation of the present seems natural since it takes place as things happen, whereas improvising the past seems a contradiction in terms since it has already taken place. But that is what their films do, even in *Raging Bull*, where there is the pre-given structure of the biopic with its set outcomes. But all the films have an outcome and here there is an interesting variation. The present-ness of *Wild at Heart* offers the hope of conspiracy override. Cage and Dern eventually outwit their conspiring enemies and live happily ever after. The living past, by contrast, is resonant with fatality. Beatty is doomed to go under to the Company, Sheen to be caught on the open road, Gere to be shot in flight, De Niro to be a commodity of the Mob. Each lives under a shadow of conspiracy and mistrust which is partly their own. The shadow can never be escaped so that Pasolini's aesthetic is transformed into an ecstatic mirage of borrowed time. But mirage is lived with a power and an immediacy which impact on its viewer because its history is so well defined. Thus Malick's title says it all – past tense, present image – *Days of Heaven*.

Chapter 7

ANXIETIES OF THE MASCULINE SUBLIME

Here follows the first reading. The 1980s increasingly saw a crisis in film masked by technical innovations in American genre. In Europe, the advances of the 1960s ebbed away, suffering from the declining audiences for a national cinema and the increasing flood of Hollywood imports. Tarkovsky remarked during his visit to Italy in 1980 on the apparent loss of nerve among its greatest directors.[1] The vitality of the New German Cinema of the 1970s was clearly on the wane, adversely affected by audiences and money while in France the New Wave seemed exhausted and despite the startling debut of Jean-Jacques Beneix with *Diva*, the so-called 'cinéma du look' never lived up to the qualities of its great predecessor. The exception to all this, though in a minor key, was the UK with its new strategic links between cinema and television. Through its ambitious funding programme Channel Four became a conduit for exciting new low-budget productions like *Angel*, *The Draughtsman's Contract* and *My Beautiful Launderette*. It also invested astutely in major international films like *Paris, Texas, Vagabond* and *The Sacrifice*.[2] But in American terms this late British conversion to modernist cinema was a drop in the ocean. After the debacle of United Artists and its greatest albatross *Heaven's Gate*, the studios began to reassert themselves against the power of the independent producers of the 1970s and to buy world-wide into theatrical exhibition, often through multiplex cinemas.[3] New stars, new cameras, new special effects helped to renovate horror and sci-fi genres, police and avenger movies resurrecting old-style macho heroism in new settings, old wine in new bottles. Realism was out. The key to resurrected genre was spectacle. Filmmakers like George Lucas, Steven Spielberg, Clint Eastwood,

John Milius, Brian de Palma, James Cameron and Ridley Scott attracted audiences throughout the world and as the decade came to a close, even made inroads into the communist world. In the 1990s with the fall of the Soviet Union, American cinema became almost universal. Reagan's decade had paid off. At the apex of the brutal, sensational and reactionary features of the period were its central male icons, Stallone and Schwarzenegger. They were offset by wacky comedies and bland family entertainment which also sold well in the new home-video market. Needless to say, Hollywood's idea of irony was to have its most bankable macho stars, Stallone and Schwarzenegger, send themselves up in films like *Twins* and *Stop, or My Mom will Shoot You!*

This conservative retrenchment mirrors the political turn in American life after the trauma of Vietnam, the Republican return to aggressive Cold War ideology. We cannot however be completely reductive. Despite the special relationship of the UK to the US this was, after all, a period of greater excitement and innovation in British cinema, whose features began to show in new film forms a wide range of social and political engagement fast disappearing off American screens. Many American movies now seemed like reruns of Vietnam in different global locations where Uncle Sam wins the replay, or else rehearsals like *Top Gun* for that supreme miracle of modern technology, the Gulf War, where Americans could conquer all (with a little help from unnamed Allies) and suffer minimal casualties. On the ground, a series of gung-ho movie Americans were fighting terrorists, psychopaths, anti-Americans with foreign accents, would-be destroyers of worlds with a battery of weapons more appropriate then to the streets of Beirut. Bruce Willis, Chuck Norris, Jean-Claude Van Damme, Rutger Hauer, Mel Gibson, Steven Seagal all followed in the footsteps of Stallone and Schwarzenegger. Where was the studied angst of the 1970s? The sharpness of social observation? The sense of identity crisis? The critical sense of life's modern hypocrisies? The answer was, largely in the movies of Woody Allen, whose Manhattan became a critical mass for social awareness during its conspicuous absence from the Hollywood production line, and who, predictably, was better box-office in Europe than in his own country.

The New Right had clearly set a political agenda for the decade and Hollywood did not rock the boat. While independent filmmakers continued to do so in their own way, the films of Jim Jarmusch, John

Sayles, Spike Lee and Donna Deitch creating their own distinctive challenges, there was no longer a critical movie discourse fuelled by the legitimacy crisis of Vietnam and Watergate. In his excellent study of recent American film, Kolker has pointed to the relationship between that crisis and the implied audience of 1970s cinema, and how in the next decade the new conservatism vitiated the power of key filmmakers while opening the door for others like Spielberg whose work is seen by many as a conservative politics of recuperation.[4] Even some of Allen's work which followed the great classics *Annie Hall* and *Manhattan* seemed like a thin pastiche of Bergman or Fellini. The box-office icon of contemporary male anxieties in the 1980s was certainly not Woody acting in his own movies. It was Michael Douglas for whom *Fatal Attraction, Wall Street, The War of the Roses* and *Basic Instinct* established a bankable line in strong anxieties for the male professional. The 'Douglas' challenge came from two redoubtable sources: predatory women – also professional – and serious money. The new naturalist monster of Hollywood, the monstrous feminine, is quite clearly the ambitious lusting professional, Glenn Close in *Fatal Attraction*, Sigourney Weaver in *Working Girl*, Sharon Stone in *Basic Instinct*, Greta Scacchi in *Presumed Innocent* and Demi Moore in *Disclosure*. While the monstrous masculine comes to operate outside of a naturalist remit, the female monster inhabits the hyper-naturalist universe of rich corporations situated in superior skyscrapers. It's interesting to note that working girl Melanie Griffith fights her way to the top courtesy of Harrison Ford's love and the support of her male Board of Directors and at the expense of her Waspish female boss, Sigourney Weaver. The mythic incorporation of the faithful servant of the firm is a theme also found with its own variations in the sentimental *Philadelphia*, where Tom Hanks may be a gay eccentric whose odd brief encounter has given him AIDS but who is equally a devoted company executive and therefore worthy of our reverence in his distress. In the same film Denzil Washington plays out the new Hollywood role forged for the mythic black male professional, devoted father and husband within the cherished nuclear family copied from models of conservative white America.

A more intriguing return of male anxiety on the naturalist register comes in film noir, post-Watergate and post-political. It is a feature of the strongly stylised narcissism in Schrader's *American Gigolo* with

Richard Gere, and Kasdan's *Body Heat* with William Hurt. Both films introduce a new variation into the genre, the fall-guy as explicit object of desire, not only for the femme fatale but for the gaze of the female spectator. This reversal indicates not so much the triumph of male sexuality as its weakness. The problem for the sexy noir fall-guy is not so much forbidden desire as the surfeit of desire, the male body in constant demand, working sexual overtime. It is the body as commodity on short loan, to be consumed as a good ride but having built-in depreciation. Women are desiring but no longer adoring. They cannot be guaranteed to stay around, hence the sudden disappearance of Kathleen Turner in *Body Heat* after Hurt has killed her husband as requested. Her dramatic reappearance at the very end, still desirable but no longer available, is the nightmare of the bemused and by now paranoid fall-guy. The audience too retains the visual iconography of the beautiful woman who has mysteriously walked away yet triumphed. In *American Gigolo*, Gere's fate is similar. No matter how many Armani suits, shirts and ties he can lay out in the bedroom of his lush apartment, he offers little more than sex for sale. In harness to Nina van Pallandt, his ruthless female boss, he is all too vulnerable to manipulation and blackmail. The new age of male narcissism ushered in by the 1970s and so well dissected by Tom Wolfe and Christopher Lasch was a false alternative to the perceived tedium of political agendas. Moreover it flattered to deceive. Clear attributes of male sexuality were threatened in the new world of aggressive females a loss of male power.

By the mid-1980s this was taken further in two key New York noirs, *After Hours* and *Someone to Watch Over Me*.[5] In Scorsese's film there is a dreamlike disconnection between attraction and desire. Uncharismatic Griffin Dunne as a Manhattan computer operator strikes a very different pose from Richard Gere as LA gigolo. His nocturnal foray into SoHo is a paranoid litany of misfortunes in which all women he encounters are potential femmes fatales, sources of threat and temptation. This is free indirect subjectivity as castration anxiety in which every woman seems to want him and then just as quickly seems to want to destroy him. His derealised journey through the SoHo of the 1980s is a form of active passivity, hypercharged motion where things and women happen to him while he significantly fails to make things happen at all. All women are extensions of type, the mythic femme fatale diffused through a series of voices and figures and faces who start off friendly, smiling and available yet quickly become bored, suspicious and angry. He finds no obvious obstacle to his desire, yet equally no real interest in the nature of his soul, giving rise to another fear which complements that of bodily castration, the fear that he has no soul at all. As he wends his frantic way through the punk underground of downtown Manhattan, polymorphous sexualities further undermine him. Just as Welles had given the found realities of Zagreb and the disused Gare d'Orsay in Paris to the nightmare journeys of Josef K in his version of *The Trial*, so Scorsese recreates his own city of night out of the city in which he was raised.[6]

In contrast, Ridley Scott's city thriller gives us a definite intimacy but again picks on the vulnerabilities of the male subject. His married New York detective (Tom Berenger) is assigned to protect a wealthy socialite (Mimi Rogers) who has witnessed a Mob killing, a plot motif pillaged several times since by the TV series NYPD *Blue*. The average guy and family man from a seedy neighbourhood in Queens is confronted by the luxury apartment of the Manhattan socialite and is immediately out of his depth. The variant on genre is interesting – the fall-guy as married, not single – and explores the same terrain as the Michael Douglas movies, the nuclear family under threat. It does so with more interesting and powerful variations – on class and status where Berenger feels himself to be Rogers's inferior when she seduces him and in the matters of family life where wife Lorraine Bracco is also his tough superior. The tough cop is thus threatened from both sides by psychologically tougher women who point up his own vulnerability. His life is not only a tale of two women but a tale of two homes, upper-class Manhattan and working-class Queens, where he is always the outsider looking in. In the silky labyrinth of Rogers's plush apartment, Berenger is both literally and metaphorically out of his depth. In one sequence where he tracks down the Mafia hitman, the apartment literally becomes a maze in which he has lost his bearings. Psychological lostness is converted into spatial vertigo by Scott's brilliant *mise-en-scène*. In both films, the gloss on male anxiety works cinematically through derealisation. That most familiar island city of film, Manhattan, is made thoroughly unfamiliar, Scott's picture created through intricate studio interiors and Scorsese's through eerie nocturnal locations. The loss of one's bearings, agoraphobic for Dunne, claustrophobic for Berenger, becomes the correlative of acute sexual anxiety, an identity angst in which classic forms of tough guy recuperation are not viable. The strength of Scott's film lies partly in the acting of Berenger who can and does act tough, yet who evokes a vulnerable side as the servant of two mistresses which, bereft of any saving voice-over, goes far beyond the fall-guy of classic noir.

Finally we can add two more city noirs which reflect obliquely on the changing role of women and consequent male paranoia, Becker's *Sea of Love* and Pakula's *Presumed Innocent. Sea of Love*, with an impressive screenplay by novelist Richard Price, concerns the attempt of divorced cop Al Pacino to trace a Manhattan serial killer of unfaithful husbands, whose common link is a passing liaison with divorcée Ellen Barkin. Pacino in turn has a steamy affair with Ms Barkin. Barkin is framed as a challenge to convention, an independent working woman with a young child whose sensuality dominates her male partners. Pacino's paranoia is to make the wrong connection between these qualities and murderous intent by thinking himself in line as the next victim. He falls for the perceptual stereotype of the femme fatale in the instant where it no longer holds. *Presumed Innocent*, adapted from Scott Turow's best-seller, links adultery and the machinations of femme fatale Greta Scacchi to the corruption of city politics from which lawyer Harrison Ford tries vainly to extricate himself. Here the punishment of adultery is itself lawless but finally goes unpunished. Ford's nuclear family saves itself but at the price for husband and wife Bonnie Bedelia of secret, irrevocable guilt over Sacchi's slaying. In the refashioned noir of the 1980s and 1990s civic division between public and private realms, sacrosanct for classical liberalism, is finally dead.

Here endeth the first reading. The second now begins, for something is missing. In noir, for sure, we have male sexual angst, the nuclear family under threat and the single independent woman, but outside of genre the critical and artistic challenge to public discourse has gone. When the public crises of the post-Vietnam US had run their course, something else had to emerge, and it did. In a country where the romance of the sublime as the magnitude of the 'absolutely great', to use Kant's phrase, has had so much to do with its vast landscapes and its powerhouse of industrial energies, the sublime must make its return to an age of advanced electronic technologies. Hollywood has duly redefined box-office as the techno-sublime. Part of this is purely technical, the power-surge in special effects which radically changed studio shooting and post-production. From the point at which the Dykstra lens soared through outer space in the inner space of the studio's miniature galaxies in *Star Wars* up to the point where computer manipulation of the image allows Forrest Gump to shake hands with President Kennedy, we are already in the land of Oz, a place of ineffable marvels whose behind-the-scenes techniques spectators barely question. But then neither film really transforms by special-effects into the authentic sublime. That perhaps is the fate of a small handful of significant sci-fi and horror features starting with Kubrick's defining journey through the galaxies in *2001*. After that the films which come to mind are *Close Encounters of the Third Kind, The Shining, Alien, Blade Runner, Barton Fink, Fire Walk with Me, Jurassic Park* and *12 Monkeys*. No list could be complete however without that surprising and extraordinary anomaly, Stone's *JFK* which rewrites recent history not so much as a form of myth but as an investigative sublime bordering on science fiction.

Here history has its own ironies. The American space programme and the first moon flight coincided with the pastoral cool of the New Left counter-culture which then regarded it as the crewcut technology of the uncool. Subsequent developments in the space race were sidelined from public discourse during the furore over Vietnam and Watergate. Thus it was that the docudrama reconstruction of *The Right Stuff* by Philip Kaufman from Tom Wolfe's study of one of the early space launches should make little impact compared with the futuristic science fictions of Lucas and Spielberg. While the latter were an oblique comment on the former, space is futuristic, returning to the American screen primarily at the level of fantasy scenarios and indebted to Kubrick's exploratory *2001*. Both *2001* and more recently *12 Monkeys* have made self-conscious reference to the sublime which they evoke in different ways, Kubrick through one shot where his spaceship appears to be heading over the familiar buttes and peaks of Monument Valley, Gilliam through the Rocky Mountain landscape painting placed over Bruce Willis's time-travelling pad in his futuristic laboratory. Meanwhile in *Total Recall* the mountainous rust-red landscape of the imaginary Mars to which the programmed Schwarzenegger travels, seems a clear pastiche of the Grand Canyon. Extra-terrestrial is the vital magnitude which allows American cinema, with the help of its popular science fiction, to reinvent the sublime, a dominant motif of its culture on a galactic scale. What we witness then is a form of Nietzschean return to the supersensible of a materialist culture which in fact has never died. Beneath the metaphysical level of the image which inspires awe and wonder, fear and horror, and touches our raw cosmic nerve, is a set of material dilemmas which the picture's look more than its narrative mythically resolves. Not only is there the usual threat to public order and the body politic, there is also the adjacent threat to romance, family and sexual identity, two adjacent layers of dysfunctional threat. The public and personal again come together, and stand or fall together. They are saved in the absence of God by evoking the sublime, by evoking the imaginary encounter of human technology and the infinite.

The techno-sublime has one vital ingredient. It is a mythic re-ordering of the non-places of 'supermodernity' as futuristic and extra-terrestrial. It creates imaginary places even when it confers upon them real names, so that in sci-fi cinema space and place are virtually indistinguishable. As Bukatman notes, however, the confrontation is not really with the cosmos but with the artificial infinite, the new world of special effects, spearheaded by Douglas Trumbull, which is able to create through its mattes, electronic miniatures and computer-controlled cameras the cinematic illusion of infinite space.[6] In Kubrick and Spielberg this focused upon the artificial intensities of light which signify the infinite, in the famous Stargate sequence of *2001* and the earth landing of the Mothership in *Close Encounters of the Third Kind*. The miracle of infinite light is typically cued by Spielberg for his audience through the rapture reaction shot. The most famous of these is in *Close Encounters* where the rapt, collective gaze of the assembled technicians at the mountain site in remote Wyoming awaits the Mothership. Visual marvel that it is, Spielberg's rapture shot is thus the sublime sutured into the spectator's gaze as Hollywood spectacle and recently spoofed as such in Burton's abrasive *Mars Attacks!* It is also the flipside of a chaotically democratic culture which prides itself on individualism, collective submission sealed into the collective gaze where submission to the unknown operates in the absence of submission to the actual. The sublime is the third meaning beyond earthly or divine authority, a close semiotic encounter of the third kind. Here masculine anxieties of the earthly kind are resolved by sublime spectacle. As Roy Neary

(Richard Dreyfuss), the embattled all-American male of mid-West suburbia, is left behind by his resentful family to pursue his undying
obsession, his mountaintop vision of the place where the Mothership
will land on earth. When it does finally appear, the quest for the sublime is triumphantly vindicated, even when the family unit becomes its
sacrificial victim. The mythic resolution of real contradiction is baldly
authoritarian as friendly aliens, here and in ET, symbolically recreate
motherhood and fatherhood for a culture which has irrevocably damaged them.[8] Damaged them, that is, for the typical man-child of the
Spielberg opus who is stranded between innocence and experience
and thus submits so easily to the distant sublime.

The prototype of Spielberg's 'manchild' is clearly Dreyfuss as Roy
Neary. But it is reincarnated generally in a number of Hollywood
features from *Back to the Future* to *Forrest Gump* and a new crop of
actors like Tom Hanks, Robin Williams and Michael J. Fox who create
subworlds for themselves devoid of adulthood. Here, out of Spielberg's
hands, the sublime has gone absent without leave and nothing is left
save a battery of hyperactive mannerisms and cute special effects.
Meanwhile, the flipside of the sublime had taken a very different turn
in *The Shining* and *Blade Runner*. We are back on earthly terrain in the
genres of horror and film noir. Yet the dystopic effects of both films play
on an enduring tension between the material and the sublime. The
sublime is now introjected back into the material world, occupying
an elusive inner space and not the outer space of pure science fiction.
Yet the dimensions of inner and outer space are analogous and the
monumentalism of design stunning to the eye. The material world is
portentously wrapped in a metaphysical cloak, unamenable to naturalist
formatting.

There are two minor links between *The Shining* and *Blade Runner*.
The first was the casting of Joe Turkel, he of the bespectacled flint-like
face, as the imaginary bartender of Kubrick's hotel, and then as the
patriarchal head of Scott's Tyrell Corporation. The second was the use
of outtakes from the start of Kubrick's film to end the International Cut
of *Blade Runner*. Thus the forbidding helicopter shot of the Torrance
family's Volkswagen wending its solitary path through mountain
wilderness to the coming nightmare of the Overlook Hotel was
trimmed in Scott's post-production formatting to frame the romantic
'Ride into the Sunset' of Harrison Ford and Sean Young in an American

sedan.[9] The differences are major ones. In adapting Stephen King's novel, Kubrick plays on the convention of an imaginary supernatural force which informs the fraught lives of the hapless family wintering at the unoccupied hotel. Scott's focus is on the techno-disaster of human futures where scientific corporations have created the time-bomb of rebellious replicants through their use of genetic engineering. As Jack Torrance, Nicholson's derangement is embedded in the mythic failure of the nuclear family while Harrison Ford's failure as a world-weary blade runner lies in the mythic collapse of romantic love under the weight of social division and the horrors of replicancy. Both films take screen space into new dimensions, stressing human helplessness through expressive variations on visual scale. Those of Kubrick are clean-lined, geometric, pristine, overlit. Those of Scott are dark, labyrinthine, nocturnal, their exteriors often shot on a Warner's backlot using only the available electronic light and head lamps of its intricate street designs. Both films echo the 1920s in different ways, *Blade Runner* with its pastiche neo-Mayan look and its occasional shooting of LA's period exteriors, *The Shining* in Nicholson's deranged fantasy of a 1920s bar complete with dance orchestra and reminiscent of the hotel's better days. Both films express the metaphysical defeat of their male subjects in terms of a particular triumph, magnitude over mind, size over soul.

Both settings are non-places, labyrinths to be navigated at one's peril, where familiarity of place has gone and paranoia has grown to great size. In *The Shining* Kubrick cuts down the standard metaphysics of Stephen King's plot by limiting the scope of the supernatural Force which in the novel envelops the whole family. Here there is narrative alternation between three distinctive mindscreens, the Force which seizes Danny and invents his Evil Friend, the growing apprehension of his passive mother Wendy (Shelly Duvall) and the growing paranoia of his demented father whose writing failures lead the persecutor to feel persecuted. Where Spielberg's male obsessives are exonerated by the sublime, Jack Torrance is destroyed by its oblique resemblance. For we never see what the Overlook Hotel overlooks, so that the dread of abyss is contained within its vast clinical inhuman spaces designed at Shepperton Studios. Worse than the physical peril of a pioneering settler family facing the hostility of a forbidding landscape is a physiological peril of the modern family faced with vast interior spaces it cannot endure. This is the obverse of Frank Lloyd Wright's romantic belief in the open place, open vista woodland house which merges with its natural surroundings. For Kubrick there is no outside or if there is, it is the garden maze which merely mirrors the interior labyrinth.

Kubrick's imploding nuclear family (single child only) contrasts with the American film tradition of the ethnic family in the city apartment or neighbourhood house, voices, noise, bodies, presence. What weakens the film is its inconsistent subjectivity, man and boy possessed by supernatural forces, woman as purely reactive, avoiding the horrors that provides. The directing of Shelley Duvall is a moot case in the debate on misogyny,[10] for Duvall often seems no more than a fear-ridden appendage to an untalented paranoid writer. Yet even here male identity is on the defensive as the dread spaces of the Overlook start to overpower. Faced with the long endless corridors and the great hall which dwarfs his futile writing desk, one woman seems not enough for Torrance to control. But the female grotesques he hallucinates are beyond control too, nightmares of helplessness before which the male gaze is impotent rather than omnipotent. In any case it is the form of hallucination rather than its content which seems more important, for Torrance is desperate to populate its vast empty spaces with any human forms his fantasies can dredge up rather than be faced with the spareness of the besieged nuclear family – a demented writer with writer's block, fearful spouse and possessed child.

The size and intricacy of interior space itself took cost and design into new dimensions when Kubrick started filming at Shepperton studios. From the start the hotel becomes a character in the picture because after the opening sequence, there is nothing else. This resurrection of the studio movie was followed in England by three keynote pictures in the renaissance of British cinema, Jarman's *Caravaggio*, Jordan's *Company of Wolves* and Greenaway's *The Cook, The Thief*, all of which create their own intricately designed worlds. Note too that Greenaway's *Le Hollandais* functions in a similar way to Kubrick's Overlook. While Greenaway opted for the lateral track and the cross-section effect as the major stylistic device, Kubrick had taken up the invention of Steadicam as a defining instant of camera mobility, and the following shot is used to eat up the vast spaces of the studio. The harsh transparency of the high-key lighting with its cold, clean reds and whites – the Overlook as overlit – moved the film away from

Gothic convention and gave it an anti-noir look. The horror we expect to arrive in shadow appears in full, electric light. The labyrinth of the hotel interior is mirrored in the garden maze, another studio construct where Torrance's pursuit of wife and son mirrors the interior Steadicam tracking. This of course created the picture's major discontinuity shot. In the actual hotel exterior in Oregon, the opening long-shot reveals no maze. Thereafter in the studio reconstruction it is a standard fixture. The confusions of space abound too in Kubrick's deconstruction of point-of-view where often Duvall's fearful gaze is turned away from and not towards the stalking Nicholson.[11] Here Kubrick ironically inverts circumstance to reveal Nicholson's paranoia as he spies Wendy ever vigilant with baseball bat in hand. The persecutor instantly imagines himself persecuted.

This is a film where Kubrick tries, and sometimes fails, to tread a fine line between paranoia and pastiche. The acting is made to mimic the horror genre while the psychotic threat must seem all too real. It is the same structure of feeling and same risk-taking which Lynch takes back into the more naturalistic location shoot of *Blue Velvet*. In both films there is also the same self-conscious evocation of Freud. Kubrick and Diane Johnson, his screenwriter, had read Freud's essay on 'The Uncanny' and decided to make the hotel a prime source. The 1920s hallucination, complete with ballroom music, which has since been fodder for a high-budget commercial, is one such instant, a revisiting in Jack's mind of the hotel's past which ends after his death with the shot of the photograph showing him at a social event of the time. Unlike Hitchcock, however, Kubrick cannot bridge the gap between horror and the uncanny, the psychic and the supernatural, and the film suffers as a consequence. The same quandary appears a decade later in two key films, *Fire Walk with Me* and the horror-history pastiche by the Coen Brothers, *Barton Fink*. Lynch's film has a clear continuity with *The Shining*, the North-West setting, the interior sublime where Lynch's prequel to *Twin Peaks*, *Fire Walk with Me*, makes less use of exteriors, and the horror of the deranged and paranoid male. This is Kant for the horror genre, the point at which the sublime is an erroneous projection of nature. Instead of the romantic sublime which substitutes the metaphysical power of landscape for its detailed beauty, we have the horrific sublime in which lie the forbidding interiors within the sublime landscape, the many rooms and corridors of the Overlook and the many paths of its garden Maze, Lynch's Deer Meadow trailer park and Laura's demonised house, the Red Room, and the seedy nightclub at the Border. Leland Palmer is a copy of Jack Torrance as the paranoid hallucinating tyrant exploding male power in the instant of abusing it. The metaphysical sublime of landscape and culture turns into the sadistic sublime of the nuclear family in its festering isolation.

In the history fable of the Coen Brothers, *Barton Fink*, the sublime is again contained in confined spaces and made cruel. Here the visual imagination is startling, the historical reference ambitious. But a fault-line appears between the supernatural reworking of the sublime and the dilemmas of art and history which engage the filmmakers. This is the American reverie as nightmare but its reflexive history, that of 1930s studio-bound Hollywood, lacks the clinching detail so vital to the historic immediacy we have noted in Altman, Malick and Scorsese. It also lacks the designed sense of period so crucial to *Chinatown* or *Singing in the Rain*. The plot then ends up as a substanceless picture *à clef*. John Turturro as a radical New York playwright heads to Hollywood, much like Clifford Odets, where he meets a drunken Southern novelist turned screenwriter, much like William Faulkner, who is having an affair with a studio secretary (Judy Davis) much like Meta Carpenter, Howard Hawks's secretary with whom Faulkner did have an affair. The skin-deep level of pastiche is sustained in the caricatured studio mogul to whom Turturro constantly reports his non-existent progress. Meanwhile the imprint of *The Shining* is everywhere. Turturro, like Nicholson, has writer's block and is trapped in an LA hotel whose bedroom walls appear to crack and sweat as paranoia takes hold. Later, paranoia turns back into guilt again as Turturro discovers the murdered body of Davis in his bed the morning after he has made love to her. Having failed to convey anything of the Hollywood of the period, the Coens thereafter regale us with superb visual effects. John Goodman, the cheery German-American killer rushing down the hotel corridor in flames, is the most clinching image of the Coens' claustrophobic sublime. But his function is contrived, not only to let Turturro off the hook but also to evoke the dead weight of allegory which the film is too flimsy to hold. Is the rotund Germanic Goodman an allegory of the Nazi fury about to descend on the world? A one-man Holocaust? The Coens' claustrophobic hotel is even less well equipped than Kubrick's agoraphobic hotel to provide any real answer to its implicit imaginary. Here the oscillation between the pastiche of 1930s Hollywood and the paranoid premonition of global disaster – Goodman as a paranoid projection of Turturro's fear of racial catastrophe – spins out of control. The film becomes a horror cartoon from which we can easily awake rather than a nightmare from which we cannot. In rejecting the naturalistic psychology of *Chinatown, Fire Walk with Me, Barton Fink* and *The Shining* seek to replace the all-too-human by the horror which lurks within the sublime. That is precisely the unease of form they cannot resolve.

Blade Runner, by contrast, was a commercial failure in 1982 which became a widespread cult on its re-release in 1991, and is now cut in five different versions which cultists constantly debate. It is *Metropolis* for the late-twentieth century yet it came via the prolific pen of Philip K. Dick out of the political crisis of the late 1960s. Dick's novel *Do Androids dream of Electric Sheep?* was a brilliant paranoid response to the wilful repressions of a besieged American Establishment. With its prophetic vision of genetic engineering as a source of political control, Scott's film turns Dick's fiction into an apt fable for the American future. *Blade Runner* thus contains an inexhaustive visual abstract of the new cultures which emerged in the latter part of the century. While special effects elsewhere have dated, we now seem to have grown into the world which *Blade Runner* prophesied. Yet *Blade Runner* also goes back to the past in its visual debt to *Metropolis* and through the image of its cynical private eye, its formulaic debt to *The Big Sleep.* The replicant theme recalls the doubling of Maria as madonna and robot in Lang's epic and the amnesia of weary romance in Hawks's thriller where the dark criminal side of Bacall's femme fatale is conveniently forgotten. At the same time the bobbed, swept-back hair of Rachael (Sean Young), her *Blade Runner* equivalent, is a clear 1940s pastiche, Joan Crawford-style. Rachael's attraction for Deckard seems to be that of a nostalgic icon, his dream a longing for a golden age before the curse of replicancy, where flawed women were redeemed by the call of romance. Thus Deckard falls for a woman he knows has no real past but who conveys so radiantly the illusion of belonging to a past for which he secretly yearns.

As in Hawks's film, *Blade Runner*'s Los Angeles was shot on the main city street of the Warner backlot in Burbank, its Animoid Row. Crucially it reverses the norm of location pictures where you move into the studio for specific scenes which demand greater finesse. Scott uses a select handful of LA locations and integrates them into the look of the designed backlot, among them the Second Street Tunnel, a Blade Runner office in the middle of LA's Union Station, and various interiors and exteriors of the downtown Bradley Building, which is transformed so evocatively into Sebastian's crumbling apartment block.[12] As in *Touch of Evil* Scott goes literal on the noir convention. Nearly everything is shot at night. The use of available light and the simulation of a constant acid rain lend a new gloss to dystopian studio realism. As in *The Big Sleep* this is detection littered with non-sequiturs. There is no sixth replicant, while the image of Zhora which the Esper blows up for Harrison Ford is not that of Joanna Cassidy who plays her in the movie but a stand-in, as is the stunt-double who explodes clearly in slow-motion through department-store glass after Ford has shot her in the back. While Zhora never gets to do her snake-dance and Roy Batty practically disappears from the first half of the film, the live unicorn of the Director's Cut is Scott's own speciality, not in the script, which left the other filmmakers bemused. The lame voice-over by Ford tacked on to illuminate the story over the continuity cracks after bad previews, had the paradoxical history of repeating itself, being in the original screenplay before being jettisoned in the favour of the film's sublime visuals, put back in for commercial release and then taken out again for the 1992 Director's Cut which film buffs lovingly enshrined in the annals of movie history.

While the city model of Lang's picture was clearly a major spur to Scott and his design team, they replaced Lang's vast industrial prison by a post-industrial wasteland. Los Angeles in 2019 is a foreign city speaking a hybrid language, populated by an Asian underclass topped up by a sprinkling of Anglo punks, and surrounded by huge electronic billboards with smiling Asian faces. The vertical structures are those of *Metropolis* with more complex and sophisticated special effects. Here we travel with and through Deckard's mindscreen. The Spinner is the source of ascent out of the urban underworld into the Ziggurat temple of genetic engineering, the Tyrell Corporation Pyramid. The Corporation is both laboratory and temple, the two mythic homes of the sacrificial unconscious joined as one. It rises above the post-industrial wasteland of greater LA we see at the start which in turn, one suspects, doubles the industrial wasteland of South Shields in whose abrasive landscapes

Scott grew up. Less than three feet high, the Pyramid's neo-Mayan design echoes an architectural fad of 1920s Los Angeles, but the sublime is evoked by Douglas Trumbull's studio miniatures, six-feet skyscrapers navigated by a computer-controlled camera system called the Icebox which could mimic the Spinner's flight and constantly repeat the exact move on the miniature, allowing multiple layers of special effects to be built up on the same negative.[13] This is one of modern cinema's supreme illusions, the tiny detailed miniature blown up on the screen to suggest a sublime and limitless space. Tired perhaps of his imitators in Hollywood, Trumbull was later to commodify his genius for the sublime through his IMAX Ridefilm corporation which has developed virtual rides for Universal's Theme Parks in Florida and California.[14]

Unlike many of its many imitators, the special effects of *Blade Runner* are seldom arbitrary. Crucial to the film is the relationship between technology and desire. Here the feminine doubling of *Metropolis* with its robotic Maria and *Vertigo* with its surreal impersonation are fused and transformed. Rachael inhabits the upper world of the Tyrell Pyramid while the other replicants are Off-World rebels who must negotiate the asphalt underworld of Los Angeles. The female images are drastically polarised between the 1940s femme fatale, softened to a romantic hue, and the New Wave style of punk dominatrix. Deckard is thus divided between the lure of sado-masochism and the lure of romance. It is the former which wins. The film's weakness, if there is one, lies in the failure to balance equally the dilemmas of love and pain. It is clear the sexual charge of female violence triggers the male masochism of Deckard who involuntarily repeats the humiliation he suffers from the powerful Zhora at the hands of waif-like Pris. This is less the sado-masochism of Sadean writing and more a new convention, the filmic nightmare of the maso-sadist who must awake to the flaky rituals of romance. The nightmare, the twice-over killing of the dominant punkette, entails both fear and guilt as the twin forms of male anxiety. Fear of the monstrous but beautiful feminine, guilt at her ruthless killing. Such anxiety thus taints the dream of romance and Deckard's sadistic kissing of Rachael in which passion seems inseparable from hate is the flipside of his beating. At the end too Deckard's compassion for the gentle replicant is mingled with contempt for her passivity. She is no match for the child-like but athletic Pris whom he has brutally shot, whose terrible beauty matches the forlorn spirit of the discarded to the erotic power of strangulation.

Since 1982, mediocre screen versions of Dick's paranoid fictions have surfaced in *Screamers* and *Total Recall* and in 1992 *Blade Runner*'s new Director's Cut still seemed more compelling and more topical than all of its bankable successors in the intervening decade. Three interesting films have emerged in the 1990s, however, which go against the grain of dead-end science fiction. Tim Burton's second Batman feature, *Batman Returns*, and Terry Gilliam's *12 Monkeys* are key high-budget responses to the world according to *Blade Runner*. The third is more oblique and finally more compelling. It is Burton's *Edward Scissorhands* which absorbs gothic, surreal and sci-fi idioms into its strange suburban tale of a forlorn monster forced into the garish mores of consumer culture. Not only does it reverse *Blade Runner*'s male mindscreen by casting its mutant male hero as the object of the adoring female gaze, it explores even further the mythic sensibilities of monstrous solitude. Here Johnny Depp is not so much the blood-brother of Rutger Hauer as the lost brother of Darryl Hannah. If anything Depp's Edward is an androgynous mix of Pris and Sebastian, the designed and the designer of *Blade Runner*. The cinema of solitude, existential in Northern Europe and East Asia, comically surreal in Australia, becomes metamythic in the good old US of A. Heartbreak Hotel, Elvis's great refuge for the lost and the lonely, is now full of monstrous replicants – understandable when the box-office alternative is Michael Douglas or Tom Hanks faking domestic intimacy.

Desublimation, that dark and doleful concept which haunts the pages of Freud and Marcuse, is transformed by Burton's movie into a generic visual gag, a vast comic debagging of the techno-sublime. But its substance is to be found in the grainy detail of Caroline Thompson's superbly observant screenplay. It reminds us that in the consumer age technologies are also domestic and forsakes Off-World metaphysics for the demonisation of Good Housekeeping. Thus Vincent Price's misformed monster has been trained to his chagrin in etiquette manuals and subjected to a mad inventor's assembly line of brainless kitchen technologies. We are therefore given the answer to questions we would never dare to ask of Deckard or any other designer private eye. How does he cut the garden hedges? How does he slice the salad? How does he carve the roast? The only possible point of convergence might be: how does he pick locks? But even then in 2019, the gun and the shoulder would be judged more dramatic then the sharp scissored instrument used for the forcing of doors. Edward's mutant hands also pose the secret question which is never answered for any male hero. How does he urinate? Burton proves once and for all to Woody Allen that castration anxiety does not necessarily have to be verbal.

In the mark of the scissors' scars, Roy Orbison's 'Only the Lonely' is written all over Depp's face. Involuntary mutilation. But the scars are more, a sign perhaps of the male fear of 'feminised' technologies where being adept in the home or the hairdressing salon brings on the fear of damaging one's 'masculine' being. Thus the intricacies of the gender divide overlap those between the human and the monstrous. Edward has to run the gauntlet of suburbia's everyday surreal, the pastel-coloured homes, cars and shopping centres, local TV, predatory house-wives, bank loans with acceptable collateral, alarm systems, psychiatrists, bumper Christmas decorations and media scrums. Winona Ryder, the teenage daughter who laughs at him with her boyfriend when he gaffs around the home, falls in love with him when he first appears on TV, while her mother Dianne Wiest constantly, well, mothers him. He becomes the monstrous other as a domesticated social construct, a novelty to be feared, ridiculed, loved or laid depending on who you are. When he does not fit the construction, he is in trouble. The literal drama of *Blade Runner*'s Voight-Kampff test is replaced here by well-worn rituals of neighbourhood exclusion. The gothic sexbomb soon turns into a social misfit and Depp's mutant-designer look uncannily matches the look in his eyes and the feeling in the soul. The scis-sorhands which have done the salad, the roast, the hedges and turned the female hair of the neighbourhood into an exclusive Lopsided Look, now rip up curtains and wallpaper, puncture car tyres and cut away the artefact of clothes bestowed upon the leather-suited body. The monster returns to the solitude of the mad mansion on the hill.

The gloss on the gothic mansion and the surreal suburb is crucial. One promises the sublime by rising above the human, for the sublime always soars above, while the surreal denies the sublime by delving below the human. The surreal always digs beneath. Clearly, expres-sionism is the obvious mode of the popular sublime because its tran-scendence-as-danger transports from the banal and the everyday. By contrast, the surreal *mise-en-scène* of Burton's film picks up inexorably on daily detail and makes the sublime look ridiculous. That, after all, is what the best comedy is about. The Aussie comedy, *Sweetie*-style, of the daily surreal then seems a riposte to the portentousness of sci-fi special effects and provokes the obvious tongue-in-cheek comparison. Upwardly mobile nerds in Spinners and Spaceships are replaced by nerds in bungalows who can't cook, wash up or dress themselves in the morning. Burton joins the two worlds since Edward Scissorhands, symbol of the techno-sublime gone awry, also cannot dress himself in the morning. The daily and the gothic sublime again clash in the double life of Selina Kyle in *Batman Returns*. Selina, alias Michelle Pfeiffer, is both lonely spinster and lithe catwoman, a new update on the true and false Maria of *Metropolis* but also a composite of *Blade Runner*'s Rachael and Kris, domesticating the former and eroticising the latter, polarising in her split personality the alternate replicant attractions which so agitated Harrison Ford. In this case the lithe balletic movements in the cat-suit, leather-as-totality, involve straddling the bland virtuous Batman of Michael Keaton without making it seem boring. Danny De Vito's mutant Penguin, his circus jugglers and underground penguin army are all garish variations on *Blade Runner*'s underclass, now literally underground in the sewers of Gotham City. The Penguin too is a fantasy update of expressionist models, whose cunning evokes the wiles of Doktor Caligari, while Christopher Walken's vicious tycoon is intended to parallel the look, if not the spirit, of Murnau's Nosferatu, the name of whose actor – Max Schreck – he bears.

As *Blade Runner* is stylised LA, so Gotham City is stylised Manhattan with its centrepiece a monumentalist set, framed by blow-up sculptures which cleverly mimic the Rockefeller Centre.[15] The neat pastiche fashions of its concerned citizens are a nod to the orderly 1940s in the disorderly present, with the underground world of the Penguin an allegorical nod to the well-ensconced criminal ghettoes within Manhattan, Brooklyn and the Bronx. This is the world of stylised eros, cartoon corruption and fantasy underclass. The allegorical levels in the films of Scott and Burton appeal because the natural panorama of the city is now beyond Hollywood's aesthetic and political grasp. Tom Wolfe's coruscating novel, *The Bonfire of the Vanities*, had achieved precisely that, a naturalistic fable of the tensions between rich and poor, black and white in a divided metropolis. Brian de Palma's overpriced overbudget film of the book, however, dogged in advance by the notoriety of its literary property was anything but. Doors closed in the face of assistants scouting locations for Brian de Palma, while inept star casting and on-set resident hostility during filming in the South Bronx made matters worse.[16] At the end it is de Palma's failure to give a sense of place either to a rich Manhattan or a poor South Bronx which buries the picture and makes us realise the scale of the American retreat from the tensions of the present. Of course, films by Allen, Scorsese and Lee work well within specific contexts and neighbourhoods as do the low-budget freewheeling *Kids* or *I Like it like That*. The focus is intensely localised, but not major box-office. Meanwhile the panoramic has all but disappeared.

Of all the *Blade Runner* clones that have littered the wide screen since 1982, the recent time-travelling film by Terry Gilliam, *12 Monkeys*, is the most intriguing. Modelled on Chris Marker's short 1962 film *La jetée*, it is intriguing for two specific reasons. It uses the found realities of East Coast locations in Philadelphia and Baltimore for its major shoots, thus moving away from the stylised studio set which typifies the genre.[17] It also uses the figure of Bruce Willis to generate its own interesting subtext of paranoia which leaves us with surprisingly fertile ambiguities. The screen persona of Willis as Cole framed around the machismo daring of *Die Hard* is one which persuades us, and psychiatrist Madeleine Stowe, to believe in his incredible story of time-travel as a person come back from 2036 to reverse the catastrophe virus which first starts to destroy the world in 1996. If we are taken in by it, it is because we take in the illusion of the persecuted outsider in possession of some terrible truth which authority wishes at all costs to conceal – the paranoid fix – and we do so because the persecuted visionary is the tried and tested Willis. If we assume that Stowe is right the first time to put him away as a paranoid-schizophrenic, and wrong when she relents, then the film starts to make more sense and become more interesting. As in *JFK*, the narrative drive depends on the fix of the paranoia rush, the melodramatic movement towards revelation. But in both films of course there is no revelation, and both films are more convincing if we accept that there cannot be. In Gilliam's picture, unlike Stone's movie, there is that possibility. The future world could well be the deranged mindscreen of the deranged Willis inventing a fantasy about the underground laboratory and its time-machine, a visual invention cast out of the cartoon bric-à-brac which permeate electronic culture. Just as Gilliam's sets are found realities so their fantasy contents may be the dreamed worlds of a deranged mind where, aptly, all forms of communication have broken down. The intensely architectural look of the film, the designed use of power station, orphanage, and exteriors of Philadelphia's City Hall, the clutter of graffiti and billboards, all lend the illusion of reality to fantastic imaginings which studio sets alone would not. The search of Willis and Stowe for the virus-villains allows Gilliam, alas, to indulge his excess monumentalism and wild location switching which do not compare well with the tight epiphanic sequences in *Blade Runner*.

Yet the film still suggests a powerful reflexive reading of extreme paranoia. Gilliam's framing of sublime time-travel is itself reflected in Cole's psychotic imaginary. What Gilliam wildly imagines ends after all up as a 30-million dollar picture for Universal. What Cole imagines ends up, in the double-register of film form, as the vision of a seer or the psychotic fantasy of a paranoid-schizophrenic. The difference is on a knife-edge. Technically speaking, in science fiction, the paranoid is always the filmmaker's alter ego. Both share that fateful moment when out of a chaotic world of detritus and greed, the techno-sublime emerges both as Horror and Destiny. It imposes a grand design with its own nobility even if that design is a figment of someone's imagination. It also glosses a current American pre-occupation in which the sources of conspiracy are pushed back in a brainstorm of justified paranoia from material entities in American society to insubstantial ones which depend upon a world beyond. The conspiracies of the state against the individual which Stone uses as a lever in *JFK* incline optimistically towards some as yet unknown proof. But here the answers lead nowhere. In the cult TV serials which currently cross science-fiction paranoia with *JFK*'s conspiracy theorising, the *X-Files* and *Dark Skies*, the politics of today are pushed even further back (forward? outward?) into outer space.[18] Viruses, UFOs, political killings, are merely staging-posts in a grand cover-up by the state to conceal the cosmic truth from us, namely that the world is already run by aliens. Here the techno-sublime descends well and truly into the ridiculous and joins hands with the new American folk-lore which it has helped to create and which is now, even in such a devout religious country, becoming an article of faith.

Here endeth the second reading. The third begins and ends very briefly by repudiating both its predecessors. While our first, sublime-free reading can be seen as a worthy but uncinematic nod in the direction of political correctness, the second in which everything with major impact in the USA appears to be sublime could be challenged as a feeble excuse for a movie buff's all-American junkfest. The third reading in a way is a Barthesian third term where the sublime is identified by its geopolitical non-being. It is a distinctive match of landscape and culture which is un-American and, for that matter, not very British either. It challenges both the British nostalgia for past glories of empire seen in the pictures of Attenborough and Lean, and currently in *The English Patient*, along with the current arrogance displayed by the United States over its world-empire of the moving image. It lies, that is, outside the explicit empire which no longer is and equally outside the implicit empire which is so busy extending its power that it does not need even to speak its name.

Here we have to name films in countries whose remote landscapes are beyond the Anglo-American reach, or interest. These are just some of them: Chen Kaige's *Yellow Earth* and *King of the Children* in China, Alexander Sokhurov's *Days of Eclipse* and *The Second Circle* shot on the Arctic and Central Asian fringes of the ex-Soviet empire, the epic celebrations of landscape in Kurosawa's Siberian *Derzu Ursala* and also in *Ran*, his Japanese adaptation of *King Lear*. Other names and places suggest themselves, the Iranian people and rural landscapes of *Under the Olive Trees* and *Gabbeh*, the village lives of Burkina Faso in *Yaaba* and the mystic rituals of Mali's Bambara tribe in *Yeelen*, the cruel politics of winter landscape in *Yol*, written and partially directed from prison in 1981 by Yilmaz Gurney. All of these images, these cinematic landscapes perceived by Western eyes as remote and peripheral are indelible and reveal as well as their own nature the limitations of the Hollywood gaze in penetrating landscape and culture which is uniquely Other, and which will remain so. The tenacity of the cinematic Other gives the film image an abiding mystery in which object and image cannot be separated or subsumed. Cinema will always produce such images, out of sight certainly of most of the commercial audiences through the Americanised world. To do justice to them in their diverse entirety would not be the task of another chapter in his book, however. It would be the task of another book altogether.

Chapter 8

THE ROAD TO NOWHERE:
1990s Noir

—————⊃⊂—————

'The very concept of genre is as cold as the tomb', Tarkovsky once said, yet sometimes it isn't. Film noir still remains an important form on the edge of American filmmaking, a low-budget needling of the culture of the Hollywood studios. It is the one genre which challenges the continuing power of money in the mythology of the American Dream. It has to be seen, therefore, as something more precise than mere house-style with intimations of dark motive in its familiar, stylistic motifs, low-key lighting, flashing neon, fog, rain and cross-hatched blinds. It has to be seen as a relationship between money, passion and murder, which form the points on a deadly triangle. Just as the forms of murder vary, so do the material emanations of passion and money. The former can be adulterous, interracial, lesbian, homoerotic, incestuous or if just plain straight, will inhabit places other than mattresses. Whatever it is, passion is always a source of betrayal while money is variously expressed through kidnapping and ransom, drugs, cars, gambling or Acapulco, all iconic signs of the power of the greenback. Whatever it is, the stash of stolen bills in the black suitcase bypasses the anonymous world of plastic and the invisibility of credit. It is there for all to see. The combination of money, murder and sex then gives us that darkly ambiguous epicentre of all good noir – the conspiracy of passion.

Noir in the 1990s is notable for the way in which filmmakers play self-consciously upon the theme which nourishes them. The fall-guy's ordeal is by now as pre-ordained as much by film history as by plot. Yet at the same time the style of noir has become more existential, more digressive, less tightly melodramatic. The greatest cross-over in 1990s noir is its absorption and reworking of the 1970s road movie, to create what some have called the new hybrid of country noir. The cross-over can be seen in the trilogy of John Dahl, *Kill Me Again, Red Rock West* and *The Last Seduction*, in Carl Franklin's racial thriller *One False Move* in the Texas oil-towns of *Rush*, the cheap motels of *The Grifters* and the desert landscapes of *After Dark, My Sweet*. The fragmented and sometimes circular journey of the 1990s fall-guy is one which matches freedom of action and confusion of motive to necessity of plot. The cinema of poetry lies in the formal composition of indeterminacy. But noir is never fully indeterminate. As even Altman showed us in *The Long Goodbye*, finally a plot's gotta do what a plot's gotta do. 1990s noir, I want to argue, should be seen as *unfree* indirect subjectivity as the fall-guy journeys and flounders through the hazy recognition of the unfreedom which defines his fate.

In its mythic form, its resolving of social contradiction, 1990s noir further updates male anxieties in the period of gender crisis. Where sexuality is in flux, roles are shifting rapidly, and marriage is no longer sacred – though perhaps divorce is – things change. Females compete with males not only in the marketplace but in all spheres of carnality and knowledge. At the same time the new forms of agonistic tussling sit uneasily with a solemn discourse of women's rights which periodically exalts victimhood. Noir picks up on this contradiction. The new femme fatale eroticises the enterprise culture by making the money currency of commodities and the sexual currency of the male body exchange equivalents. Money is to be made, the body to get laid, but no longer just as in the classic idiom, to gain release from the tyranny of a dead marriage. Money and body are desirable objects in themselves. As it kicks over the traces of the old adultery code, noir treads the same ground as box-office like *Pretty Woman* but reverses the relationships. We may recall Julia Roberts as the Pygmalion hooker with a heart of gold who makes it from the streets of West Hollywood to Beverly Hills courtesy of Richard Gere, the businessman with table manners and gold credit cards. The complete opposite of Roberts is Linda Fiorentino in *The Last Seduction*, the married woman with a heart of glass whose idea of a happy ending is to destroy all the men around her.

The femme fatale is the centre of commodities at their most

addictive. In *Pretty Woman, Working Girl* and *Philadelphia*, serious corporate money is made but the methods never questioned. In 1990s
noir, however, money is streamlined original sin, stolen as cash or
commodity with its own circular economy spun like a web around its
hapless subjects. Its commodities are highly addictive, gambling in *The
Grifters* and *Kill Me Again*, narcotics in *Rush, One False Move, Light
Sleeper* and *The Last Seduction*. In all of them, sex is also addictive but
only when combined with one of the other forms. If this is a decade of
addiction culture then noir is surely a confederate, celebrating the
perfidy of risk. In the Dahl trilogy, the addiction culture fuses with the
reflexive fix of genre play to give noir a distinctly comic edge. But even
here the predominance of rural landscape gives noir a new edge.
Traditionally it was the form of the city, and while this has been carried
on in *Sea of Love* and *Light Sleeper*, it seems to work now within a
knowable community, the small town no longer immune from the
predations of the city. In the 1980s, *Body Heat* and *Blue Velvet* had established the small town as the fulcrum of dark conspiracy, but the 1990s
format goes further in its embrace of the open road and the horizontal
contours of the American West. *Kill Me Again* is set in Nevada, *Red
Rock West* shot in Arizona posing as Wyoming, *After Dark, My Sweet*
in the arid Californian landscapes also used in *Delusion, Rush* in small-
town Texas. *One False Move* leaves south-central LA for South-Central
USA as its murderous trio of drug dealers drives through New Mexico
and Texas to the home town of Cynda Williams in rural Arkansas. In all
these movies the motel acts as the staging post to close encounters of
a transient kind, a crucial nexus of flight.

So it is that Lara Flynn Boyle breaks off her escape with Nicholas
Cage at the Comfort Inn outside Red Rock West to use his unresisting
body for her own pleasure. She has after all just shot her previous lover
and no-one else seems readily available for the sacred cause of adultery. As the gender wars hot up, it also becomes clear that political noir
only operates in the past tense. In adapting Walter Mosley's *Devil in a
Blue Dress*, Carl Franklin looks back to the corrupt post-war politics of
a racially segregated LA, where Denzil Washington must tread warily to
uncover a conspiracy with racial overtones. *Rush* starts in 1975, the year
of Watergate, which is duly mentioned on the car radio in the opening
sequence of the film. It cues the enveloping paranoia of Jason Patric as
undercover narc who gets lost in his own heroin addiction. His target

Gregg Allman, as a suspected dealer controlling the flow of all kinds of decadence to the town, also provides with his own drugs history as a big rock star of the period, something of a knowing reference. For this is a metaphorical dating of America's loss of narcotic innocence as the flood of hard drugs flows on apace. By the 1990s, in *The Last Seduction*, drug-dealing has become a form of moonlighting by city professionals.

Less remarked, but equally clear, is the antidote noir offers to the carnage genre of serial killing. For mass audiences who wish to exorcise their fear of evil by feeling helpless before it, serial killings are a form of serial sensation of the monstrous, goring by numbers. This sets up a double audience addiction – addiction to the monster as icon and addiction to the mechanism as sequence. The pattern links *Manhunter* and *Silence of the Lambs* to *Heat* and *Se7en* but reaches its nadir of sentimental brutality in *Natural-Born Killers*. The myth of serial killing, that of the true-life case history of the invisible monster who roams the country at will looking for arbitrary victims, is a form of decadent reason. It predicates rational scientific investigation of the unspeakable in which investigators must be seen using the latest forensic science and computer technology. The fantasy of the monster is freed from such stringencies. As science or pseudo-science provide an anchor, homicidal fantasies run riot. Noir by contrast is existential. *One False Move* may have nine brutal murders to *Se7en*'s seven, but its plot is not a mechanical feeder in which killing is a form of punctuation. Its murders are bunched and though always likely, are unpredictable when they come. There is also a strong sense of fatality which runs counter to the pseudo-science of the serial killing investigation. Here *One False Move* (tragically) and *Red Rock West* (comically) involve spirals of descent, whose subjects seem to be instruments of fatality which transcend circumstance. Here country music, never used on soundtrack, is a grey eminence, the familiar wail of cheating hearts wafting up from the car radios tuned to local stations the length and breadth of the American highway. For noir too is about cheating hearts but only when the circulation of blood through the aorta matches the circulation of money through the black economy. If noir reinstates the power of passion now unfashionable in other genres, it reinstates it as pure commodity. Therein lies its predictability. With passion comes betrayal, real or imagined, and something existential is suddenly a form of destiny.

One False Move is a series of false moves, of mishaps, wrong encounters and mistakes all governed by a dread serendipity which subverts the melodrama it creates. After the butchery of the botched robbery in LA there is understatement amidst Jacobean horror. The killers' captioned flight through the small towns of New Mexico, Texas and finally Arkansas is an eastward flight which is also a return to the South, that freak of naming in American geography whereby West and South, capitalised, work on the same latitude. The psychopathic ex-cons, Ray and Pluto, one white, one black, one histrionic the other ice-cool, are heading for Houston to sell off their stolen cocaine with Fantasia (Cynda Williams) their accomplice fast regressing into her first identity as Lila, a black girl of the South, making the trip back to Arkansas to see her young son. This double flight, chaotic and tragic, suggests a Nietzschean descent towards origin, but also echoes the African-American search for roots, the movement back South. It is the tension between the two, homecoming and descent, which gives the film a mythic power far in excess of its modest production values. As the Fantasia of LA and the Lila of the ironically-named Star City, Williams has the double identity of West Coast wannabee and small-town girl. But she also has mixed blood and is fatally linked with two white men, the Law and the Psychopath.

Repetition is the key to nemesis. Her secret return home reveals her chequered past, the disaster of teenage sex with the Sheriff (Bill Paxton) who is the father of her child. As lawman and lawbreaker, the sheriff and killer Ray are doubles of one another, one repeating the forced relationship of white man and black woman the other has instigated. But the second time around Lila is a willing accomplice. She betrays her black friends in LA, shoots the highway patrolman who tries to arrest the gang, but finally betrays her current lover to her former lover in the film's gruesome ending. The film transforms the role of the gangster's moll into femme fatale and femme fatale into femme fataliste. Fantasia acts while appearing to react, determines while appearing to submit, and becomes an instrument of the bloodbath which finally consumes her. The narrative turns upon three defining actions. First her refusal to tell the killers of the child she has found hiding in the dealer's house in LA because it reminds her of her own. Second, her shooting of the patrolman as he arrests Ray and Pluto, filmed by an elliptical cut to a brief long-shot of her firing on the edge of the nocturnal highway. Third, her stealing of Ray's money from the drugs heist to give to her own son which draws the killers back to Star City and their own death. Lila is thus the orchestrator of nemesis, including her own, and we do not know at the end if Paxton, wounded bloodily in the shoot-out, will survive her. 'Are you dead, mister?' his black son asks him, standing by his prone body, as the LA detectives arrive tardily to witness the gunfight they were unable to prevent.

Country noir deals here not in the dumbing of America which we can readily find in box-office hits such as *Pulp Fiction*, *Forrest Gump* and the aptly named *Dumb and Dumber*, but in the simulation of dumbness, a feature which links Paxton to the fall-guys of *Kill Me Again*, *After Dark, My Sweet* and *Red Rock West*. Their professed naivety is ambiguous, and only in *The Last Seduction* does Dahl give us in comic vein a purified male idiocy. Otherwise naivety disconcerts us because, we suspect, it may be something of a pose. If the true sheriff of Star City is not all that he seems this applies elsewhere in noir too. Though two years apart in the making, three things link *Kill Me Again* and *After Dark, My Sweet*. First, both films cue the agoraphobic nature of the new noir. The credits roll over a montage of panning shots across desert hills and shrubland in twilight, linking distortion to distance. Second, both femmes fatales are called Fay and played by English actresses, Rachel Ward in Foley's Californian thriller, Joanne Whalley-Kilmer in Dahl's Nevada pastiche. Third, and most important, the naivety of their fall-guys, Jason Patric and Val Kilmer, is itself suspect and their mindscreen flashbacks are sources of ambiguity, not revelation. As an ex-boxing champ Colley (Patric) appears to recall obsessively the fight in which he killed his opponent. As a private eye whose wife has tragically died, Kilmer appears to recall her drowning after their car has swerved off the road and crashed into a lake. Initially, we take the flashbacks to be real. But after Resnais and Buñuel, there is always the lingering doubt. Thus both films go beyond the *locus classicus* in noir to which they are both indebted, Jacques Tourneur's *Out of the Past*. Here we assume Robert Mitchum's extended flashback to be the true account of his shady past, aided by his defining voice-over. His Bridgeport refuge on the Californian border near Lake Tahoe is a landmark, too, for country noir. But it is a place of innocence and retreat, idyllic, untouched by the corrupt life of the city. In 1990s noir, there is no rural hiding place. After Lynch, each small town opens up to the

prying camera lens its can of worms. Patric stumbles out of the mountains near the Mexico border to become involved in a kidnapping
conspiracy. *Kill Me Again* starts with Vince (Michael Madsen) and Fay's
robbery at a desert mining depot. In *Red Rock West* Nick Cage is a
penniless drifter mistaken by the saloon-bar owner for a contract killer
who has come to murder his wife.

In the age of the designer jeep and four-wheel drive, the noir
automobile is the flash used car which has seen better days – the
white-finned Cadillacs favoured by Dahl or beat-up 1970s saloons and
station wagons suggesting well-preserved decay. The car's transient
identity matches its owner's. It is traded in, its number-plates changed
and it never musters respectability, though hi-tech inventions can
always lend themselves to a good twist in the plot. Linda Fiorentino in
The Last Seduction spots the airbag – driver-side only – sign as she
sits alongside the New York detective sent by husband Bill Pullman to
track down his drugs money. Her shiny black jeep becomes an instant
wreck, the unprotected and unwanted passenger dead, and the femme
fatale survives courtesy of the latest safety device. Cars are transient
possessions and country noir follows road movies and the commercials
which copy them in cannibalising the West as the landscape of the
open road. One of Dahl's favourite shots is the 'front-wheel' shot, the
low-angle deep focus of the four-wheeled rectangle, a slick monster of
mayhem elongated on the angle and given even greater depth by an
empty desert highway. This is the shot which frames Vince and Fay's
desert hold-up at the start of *Kill Me Again*. But country noir also
sees the moving car as a medium of circles and detours, not straight
lines, despite the flat Western roads. Like money and drugs, cars are
circulating commodities.

Repetition also aligns itself with the doubling of identity. 1990s noir
is a coda to the split screen of the expressive double. Jack Andrews is
as close to Scottie Ferguson as he is to Philip Marlowe. *Kill Me Again*
is more indebted to *Vertigo* than *Out of the Past* and closer in style to
Liebestraum where Kim Novak is femme fatale twice over, having
ordered the killing of the first couple and now willing on her deathbed
for the death of the second, that of her son and his married lover, the
movie's other femme fatale played by Pamela Gidley, to be enacted
by the enraged husband. To make the point, Figgis has the two couples
of different decades played by the same actors. To stress the close

identity of Fay and Jack's dead wife, Dahl twice cuts early on from a close profile shot of Fay to the shattered frame of the honeymoon photo in which Jack stands with his wife under a blurred motel sign. The frame has been shattered by the marauding loan sharks who have broken his finger for late payment but the action, typical of the physical knocks of the private eye, also cues us into the spiral of shattered glass which blots out the woman's face. In the reprise of this cut Jack is looking at the shattered photo just as Fay walks into his ramshackle office with the plan to fake her murder and thus escape the clutches of the casually psychotic Vince.

As in *Liebestraum*, Dahl drives his plot forward to link death and eros in the spirit of *Vertigo* and here the faking of the murder, using a bag full of Fay's blood type, itself becomes an erotic *mise-en-scène*. The ubiquitous motel, hypostatic double of the circulating car and familiar scene of nocturnal seduction, is the scene of the mock crime. The couple wrestle at Fay's command to make the death-struggle real. Jack sitting over her, cuts the blood-bag to leave tell-tale traces on the bed but his knife slices too hard and the blood drenches her on the bed. It is a good comic touch with a chilling edge, the spilt blood connoting spilt semen, the slicing of the bag done with swift arousal and intimating premature ejaculation. The fake murder is thus a form of sexual desire out of control. But the mystery deepens, aided by the film's title. Fay is a look-alike for the dead wife so that her fake dying could be a re-enactment of the spouse's real death by drowning, a retrojection of intent in which Jack, beset by guilt, feels himself to be the murderer. Or maybe he was a murderer by default, by swimming in too late to save her.

Jack's sinking of the 'murder' car in the Indian lake with Fay's blood-stained clothes in the boot triggers the flashback of his wife's drowning, but Fay has already vanished. She rings the identity changes of name, hair and clothes which see her as a high-roller at the gambling tables. The red-tinted hair, the tight dresses and high heels intimate the world of glamour she seeks as an independent woman, but when she flees for the second time with Jack after murdering the mobsters who seek revenge for the original heist, she is once again transformed, and the role of Andrews himself becomes suspect. He takes her to Echo Bay, Dahl's self-referential title for the drowning lake and the motel under whose sign the original photo had been taken. 'Ain't I seen you before?'

the motel clerk asks as Andrews hides behind shades. He is now homme fatale to her femme fatale and the agonistic game has a perverse parity. As Dahl cuts after love-making to a breakfast scene in the motel Fay, the glamorous gambler, has changed into a domesticated woman cooking in dowdy dress and apron. The dress replicates that of Andrew's spouse in the flashback, and inverts the making-over process of *Vertigo* where Scottie makes Judy over again into the glamorous Madeleine. Jack here makes Fay over by turning her from glamorous moll into plain domestic, the image of the mourned spouse. Thus when Fay suggests a second faking of her murder the phrase 'kill me again' resonates with an erotic edge and chill double-register. Andrews suggests a fake mutual drowning in the lake to fool the Law before they collect the loot which he will bury on Indian land. In the double-cross that follows, it is he who plunges into the lake, shot by the duplicitous Fay. Yet the ending where he is saved by Indians on the reservation and leaves for Arizona with the loot suggests something else. It is the man who gets away with it through the power of his own distrust and his own forms of unresolved duplicity, a triumph for the homme fatale who, in his own way, did kill her again. This triumph is echoed with self-conscious irony in the ending of *Red Rock West* where Cage flings the treacherous Boyle from the freight train during their big escape and tosses the tainted money out with her. Here Cage, stoic through all tribulation, is given the cachet of a justified sinner, his failing borne out of a perverse strain of virtue which lifts him above husband, femme fatale and contract killer Dennis Hopper, the fall-guy who constantly stumbles but never falls. Cage and Hopper in part reprise their respective roles in *Blue Velvet* and *Wild at Heart*, understandable in a director whose movies were produced by Propaganda Pictures, the offbeat offshoot of Polygram which had previously come up with *Wild at Heart*. That there should then be a kind of sneaky in-joke when one Lynch icon is mistaken for the other by Red Rock's no-good sheriff (J. T. Walsh) is predictable. If Cage goes with the mistake, however, he also resists its package of temptations. If Cynda Williams is fatalistic and deadly then so is he, giving stoicism a bad name and being knocked back and forth like a tennis ball by cheating players. When the sheriff asked him to kill his unfaithful wife, the wife then promises to double the amount if he kills her husband. In a sustained visual gag on wishful thinking his car unwittingly runs down Boyle's bimbo lover after she has shot him, without of course Cage knowing that she has shot him. Aptly named Michael, one presumes, after the bumbling Mike O'Hara whom Orson Welles had played in *Lady from Shanghai*, Cage's alter-ego contract killer (Hopper) is called 'Lyle from Dallas' so that Dahl can stress, perhaps, his film's affinity with the dry humour in the lyrics of Texan singer Lyle Lovett. This is, after all, country noir.

If Michael as drifter is a reinvention of Frank, the drifter in *The Postman Always Rings Twice*, the plot of this movie reads more like *Double Indemnity* crossed with *Waiting for Godot*. Just as Didi and Gogo resolve to leave the stage and never do, Michael resolves to leave Red Rock West and ends up driving back into town past its welcome sign, in an endless series of departures and arrivals. Mexico, the common pipe-dream of 1940s noir, is given short shrift. 'Fuck Mexico!' the exasperated Cage shouts at Boyle. Dahl reduces Lynchian dynamics to comic and lugubrious stagnancy. The vertical descent of Frank Booth into living hell and the horizontal flight west of Sailor, a natural-born romantic, are transformed into a different pattern for Hopper and Cage, a series of overlapping circles which eventually merge. Dahl and Cage show us, like Woody Allen, that the mindscreen's existential dread can be seriously funny, but the whole conceit would be lost without Cage's virtue, or rather his morally virginal state which no one is able to violate. He can be beaten up and shot at. He can be easily seduced. But he can still say at the end to Hopper, the dumb psycho on auto-pilot, who has sneered at his professed goodness: 'You know what. I am better than you.' And mean it. Better, though, offers no chance of moral ascent. It simply means going round in circles and staying above the level of those beneath, never quite descending to their level. It is a tactic which is seen to work, perverse to the end, but just as the auto-mobile now offers no way out, the freightliner and the rail track are in the end the only means of escape. All roads, it seems, lead to Red Rock West.

The Last Seduction, the third of the trilogy, is the best-known but the least complex, remarked on for its virtuoso performance from Linda Fiorentino. The trick of the film is a 1990s first, even in the fast-changing play upon genre for which noir is known. The mindscreen here belongs uniquely to the femme fatale, no longer the figure of mystery or opaque deceit but shamelessly transparent, our guide through the labyrinth of double-dealing and double-crossing at which she is the champion. Dahl's camera, it has to be said, is in love with its subject who outwits every witless male in sight. The cross-over effects of gender, never far from contemporary thoughts, are turned by Dahl into instances of wicked fun. In the small town in upstate New York where Wendy (Fiorentino) changes her identity to escape from her dealer-husband back in NYC – 'Cowtown' as the private eye tracking her calls it – she scores with an ex-married man, married as she soon finds out, by mistake to another man. While the local fall-guy's past mistake had been to fall for a man trying to pass as a woman, his present mistake is to fall for a woman whose ruthlessness would be defined as male. Fiorentino has claimed to inject into her character many of the characteristics she had observed in male Hollywood producers of her acquaintance, but to make them convincingly female. The camera lovingly goes with the charade. It observes the body-language of existential deceit, which is not however a sign of the weak trying to manipulate the strong, but rather a sign of strength itself eroticised in a sexually charged performance. The fall-guy by comparison is a repository of all those open sensitivities which are supposed in the 1990s to be the hallmark of the New Man. Dahl, however, gives us a version of the New Man as village idiot, prattling on about 'feelings' and 'relationships' in a vacuum to a woman whose interests are money and power. The female mindscreen is notably anti-paranoid, not fearful of what is being plotted, too busy plotting itself, probing and second-guessing the weak spots of all its male victims. The existential recognition of weakness, Fiorentino's body-language conveying instant awareness of the Achilles Heel, is one of the film's visual joys. And the ending thus becomes obvious. If you are that sexy and that larger-than-life, you can't be punished. You get away with it, whatever it is. And in the end, it doesn't matter what it is at all.

In the same way, the freedom of the open road is the freedom to go nowhere in the pursuit of wealth and money, to visit non-places with meaningless names and no nature so that nature is conveyed by the speed of movement into them and out of them again. Here the automobile becomes an imaginary character like its occupants with its special look, its own charm, its own menace. That which exists is that which moves, the country noir's version of primary experience. That still place, the small town or short stop on the road which movement confronts, is merely a secondary experience of being. Yet the freedom of primary experience is an illusion, an illusion of the car that is going nowhere. Transience, solitude, rootlessness: all part of the spin-off from the lust for greenbacks and the prelude to violent death. In noir, killing and conspiracy and those alone translate the expectation of going somewhere into the reality of going nowhere. In this low-budget incessant movement, all small towns are ghost towns formed on the axis of perennial motion. Their absurd names come from a different time, the past, and their nature from a different space, a zone of transition where no-one relies on the kindness of strangers. In country noir, the road to nowhere is circular but not tragic, a violent but comic fate.

ENDNOTES

———◦———

CHAPTER 1 A CINEMA OF POETRY

1. Pasolini, Pier Paolo (1988) *Heretical Empiricism*, translated by Ben Lawton and Louise Barnett, Bloomington: Indiana University Press, 176. The standard translation of *discorso libro indiretto* is 'free indirect discourse' but the translation by Naomi Green in her excellent study of Pasolini is 'free indirect subjectivity', while Gilles Deleuze suggests 'free indirect vision'. Both of these translations stress more effectively the visual meaning in film language as opposed to the grammatical meaning of the term in prose. For Green's discussion of Pasolini's poetics, see *Pier Paolo Pasolini: Cinema as Heresy* (1993), Princeton: Princeton University Press, 92–127.

2. Deleuze, Gilles (1989) *Cinema 2: The Time-Image*, translated by Hugh Tomlinson and Robert Galeta, London: Athlone Press, 128–9.

3. Pasolini op. cit. 178.

4. Orr, John (1993) *Cinema and Modernity*, Cambridge: Polity Press, 83–5.

5. Pasolini op. cit. 172–3.

6. ibid. 180.

7. Deleuze op. cit. 72–3.

8. Sartre, Jean-Paul (1978) *What is Literature?* Bloomington: Indiana University Press, 142.

9. Banfield, Ann (1984), *Unspeakable Sentences: Narration and Representation in the Language of Fiction*, Boston: Routledge & Kegan Paul, 65–76. See also the interesting study of the free indirect mode in Flaubert by Vaheed Ramazani (1988) *The Free Indirect Mode: Flaubert and the Poetics of Irony*, Charlottesville: University Press of Virginia.

10. Freud's key essays on neurosis and psychosis are to be found in *The Standard Edition of the Complete Psychological Works of Sigmund Freud*

(1961) London: Hogarth Press, Vol. 19; 149–53, 183–7. For a recent critique see Teresa Brennan (1993) *The Interpretation of the Flesh: Freud and Femininity* London: Routledge & Kegan Paul, 89–110.

11. Deleuze in fact sees Godard's cinema as the chief exemplar of free indirect vision. See Deleuze op. cit. 180–4.

12. Thomas Elsaesser analyses Fassbinder's episode in the film in *New German Cinema* (1989) London: Macmillan, 267–8.

13. Quoted in Peter Cowie (1992) *Ingmar Bergman: A Critical Biography* London: André Deutsch, 276.

14. Geoff Eley analyses Davies's filmic use of history in 'The Family is a Dangerous Place: Memory, Gender, and the Image of the Working-Class', in Robert Rosenstone (ed.) *Revisioning History: Film and the Construction of a New Past* Princeton: Princeton University Press, 1995, 17–43. For a related discussion of *The Long Day Closes* see John Caughie 'Halfway to Paradise', in *Sight and Sound* May 1992.

15. Kawin, Bruce (1978) *Mindscreen: Bergman, Godard and First Person Film* Princeton, New Jersey; Princeton University, Chapter 1.

16. Tarkovsky, Andrei (1987) *Sculpting in Time* London: Faber & Faber, 26ff.

17. Trainor, Richard 'Black and White Light; Interview with Henri Alekan' in *Sight and Sound* July 1993.

18. Kim Worthy comments adversely on the subject in '*Hearts of Darkness*: Making Art, Making History, Making Money, Making "Vietnam"' in *Cineaste* Vol. XIX, 2–3, 24–32.

19. Chute, David 'Golden Hours' in *Film Comment* 27; 2. March–April 1991, 68.

20. Stok, Danusia (ed., 1993) *Kieślowski on Kieślowski* London: Faber & Faber, 160–1, 170–1.

21. See Stig Bjorkman's interview with Von Trier 'Naked Miracles', in *Sight and Sound* October 1996.

22. Bazin, André (1967) *What is Cinema?* Berkeley: University of California Press, Vol. 1, 9–12.

23. On the specific composition of the tracking shots, see Susan Hayward 'Beyond the gaze and into femme-film écriture: Agnès Varda's *Sans toit ni loi*', in Susan Hayward and Ginette Vincendeau (1990) *French Film: Texts and contexts* London: Routledge & Kegan Paul, 288.

24. For a more detailed examination of Deneuve's acting, see Ginette Vincendeau 'Fire and Ice' in *Sight and Sound* April 1993.

25. Denise J. Youngblood sets the historical context for Abuladze's film in '*Repentance*: Stalinist Terror and the Realism of Surrealism', in Robert Rosenstone (1995) *Revisioning History: Film and the Construction of a New Past* Princeton: Princeton University Press, 139–54.

26. For a more detailed analysis of the closing sequence of the film, see Robert Kolker and Peter Beicken (1993) *The Films of Wim Wenders; Cinema as Vision and Desire* Cambridge: Cambridge University Press, 154–60.

CHAPTER 2   THE SACRIFICIAL UNCONSCIOUS

1. Pasolini's resurrection of the idea of myth is discussed by Green, op. cit. 126ff.
2. Ruiz, Raul (1995) *Poetics of Cinema* Paris: Editions Dis Voir, 57–66.
3. Nietzsche, Friedrich (1973) *Beyond Good and Evil* translated by R. J. Hollingdale, Harmondsworth: Penguin 63.
4. Zizek, Slavoj (1989) *The Sublime Object of Ideology* London: Verso, 110f.
5. ibid. 115.
6. Girard, René (1979) *Violence and the Sacred* Baltimore: The Johns Hopkins Press, 39–67.
7. O'Brien, Tom 'Jesus of Montreal', reviewed in *Film Quarterly* 44/1, Fall 1990, 47–50.
8. Turovskaya, Maya (1989) *Tarkovsky: Cinema as Poetry* London, Faber & Faber, 139–42.
9. Von Trier has stated: 'My intention has not been to criticise a particular religious community, such as the one that exists in this Scottish environment . . . It is just that, if you want to create a melodrama, you have to furnish it with certain obstacles. And religion provided me with a suitable obstacle.' in 'Naked Miracles', op. cit. 14.
10. Hayward op. cit. 292–3.
11. See 'Imitation as Mastery', the recently translated essay in Ian Christie and Richard Taylor (eds) *Eisenstein Rediscovered* London: Routledge & Kegan Paul, 1993, 68.
12. Calasso Roberto (1994) *The Ruin of Kasch*, translated by William Weaver and Stephen Sartarelli, Manchester: Carcanet, 248.
13. *Sculpting in Time*, 151.
14. For the best discussion of Antonioni's use of colour, see Ned Rifkin (1982) *Antonioni's Visual Image* Ann Arbor: UMI Research Press, Chapter 2.
15. Sculpting in Time, 21.
16. The similarities between Mayak and Chernobyl are analysed by Piers Paul Read in *Ablaze: The Story of Chernobyl* London: Mandarin, 1993, 14–20.
17. Hobson's physiological study, which stresses the continuity between dream-work and the waking consciousness, provides a strong challenge

to Freud's theory of dreams. See J. Allan Hobson (1990) *The Dreaming Brain* London: Penguin.
18. Turovskaya op. cit. 106–7.
19. Don Shiach discusses the Anglo-Australian relationship in the film and in recent history in *The Films of Peter Weir* London: Letts, 1993, 51–2; see also Brian Hirst *A Republican Manifesto* Oxford: Oxford University Press, 1994, 63–4.
20. Hughes, Robert (1987) *The Fatal Shore* London: Collins Harvill, 16–17.
21. See Stella Bruzzi 'Bodyscape' in *Sight and Sound* October 1993, which includes Mary Colbert's conversations about the movie's look with its costume designer Janet Patterson.
22. Palley, Marcia 'Order vs. Chaos: The Films of Peter Greenaway', in *Cinéaste* XVIII:3:1991.
23. Greenaway, Peter 'Just place, preferably architectural place', in John Boorman and Walter Donohue (eds) *Projections 41/2* London: Faber & Faber, 1995 79–80.
24. Sennett, Richard (1993) *The Conscience of the Eye; the Design and Social Life of Cities* London: Faber & Faber, 159–63.
25. 'Peter Greenaway interviewed by Brian McFarlane' in *Cinema Papers* Vol. 78, March 1990, 42.
26. See the crucial difference in the reading of Egoyan's 'neurotic family romance' between two excellent essays by Jacinto Legeira 'The Recollection of Scattered Parts', in *Atom Egoyan* Paris: Editions Dis Voir, 1993, 29f; and Peter Harcourt 'Imaginary Images: An Examination of Atom Egoyan's Films', in *Film Quarterly* 48:3, Spring 1995, 2–10.

CHAPTER 3 THE SCREEN AS SPLIT SUBJECT 1:
PERSONA'S LEGACY

1. Girard op. cit. 57.
2. On this particular debate see Charles Taylor (1989) *Sources of the Self: The Making of Modern Identity* Cambridge: Cambridge University Press, 456–523, and Anthony Giddens (1991) *Modernity and Self-Identity* Cambridge: Polity Press.
3. Discussions of Hollywood stardom are to be found in Richard Dyer (1986) *Heavenly Bodies; Film Stars and Society* Basingstoke: Macmillan, and Christine Gledhill (ed.), 1991 *Stardom: A History of Desire* London: Routledge & Kegan Paul.
4. Girard, René (1984) *Deceit, Desire and the Novel,* translated by Yvonne Freccero, Baltimore: The Johns Hopkins Press, 1–52.
5. Marilyn Blackwell gives a detailed breakdown on the film's opening

sequence in *Persona: The Transcendent Image* Chicago: University of Illinois Press, 1986, 11–37.

6. For a discussion of the literary developments, see John Herdman (1990) *The Double in Nineteenth-Century Fiction* London: Macmillan.

7. Kundera, Milan (1995) *Testaments Betrayed* London: Faber & Faber, 57.

8. Corrigan, Timothy (1994) *New German Cinema: The Displaced Image* Bloomington: Indiana University Press, Revised Edition, 43–5.

9. On Altman's problem of finding a coherent design, see Robert Philip Kolker (1988) *A Cinema of Loneliness* Oxford: Oxford University Press, 2nd Edition, 375–7.

10. Seiter, Ellen 'The Personal is Political: Margarethe von Trotta's *Marianne and Juliane*', in Charlotte Brunsden (ed.) *Films for Women* London: BFI, 1986, 112. See also E. Ann Kaplan, 'Female Politics in the Symbolic Realm; Von Trotta's Marianne and Juliane', in *Women and Film:Both Sides of the Camera* London: Methuen, 1983. NB: *Marianne and Juliane* is the American release title of *Die Bleierne Zeit*.

11. The key modern text on the topic remains Christopher Lasch (1994) *The Culture of Narcissism* 2nd edition, New York: Norton.

12. Stefan Aust has written a detailed study of the incarceration of the Baader-Meinhof group, *The Baader-Meinhof Group: The Understanding of a Phenomenon* London: Bodley Head, 1987, based upon his screenplay for the feature film *Stammheim* (1986) directed by Reinhard Hauff.

13. Zizek op. cit. 117.

14. Peter Wollen gives a fascinating account of the circumstances surrounding the making of the film in 'Possession', *Sight and Sound* September 1995.

15. Guy Austen assesses the pivotal 1970s role of Rivette's film in *Contemporary French Cinema* Manchester: Manchester University Press, 1996, 64–8.

16. Bérénice Reynaud examines the close links between Rohmer's film and Girard's concept of 'triangulated desire' in 'Representing the Sexual Impasse; Eric Rohmer's *Les nuits de la pleine lune*', in Hayward & Vincendeau op. cit. 270–4.

17. Deleuze describes Rohmer and Bresson as the two main exponents of the variant of free indirect vision which he terms 'atonal cinema'. Here he argues, somewhat mysteriously, 'the character acts and speaks himself as if his own gestures and his own words were already repeated by a third party.' Deleuze op. cit. 183.

CHAPTER 4   THE SCREEN AS SPLIT SUBJECT 2:
INTO THE 1990s

1. Laura Mulvey discusses the film with Tlati in 'Moving Bodies' in *Sight and Sound* March 1995.
2. Chow, Rey (1995) *Primitive Passions: Visuality, Sexuality, Ethnography and Contemporary Chinese Cinema* New York: Columbia University Press, 170.
3. See the illuminating interview with Wong by Tony Rayns, 'Poet of Time' in *Sight and Sound* September 1995.
4. Larry Gross sees this spatial doubling as a crucial feature in the revolutionary language of Wong's films: 'Nonchalant Grace', in *Sight and Sound* September 1995.
5. Tony Rayns details this sequence at first hand in his article on the shooting of the film in 1995: 'The camera is mounted on an assembly manoeuvred by three grips and its focus and angle of vision are radio controlled. Not surprisingly it takes several attempts to get the shot right.' See 'Here and Now', in *Sight and Sound* April 1995.
6. In the impressive 1996 *Virgin International Film Guide* London: Virgin Books, 1996, for example, there are no entries for the three American films in a book of 828 pages with nearly 30,000 entries, while the abrupt entry for *Exotica* dismisses Egoyan as 'a pretentious bore'. All four films, however, get enthusiastic notices in the 1997 *Time Out Film Guide* Harmondsworth: Penguin, 1997, while there is an excellent review of *Liebestraum* by Mark Kermode in *Sight and Sound* April 1992.
7. Michael Chion assesses the thematic difference between the TV serial and the feature film in *David Lynch* London: BFI, 1995, 124–7.
8. The film's directors discuss the 1960s models at greater length in *Projections Four and a Half* (1995), 272–5, while Jonathan Romney analyses the film itself with them in 'How did we get here?', in *Sight and Sound* February 1995.

CHAPTER 5   THE CAMERA AS DOUBLE VISION

1. Greenaway's use of static camera framing around the perspective frame in *The Draughtsman's Contract* is discussed by Alan Woods in *Being Naked Playing Dead: The Art of Peter Greenaway* Manchester: Manchester University Press, 1996, 45–7.
2. The design and use of the Esper are discussed by Paul M. Sammon in *Future Noir: The Making of Blade Runner* London: Orion Media, 1996, 258–60.

3. Jameson's dubious distinction between visual modernism and aural post-modernism is made in *Signatures of the Visible* London: Routledge & Kegan Paul, 1992, 194.

4. Among the controversies surrounding *JFK*, see the debate in *Cinéaste* on the issue of fascism and homophobia surrounding the arrest of Clay Shaw between screenwriter Zachary Sklar, 'Getting the Facts Straight; An Interview with Zachary Sklar.'Vol. XIX, No. 1 and David Ehrenstein, 'Jim Garrison as Gaybasher?'Vol. XIX No. 2. For the wider culture of conspiracy surrounding the killing see John Orr, 'Paranoid Fictions: *JFK*, Conspiracy Theory and Nightmare on Elm Street Revisited', in Norman Denzin (ed.) *Cultural Studies: A Research Annual* Vol. 2 Greenwich, Connecticut JAI Press, 1997.

5. The director's own comments on the film are in Kieślowski op. cit. 110–13.

6. Janda compares her very different roles in *Man of Marble* and *The Interrogation* in an interview with Michael Szporer in *Cinéaste* XVIII, 3, 1991, 12–16.

7. Chion has a different reading of the film and the role of its mysterious Red Room in *David Lynch* 105–6, 142–59.

8. Scott Bukatmen, 'Who programs you? The Science Fiction of the Spectacle', in Annette Kuhn (ed.) *Alien Zone* (London:Verso, 1990, 200.

9. See Lageira op. cit. 34–9.

CHAPTER 6 AMERICAN REVERIES: ALTMAN, LYNCH, MALICK, SCORSESE

1. This is the Lyotardian viewpoint on the post-modern put forward by Dudley Andrew in his introduction to Godard's screenplay of *Breathless* New Brunswick, New Jersey: Rutgers University Press, 1987, 19.

2. *Signatures of the Visible* 206–7.

3. Gane, Mike (ed.), 1993 *Baudrillard Live; Selected Interviews* London: Routledge & Kegan Paul, 21–2.

4. ibid. 161.

5. See the exchange of video letters between Virilio and Egoyan during the summer of 1993 in the Dis Voir symposium on Egoyan, op. cit. 105–15.

6. Augé, Marc (1995) *Non-Places: Introduction to an Anthropology of Super-Modernity*, translated by John Howe, London:Verso, 116–20.

7. Michel de Certeau discusses the meaning of spatial narrative in *The Practice of Everyday Life* Berkeley: University of California Press, 1988, 115–25.

8. Augé op. cit. 82–6.

9. Jameson's reliance on key aspects of Adorno's modernism can be seen in *Late-Marxism: Adorno or, The Persistence of the Dialectic* London: Verso, 1990.

10. Jameson, Fredric (1991) *Postmodernism or the Cultural Logic of Late-Capitalism* London: Verso, 283–97.

11. Mulvey, Laura (1995) *Fetishism and Curiosity* London: BFI, 147–9.

12. Chion op. cit. 123–4.

13. Jameson, Fredric (1992) *The Geopolitical Aesthetic: Cinema and Space in the World System* London: BFI, Part I, 9–82.

14. Zsigmond describes the pre-fogging or pre-flashing technique in Dennis Schaefer and Larry Salvato (eds) *Masters of Light* Berkeley, University of California Press, 1984, 315.

15. In her study of Altman, Helene Keysaar cites the use of free indirect subjectivity in *3 Women*, but it seems to me the analysis is equally appropriate, for example, to the final gunfight in *McCabe*, which she discusses in some detail. See *Robert Altman's America* New York: Oxford University Press, 1991, 193–7, 217–18.

16. Schaefer and Salvato op. cit. 33–4.

17. Barbara Novak examines the relationship between the sublime and landscape painting in *Nature and Culture: American Landscape and Painting, 1825–1875* London: Thames & Hudson, 1980.

18. Leo Marx discusses the cultural legacy of the technological sublime and the pastoralism of New Left counter-culture in *The Pilot and the Passenger: Essays in Literature, Technology and Culture in the United States* Oxford: Oxford University Press, 1988, 113–39, 291–315.

19. Nestor Almendros details the twilight hour sequences and the use of Steadicam for the fire sequence in *A Man with a Camera* London: Faber & Faber, 1985, 167–86.

20. Bach, Steven (1985) *Final Cut: Dreams and Disaster in the Making of Heaven's Gate* London: Jonathan Cape.

21. ibid. 163–6.

22. Lesley Stern compares the ring sequences to the dance sequences of *The Red Shoes*, one of Scorsese's favourite movies, in *The Scorsese Connection* London: BFI, 1995, 26–31; cinematographer Michael Chapman comments on the picture's use of Renoir in Schaefer & Salvato op. cit. 124.

CHAPTER 7   ANXIETIES OF THE MASCULINE SUBLIME

1. Tarkovsky, Andrei (1991) *The Diaries: 1970–1986* Calcutta: Seagull, 255.

2. John Pym gives a detailed breakdown of Channel Four'cinema' in *Film on Four: 1982–1991* London:BFI, 1992.
3. Janet Wasko assesses the position of studio expansion at the start of the 1990s in *Hollywood in the Information Age: Beyond the Silver Screen* Cambridge: Polity Press, 1994, 41–71.
4. Robert Kolker in fact wrote a new chapter on Spielberg for the second edition of *A Cinema of Loneliness* to assess his political significance for the 1980s. See Kolker op. cit. 237–302.
5. For the place of Scott's film in 1980s noir see Leighton Grist,'Moving Targets and Black Widows: Film Noir in Modern Hollywood', in Ian Cameron (ed.), 1992 *The Movie Book of Film Noir* London: Studio Vista, 267–85.
6. For a detailed commentary on Dunne's paranoia see Stern op. cit. 69–115.
7. 'The Artificial Infinite' in Lynne Cooke and Peter Wollen (eds, 1995) *Visual Display* Seattle: Bay Press, 282–6.
8. Kolker op. cit. 289–92.
9. Sammon op. cit. 301–4.
10. David Thomson writes of Duvall:'She is meant as a parody of helplessness, and felt as the casting coup of misogyny... Like Torrance, Kubrick seems to regard women as children, hags and silent beauties – no characters allowed.'From *A Biographical Dictionary of Film* London: André Deutsch, 1994, 218.
11. Kolker op. cit. 84.
12. Sammon op. cit. 138.
13. ibid. 255.
14. See Janet Abrams,'Escape from Gravity', in *Sight and Sound* May 1995.
15. Wollen, Peter'Delirious Projections', in *Sight and Sound* August 1992.
16. On the movie's many location misadventures in New York, see Julie Salomon (1992) *The Devil's Candy:The Bonfire of the Vanities goes to Hollywood* London: Jonathan Cape, Chapter 3.
17. Gilliam discusses the film's locations with Nick James in'Time and the Machine', in *Sight and Sound* April 1996.
18. Jonathan Romney charts the progress of this recent crossover in 'Curious Scapegoats', *The Guardian*, 27 January 1997.

SELECT BIBLIOGRAPHY

Almendros, Nestor, *A Man with a Camera* London: Faber & Faber, 1985.

Augé, Marc, *Non-Places: Introduction to an Anthropology of Supermodernity* London: Verso, 1995.

Aust, Stefan, *The Baader-Meinhof Group: The Understanding of a Phenomenon* London: Bodley Head, 1987.

Austen, Guy, *Contemporary French Cinema* Manchester: Manchester University Press, 1996.

Bach, Stephen, *Final Cut: Dreams and Disasters in the Making of Heaven's Gate* London: Jonathan Cape, 1985.

Banfield, Ann, *Unspeakable Sentences: Narration and Representation in the Language of Fiction* Boston: Routledge & Kegan Paul, 1984.

Bazin, André, *What is Cinema?* Vol. 1 Berkeley: University of California Press, 1967.

Björkman, Stig, 'Naked Miracles', in *Sight and Sound* October 1996.

Blackwell, Marilyn Johns, *Persona: The Transcendent Image* Chicago: University of Illinois Press, 1986.

Boorman, John and Donohue, Walter (eds) *Projections 4 and a half* London: Faber & Faber, 1995.

Brennan, Teresa, *The Interpretation of the Flesh: Freud and Femininity* London: Routledge & Kegan Paul, 1993.

Brunsden, Charlotte (ed.) *Films for Women* London: BFI, 1986.

Bruzzi, Stella, 'Bodyscape', in *Sight and Sound* October 1993.

Calasso, Roberto, *The Ruin of Kasch*, translated by William Weaver and Stephen Sartarelli, Manchester: Carcanet, 1994.

Cameron, Ian (ed,) *The Movie Book of Film Noir* London: Studio Vista, 1992.

Caughie, John, in 'Halfway to Paradise', in *Sight and Sound* May 1992.

Certeau, Michel de, *The Practice of Everyday Life* Berkeley: University of California, 1988.

Chion, Michael, *David Lynch* London: BFI, 1995.

Chow, Rey, *Primitive Passions: Visuality, Sexuality, Ethnography and Contemporary Chinese Cinema* New York, Columbia University Press, 1995.

Christie, Ian and Taylor, Richard (eds) *Eisenstein Rediscovered* London: Routledge & Kegan Paul, 1993.

Coates, Paul, *The Gorgon's Gaze: German Cinema, Expressionism and the Image of Horror* Cambridge: Cambridge University Press, 1991.

Cooke, Lynne and Wollen, Peter, *Visual Display: Culture Beyond Appearances* Seattle: Bay Press, 1995.

Corrigan, Timothy, *New German Cinema: The Displaced Image* Bloomington: Indiana University Press, revised edition 1994.

Cowie, Peter, *Ingmar Bergman: A Critical Biography* London: André Deutsch, 1992.

Deleuze, Gilles, *Cinema 2: The Time-Image*, translated by Hugh Tomlinson and Robert Galeta, London: Athlone Press, 1989.

Denzin, Norman, *The Cinematic Society* London: Sage, 1995.

Dyer, Richard, *Heavenly Bodies; Film Stars and Society* Basingstoke: Macmillan, 1986.

Elsaesser, Thomas, *New German Cinema* London: Macmillan, 1989.

Fanu, Mark Le, *The Cinema of Andrei Tarkovsky* London: BFI, 1987.

Gane, Mike (ed.) *Baudrillard Live: Selected Interviews* London: Routledge & Kegan Paul, 1993.

Giddens, Anthony, *Modernity and Self-Identity* Cambridge: Polity Press, 1991.

Girard, René, *Deceit, Desire and the Novel*, translated by Yvonne Freccero, Baltimore: The Johns Hopkins Press, 1984.

Girard, René, *Violence and the Sacred*, translated by Patrick Gregory, Baltimore: The Johns Hopkins Press, 1979.

Gledhill, Christine (ed.) *Stardom: A History of Desire* London: Routledge & Kegan Paul 1991.

Green, Naomi, *Cinema as Heresy* Princeton:Princeton University Press, 1993.

Greenaway, Peter, 'Just Place, preferably architectural place', in John Boorman and Walter Donahue (eds) *Projections 4 and a half* London: Faber & Faber, 1995.

Gross, Larry, 'Nonchalant Grace', in *Sight and Sound* September 1995.

Harcourt, Peter, 'Imaginary Images: An Examination of Atom Egoyan's Films', in *Film Quarterly* 48:3 Spring 1995.

Hayward, Susan and Vincendeau, Ginette, *French Film: Texts and Contexts* London: Routledge & Kegan Paul, 1990.

Herdman, John, *The Double in Nineteenth-Century Fiction* London: Macmillan, 1990)

Hobson, J. Allan, *The Dreaming Brain* London: Penguin, 1990.

Hughes, Robert, *The Fatal Shore* London: Collins Harvill, 1987.

Jameson, Fredric, *The Geopolitical Aesthetic: Cinema and Space in the World System* London: BFI, 1992.

Jameson, Fredric, *Late Marxism: Adorno, or the Persistence of the Dialectic* London: Verso, 1990.

Jameson, Fredric, *Postmodernism, or the Cultural Logic of Late-capitalism* London: Verso, 1991.

Jameson, Fredric, *Signatures of the Visible* London: Routledge & Kegan Paul, 1992.

Kaplan, E. Ann, *Women and Film: Both Sides of the Camera* London: Methuen, 1983.

Kawin, Bruce, *Mindscreen: Bergman, Godard and First-Person Film* Princeton: Princeton University Press, 1978.

Keysaar, Helene, *Robert Altman's America* New York: Oxford University Press, 1991.

Kolker, Robert Philip, *A Cinema of Loneliness* Oxford: Oxford University Press, 2nd edition, 1988.

Kolker, Robert Philip and Beichen, Peter, *The Films of Wim Wenders: Cinema as Vision and Desire* Cambridge: Cambridge University Press, 1993.

Kuhn Annette (ed.) *Alien Zone* London: Verso, 1990.

Kundera, Milan, *Testaments Betrayed* London: Faber & Faber, 1995.

Lasch, Christopher, *The Culture of Narcissism* New York: Norton, 1994, 2nd edition.

Lawton, Ann, *Kinoglasnost: Soviet Cinema in our Time* Cambridge: Cambridge University Press, 1992.

Legeira, Jacinto, 'The Recollection of Scattered Parts', in *Atom Egoyan* Editions Dis Voir, 1993.

Marx, Leo, *The Pilot and the Passenger: Essays in Literature, Technology and Culture in the United States* Oxford: Oxford University Press, 1988.

Mulvey, Laura, *Fetishism and Curiosity* London: BFI, 1995.

Mulvey, Laura, 'Moving Bodies', in *Sight and Sound* March 1995.

Novak, Barbara, *Nature and Culture: North American Landscape and Painting* London: Thames & Hudson, 1980.

Orr, John, *Cinema and Modernity* Cambridge: Polity Press, 1993.

Orr, John, 'Paranoid Fictions: *JFK*, Conspiracy Theory and Nightmare on Elm Street Revisited', in Norman Denzin (ed.) *Cultural Studies: A Research Annual* Vol. 2 Greenwich, Connecticut: JAI Press Inc., 1997.

Palley, Marcia, 'Order vs. Chaos: The Films of Peter Greenaway', in *Cinéaste* XVIII:3:1991.

Pallot, James and Levich, Jacob (eds) *The Fifth Virgin Film Guide* London: Virgin Books, 1996.

Pasolini, Pier Paolo, *Heretical Empiricism*, translated by Ben Lawton and Louise Barnett, Bloomington: Indiana University Press, 1978.

Pym, John, *Film On Four: 1982–1991* London: BFI, 1992.

Ramazani, Vaheed, *The Free Indirect Mode: Flaubert and the Poetics of Irony* Charlottesville: University Press of Virginia, 1988.

Rayns, Tony, 'Here and Now', in *Sight and Sound* April 1995.

Rayns, Tony, 'Poet of Time: Interview with Wong Kar-Wai', in *Sight and Sound* September 1995.

Rayns, Tony, 'Confrontations; Interview with Tsai Ming-Liang', in *Sight and Sound* March 1997.

Read, Piers Paul, *Ablaze: the Story of Chernobyl* London: Mandarin, 1993.

Rifkin, Ned, *Antonioni's Visual Image* Ann Arbor: UMI Research Press, 1982.

Rosentone, Robert (ed.) *Revisioning History: Film and the Construction of a New Past* Princeton: Princeton University Press, 1995.

Ruiz, Raul, *Poetics of Cinema* Paris: Editions Dis Voir, 1995.

Salamon, Julie, *The Devil's Candy: The Bonfire of the Vanities goes to Hollywood* London: Jonathan Cape, 1992.

Sammon, Paul M., *Future Noir; The Making Of Blade Runner* London: Orion Media, 1996.

Schaefer, Dennis and Salvato, Larry (eds) *Masters of Light* Berkeley: University of California Press, 1984.

Shiach, Don, *The Films of Peter Weir* London: Letts, 1993.

Stern, Lesley, *The Scorsese Connection* London: BFI, 1995.

Stok, Danusia (ed.) *Kieslowski on Kieslowski* London: Faber & Faber, 1993.

Tarkovsky, Andrei, *Sculpting in Time* London: Faber & Faber, 1993.

Taylor, Charles, *Sources of the Self: The Making of Modern Identity* Cambridge: Cambridge University Press, 1989.

Thomson, David, *A Biographical Dictionary of Film* London: André Deutsch, 1994.

Thomson, David and Christie, Ian (eds) *Scorsese on Scorsese* London: Faber & Faber, 1989.

Toufic, Jahal, *Over-Sensitivity* Los Angeles: Sun and Moon Press, 1996.

Trainor, Richard, 'Black and White Light: Interview with Henri Alekan', in *Sight and Sound* July 1993.

Turovskaya, Maya, *Tarkovsky: Cinema as Poetry* London: Faber & Faber, 1989.

Vincendeau, Ginette, 'Fire and Ice', in *Sight and Sound* April 1993.

Wasko, Janet, *Hollywood in the Information Age; Beyond the Silver Screen* Cambridge: Polity Press, 1994.

Wollen, Peter, 'Delirious Projections', in *Sight and Sound* August 1992.

Wollen, Peter, 'Possession', in *Sight and Sound* September 1995.

Woods, Alan, *Being Naked Playing Dead: The Art of Peter Greenaway* Manchester: Manchester University Press, 1996.

Worthy, Kim, 'Hearts of Darkness: Making Art, Making History, Making Money, Making Vietnam', in *Cinéaste* Vol XIX 1994.

Zizek, Slavoj, *The Sublime Object of Ideology* London: Verso, 1990.

INDEX

235